Chicana
Creativity
and
Criticism

Chicana Creativity and Criticism

NEW FRONTIERS IN

AMERICAN LITERATURE

EDITED BY

MARÍA HERRERA-SOBEK

AND

HELENA MARÍA VIRAMONTES

UNIVERSITY OF NEW MEXICO PRESS

© 1996 by

the University of

New Mexico Press

All rights reserved.

Revised edition, 1996

Library of Congress

Cataloging-in-Publication Data

Chicana creativity and criticism : new frontiers in

American Literature / edited by Maria Herrera-Sobek

& Helena Maria Viramontes. — Rev. ed.

p.   cm.

Revised edition of a collection of poetry, prose, and

essays originally given at a conference held Apr. 22,

1987 at the University of California, Irvine, sponsored

by the Mexico/Chicano Program of the university.

Includes bibliographical references (p.   ).

ISBN 0-8263-1712-X (pbk.)

1. American literature — Mexican American authors —

Congresses.   2. American literature — Mexican

American authors — History and criticism —

Congresses.   3. American literature — Women

authors — Congresses.   4. American literature —

Women authors — History and criticism —

Congresses.   5. American literature — 20th century —

Congresses.   6. American literature — 20th century —

History and criticism — Congresses.   7. Mexican

American women — Intellectual life — Congresses.

8. Women and literature — United States — History —

20th century — Congresses.   I. Herrera-Sobek,

Maria.   II. Viramontes, Helena Maria.

III. University of California, Irvine.

Mexico/Chicano Program.

PS508.M4C52   1996

810.9'86872 — dc20   96-9940

CIP

For Tomorrow's Generation

ERIK JASON SOBEK

PILAR RODRÍGUEZ

ELOY FRANCISCO RODRÍGUEZ

CONTENTS

ACKNOWLEDGEMENTS

Support for the conference on "Chicana Creativity and Criticism: Charting New Frontiers in American Literature," held April 22, 1987, at the University of California, Irvine, came from various sources. We want to thank all those individuals and institutions that made the event a success. Without their belief in the importance and significance of our project, the present study would not have been possible. Our sincere thanks go, as well, to the Chicano/Latino Colloquium Series; Campus Lectures; Terence D. Parsons, Dean of Humanities; Carla Espinoza, Affirmative Action Office; to Leslie Millard, Women's Resource Center; Julian Palley, Department of Spanish and Portuguese; Eloy Rodríguez, Director of International Chicano Studies Center; Jaime Rodríguez, Director Mexico/ Chicano Focus Research Program; Juliet MacCannell, Director of Women's Studies Program; Graduate Students Association; Robert Garfias, Dean of Fine Arts, Susana Cannet, and to Sylam and Felix Rodríguez for clerical assistance.

Our deepest appreciation go to the creative writers Lorna Dee Cervantes, Lucha Corpi, Evangelina Vigil and Denise Chávez for their outstanding dramatic performances, and to the critics Tey Diana Rebolledo, Julián Olivares, Yvonne Yarbro-Bejarano and Norma Alarcón for their perceptive essays. Without these talented individuals, the conference would not have been possible.

Finally, we are grateful to the Mexico/Chicano Program for sponsoring the conference proceedings publication and SCR-43 funding for research assistance.

PREFACE

Not since 1982 had the University of California at Irvine hosted such a fine gathering of Chicana/o writers and critics. At that time we were making history by being the first major University to sponsor a national conference on Mexican American women writers and thus recognize the creative efforts and the groundbreaking contributions Chicanas are making in literary circles, particularly in poetry and short fiction. The fruits of that symposium were harvested in a collection of articles entitled *Beyond Stereotypes: A Critical Analysis of Chicana Literature* (1985).

The present volume celebrates the second major conference U.C. Irvine has hosted on Mexican American Women's Literature. It offers recent works of outstanding poets and prose writers as well as thoughtful critical analysis of various Chicana authors whose works have appeared in the present decade. It is our position that Chicana writers continue to offer some of the most exciting works in Chicano letters.

The present undertaking began modestly enough with Helena Viramontes' idea of hosting a reading session of one or two poets at U.C.I. The idea soon germinated into structuring a panel which would encompass a dialogue between critics and poets. The response to the original concept of bringing together critics and writers was extremely positive, and funding from various sources was generous. We decided to host a full-fledged conference on Chicana literature and publish the results of the symposium chaired by Helena María Viramontes and myself.

María Herrera-Sobek
University of California, Irvine

Introduction

❈   ❈   ❈   ❈

MARÍA HERRERA-SOBEK

The 1980s decade witnessed an explosion in the literary output of Chicana authors. The initial success of vanguard writers such as Alma Villanueva, Bernice Zamora, Lucha Corpi and Lorna Dee Cervantes in the late 1970s and early 1980s encouraged Chicano-oriented publishing houses to "risk" investing in Mexican American women writers.[1] The success of these initial ventures has been greatly instrumental in helping minority women get their works in print and in the market place where they can be made accessible to the reading public as well as to academic critics. The most active Chicano presses encouraging women writers in recent years are the Bilingual Review Press/Editorial Bilingüe and Arte Público Press (which has been the most aggressively involved).[2] The 1980s was a productive decade for Mexican American women writers.

The 1990s decade has proven to be an equally exciting period for Chicana writers. A new publishing era was initiated with Random House's publication of Sandra Cisneros' second work of fiction, *Woman Hollering Creek and Other Stories.* The success of the publication and the wide mainstream recognition it received opened up publication doors for other Chicana writers such as Ana Castillo's novel *So Far From God* (1993, W. W. Norton), Denise Chávez's *Face of an Angel* (1994, Farrar Straus Giroux), and Helena María Viramontes's *Under the Feet of Jesus* (1995, Dutton).

The essays and poetry of both Cherríe Moraga and Gloria Anzaldúa have become necessary and important frameworks in any serious discussion of feminisms. The new poetry of Lorna Dee Cervantes continues to shake our very foundations of what language can accomplish, as does the recent fiction of Demetria Martínez and Terri de la Peña. University presses are opening doors to other writers like Mary Helen Ponce and Lucha Corpi, and feminist presses like Third Woman Press, Kitchen Table, Aunt Lute continue making our work available. The outstanding work of these Chicanas (and those omitted only for lack of space) is forcing a space in American letters that has never existed before. This second edition of *Chicana Creativity and Criticism: Charting New Frontiers in American Literature* will continue to expand the parameters of Chicana literature as an integral part of our American literary landscape.[3]

Both the creative works as well as the critical essays are characterized by their innovations in form and content. New images of Mexican American women surface in Roberta Fernández' short story "Andrea." Equally innovative is Fernández' combination of the literary history of a genre in the fictive world displayed. The south Texas author incorporates a historical overview of Mexican American theater within her narrative. Denise Chávez expands the frontiers of Chicano literature by introducing a new genre: the *Novena Narrativas y Ofrendas Nuevomexicanas*. This work is a combination of theater, sculpture, folk belief and folk art. In addition, Chávez skillfully renders images of Mexican American women from various walks of life: the bag lady, the factory worker, the housewife, the store clerk, the sexually abused retarded child, the tough *pachuca*.

The life of the factory worker is also explored by Helen María Viramontes in her short story "Miss Clairol." I foresee the factory worker as a protagonist in Chicano/a literature becoming more and more prominent, since a great number of Mexican American women belong to this sector of American workers.[4] The Chicana protagonist working in factories may be as important a character in future Chicano literary works as the migrant worker has been in theater and the novel.[5]

Sheila Ortiz Taylor, on the other hand, provides us with bittersweet memories of family life as seen through the eyes of a precocious young woman. Chávez' contribution in poetry explores the often forbidden terrain of female sexuality and eroticism, while Lucha Corpi ventures into the world of magic realism. Evangelina Vigil departs from her brassy, sassy poetic persona to offer us a more introspective, reflective poet.

Chicano/a literary critics offer new perspectives and new challenges in the field of literary criticism. Diana Rebolledo argues for a return to the Chicano text and for discovering our own theoretical constructs. Rebolledo's article is a call for independence from white European and American literary theoreticians who are not acquainted with the Chicano experience. This lack of historical specificity and historical context make their theoretical postulates suspect when applied to Chicano creative works. Yvonne Yarbro-Bejarano, reiterates Rebolledo's position and perceives knowledge and immersion in the Chicana experience as vital for an authentic Chicana feminist critical approach.[6]

Norma Alarcón focuses on patriarchal society's engendering of Chicanas as "women" and their inferior position with regard to the symbolic contract. Alarcón views this asymmetrical relationship in the symbolic contract as an impelling force that drives Chicanas to explore their subjectivity. This self-reflexivity stimulates the creative process and yields literary works of art.

Julián Olivares offers a specific case study in his analysis of Sandra Cisneros' *The House on Mango Street* regarding the contradictions and problems in applying European literary theories (in this case Gaston Bachelard's theories expounded in his book *The Poetics of Space*) to a Chicana literary work.[7] My article "The Politics of Rape: Sexual Transgression in Chicana Fiction" contrasts the vectors of functionality versus aesthetics in Chicana literary constructs. It posits that Mexican American women's concern for political and social oppression are primary vectors structuring many of their works. This does not detract from the beauty of the work but in fact invigorates and transforms it into a powerful work of art.[8] The elitist conceptualization denigrating confessional, autobiographical and subjective literary works should be seriously questioned in post-modernist poetics and particularly in ethnic minority literature.[9]

The unifying thread linking both creative and critical works in this collection are the daring inroads into "new frontiers" which the authors make in their writings. The poets, short story authors and critics are all taking risks; they are expanding the boundaries of Chicana literature and literary criticism, offering new vistas and new possibilities. Their courage to tread new waters and not remain stagnated augurs well for the future of Chicano literature. This, in turn, opens up new dimensions for mainstream American literature, since it is through the constant infusion of new blood, new ideas, new visions and new perspectives that a national literature is able to continue vigorously flourishing. The recent explosions in Afro-American, Asian American, and American feminist literatures have invigorated and revived the American literary scene and challenged the institutionalized canon.[10] Chicana writers, likewise, are joining in and expanding the frontiers of Americas' *belle lettres*.

POETRY

Lorna Dee Cervantes' "Bird Ave" introduces the reader to the tough world of the Chicana adolescent living on the edge of the world in a barrio street. The title, with its play on words (bird = *ave*) and multiple connotations, reiterates Cervantes' particular predilection for these winged creatures (cf. *Emplumada,* 1983) in her poetry. Bird, of course, in England's street jargon means "girl" or what Americans call "chick." The "birds" on Bird Ave are tough, indeed. Cervantes invokes the late 1960s atmosphere through her clever incorporation of lines from rock-and-roll songs symbolic of the era, such as the hit from the English rock group the Rolling Stones "I Can't Get No Satisfaction," and the Diana Ross and the Supremes childlike, high-voiced refrain "Baby, Baby, ooo Baby." This intertextuality subtly provides a reference to a specific historical period.

The representation of tough, teen-age Chicanas walking the streets on hot summer days, challenging the world with their street talk, street walk and street cunning, strikes another blow to the image of the passive, timid Chicana.[11] This is another vision of Mexican American women far removed from "Nice-little-girls-who-go-to-church-on-Sundays-in-their-starched-white-dresses-to-worship-the-Virgin-Mary."

On the other hand, "Bird Ave" conjures up another stereotype—the streetwise *pachuca*. The poetic voice narrates the world of the alienated, gang-obsessed young woman who, in order to survive, teams up with others in similar circumstances and, instead of being "screwed," do the "screwing" themselves. The visual, shocking, attention-getting costume of the *pachuca*— "teased tough hair", "teased tight skirts"—proclaims membership in the school of hard knocks. The barrio streets are not a young lady's sorority house and initiation into this exclusive club requires good dosages of sweat, blood and violence:

> She had it then
> all total control
> banging my head
> on the blacktop for effect.

Cervantes cleverly juxtaposes and inverts, subverts, Establishment institutions through their deformed association with the dispossessed. Membership in exclusive private clubs requires an initiation: the protagonist of "Bird Ave" is initiated by having her head banged on the street's hard pavement. The metaphor for military, "brass," is incongruently juxtaposed with the three young girls in the poem: "beauty, brains and brass." This metonymic association reveals the paramilitary nature of the group at war with society. The streetwise Chicanas live in a jungle and they are the "model Rambos."

Likewise the Catholics' revered religious symbol of God, the Trinity, is parodied in its blasphemous association with the tough *pachucas*. "We were the trinity," the poetic voice brags. Finally the police are ridiculed by the threesome's appropriation of the police's motto "To protect and to serve," translating it into "We're here to serve." The reader recognizes full well that the three street-wise adolescents are really not here to render essential services but on the contrary to do harm or serve as drug dealers. Through this process of slogan transformation, the police are transposed (by association) into just another tough street club, albeit sponsored by the Establishment. Cat-eyes' insistence on *ethics* ("you gotta understand / about ethics"), the darling word of a hypocritical Establishment who in the eyes of the barrio youth is perceived as not having ethics at all, is repossessed by the ghetto gang members. Ethics to barrio gangs are essential to their survival. They must have ethics, a special kind of ethics, a barrio honor code, which permits the gang members to trust only each other.

Cat-eyes, Mousie and Flaca Fea are rejects of society. They seek, therefore, to reintegrate themselves into their own space, reinventing themselves from the barrio jetsam that an uncaring society refuses to acknowledge and accept. Flowering in the midst of a sterile world, the young tough-as-nails girls refuse to capitulate, to fade, disintegrate into nothingness. They assert their right to be, to exist and, not wishing to display any vulnerability, they hide their wounds in macho body language and a rough exterior. The streets are mean and so are Cat Eyes, Mousie and Flaca Fea who have divested themselves of their humanity and welded their identity into ubiquitous urban animal survivors: cats and mice. The lessons learned off the streets have taught them well; nothing can equal the barrio's no-nonsense survival skills.

> it was tough
> to know it all
> and we haven't
> learned anything
> since

The connection between ghetto streets as an educational institution is rendered through the initiation-graduation rite of having your head banged against the concrete:

> grins and made
> lemon crap

> out of my cheeks
> before letting me up
> all righteous rage
> sin class ni pomp
> and circumstance [12]

The carefully cultivated impregnable exterior of the poetic persona and her friends hides the encoded social protest and the indictment against a society that is a knowing accomplice in the molding of such characters as Cat-eyes, Mousie and Flaca Fea.

Equally astute in depicting the world of the dispossessed is the poem "Astro-no-mía" which by its very title denotes the unprivileged position of the poetic voice that is expressed in the plural communal "we" — the Chicanas. "Astro-no-mía" encompasses the wrenching realization that for Chicanas this Earth is not theirs ("Astro-no-mía"="Planet-not-mine"). The word, of course, derives from *astronomía*=astronomy, the science of astronomy. The title, therefore, is invested with several connotations: the planet earth and the poverty-stricken Chicanas who, living in the midst of plenty, do not own any part of it. It also connotes the academic discipline of the physical sciences — chemistry, physics, mathematics, etc. — which are represented by the sinecdoque "astronomy." Chicanas/os have historically been prevented from "owning," from acquiring knowledge in the sciences through a substandard educational system.[13] A sisterly, feminist connection is made via the association of the Chicanas who, kept in inferior schools, feel: "The closest we ever got to Science / was the stars" and the Greek Goddesses

> Diana, Juno, Pleides las siete:
> hermanas, daughter, captives
> of Zeus, and the children, the children
> changed into trees, bears, scared into stars.

These Greek goddesses parallel present day Chicanas, since they too were victims of patriarchal law represented by the all powerful archetypal patriarch, the Greek God Zeus.[14] Thus the only avenue by which Chicanas could reach the stars was through psychological states of mind: dreaming, the imagination, reveries, desire. However, reality, represented by a mother's voice, rudely interrupts the dreaming and "shoots" them down from a lofty imagination:

> Our mothers would call, the fathers
> of fate, heavy like mercury, would trash
> our stomachs into our wombs. Cold
> We'd rollercoaster back down to the earth

Patriarchal law, the rule of man, is hard to escape. Orion, man, aims his shaft "shooting his shaft into my lit house from the bow," and the poetic voiced is forced to obediently reply to the command "y ya voy"="I go now" or "I am coming." Cervantes cleverly continues to display her splendid verbal dexterity in the last line "¿y yo? Hay bow. Y ya voy" ("And me? I bow. And I go.")

The strong-fisted series of poems "Bananas" (I–V) strikes at our political consciousness and wakes us up to the reality of poverty, political repression, racism and other important social issues. Through the title "Bananas" the author cleverly links such diametrically different populations, both ethnically and geographically speaking, as Estonians and Chicano/Latin Americans. While "Bananas I" centers its themes on the scarcity of food (and by extension, the drabness of life and the yearning for some exotic ray of light, for some color to brighten their lives), "Banana II" zeroes in on the political and economic oppression and exploitation of the Latin Americans who do have an "exotic" environment and "exotic" life styles. The United Fruit Company train takes bananas out of the South and Central American countries but leaves in its wake death and abject poverty. The Colombian massacres are invoked as are the epidemics, the starvation of the Indians and peasants in the land of exotic and plentiful produce. The mestizo poor serve only as fertilizers for the high yielding fields.

In "Banana III" the linkage becomes closer between addressee and poetic voice. The poem is structured through the use of the epistolary mode—a letter to I (Indrek of "Bananas I"). Here racism is highlighted. The ethnicity of the poetic voice is underscored and the "strangers in their own land" feeling overpowers the narrator as she is asked "Where are you from?"

Concerns related to ecological issues are expressed. The use of pesticides, a primary issue with Mexican American farmworkers, is explicitly discussed and underscored.

The raping of the environment dominates "Bananas IV." Here the issue is not bananas but the mining of uranium, a primary element in nuclear energy and nuclear weapons. Nevertheless, just as the harvesting of bananas brought poverty, death and hardships to the Indian and mestizo campesinos of South and Central America, the mining of Uranium in Big Mountain (Colorado?) rains destruction and suffering on the Native Americans in the western part of the United States. The local vegetation is destroyed as are the sheep, and Native Americans are left without their major economic means of survival.

"Bananas V" returns to the stark reality of the previously Russian occupied northern country, Estonia, and linkage again is weaved through the oppression of peoples. The "exiles in their own homeland" are not Chicanos in the United States or Native Americans as had been intimated in the other poems but are Estonians. Unemployment sears the soul—no-work-no-food is the mantra by which they live and die. Non-stop hunger is their lifestyle.

Toward the closure of the poem, the poetic voice returns to ecological issues. Nuclear power, nuclear weapons, nuclear testing bring forth issues of radiation and the by-products that harm the ecological systems of the world. In particular harm is wrought upon humans, be it cancerous tumors in adults or birth defects in infants. The poetic voice finds the answer in poetry. Poetry feeds the soul and ultimately is the one sustenance humans cannot do without.

Taking a different tack from the "Bananas" poems, Cervantes approaches the subject of giving birth from a personal, autobiographical mode in her poem "First Beating." Some Chicana poets have used the metaphor of birthing, as in "birthing" themselves or "birthing" a poem, effectively in their writings. Alma Villanueva and Cervantes herself have utilized this trope in the past. Previously, in her poetry collection *Emplumada* (1983), Cervantes had written a poem related to the "birthing" of self as a metaphor for the process of maturation and growing stronger. In "First Beating," the poem included in this collection, she returns to the birthing metaphor but this time it is a paean to literally giving birth to a baby. The poetic voice views the birthing of her baby as a miracle. The strength and power of the infant amazes the poet, who marvels at the miracle of birth and development.

The poetic persona is particularly astonished at the strength and energy of the new life. This new life had to struggle through all sorts of barriers in order to make it through. The poet admires the new life that she perceives as having had to come up from an old life, a bitter, lost life (mainly the mother's). The new life brings a sense of hope and strength to the old life (the mother) and makes an identification and linkage between the new and the old life. This identification brings hope and optimism for a better future.

Motherhood, then, is perceived as a creative process and equated with writing poetry, with being born again.

. . . .

Lucha Corpi's "Romance Negro" ("Dark Romance") was her personal response to the article "The Politics of Rape: Sexual Transgression in Chicana Fiction." The study was read at the conference and elicited a strong emotional response.[15] Corpi, for instance, had not intended to read this particular poem from her previously published collection *Palabras de Mediodía/Noon Words* but, because the thematic material covered in the poem coincided with the "Rape" article, she felt compelled to include it during the poetry recital session and in the anthology as well.

"Romance Negro" narrates the sexual violation of a young woman who in despair hangs herself from an orange tree, where the orange tree and the non-present flower, the *azahar* or orange blossom, symbolize the woman's frustrated future wedded life.[16] The poem is a *tour de force* in its juxtaposition of sensuality and eroticism with the negative vectors of violence and brute masculine force which destroy a budding, beautiful life. The images and metaphors, creating an atmosphere found in the *romances* of García Lorca, invoke the exotic sensualness of a tropical climate: *vainilla* (vanilla), *caña* (sugarcane), *canela* (cinnamon), *cacao* (chocolate), etc. Corpi elaborates a strong linkage between woman and nature by applying the above imagery to the young woman, Guadalupe, who is luxuriously bathing in the afternoon sun in the river just before the violation occurs. The sensualness and relaxed atmosphere contrast sharply with the male principle which suddenly and unexpectedly intrudes. The peaceful connection between woman and nature is brutally severed through the violent force ravishing the woman:

> Y en un instante arrrancó la flor
> Estrujó la leche hasta cambiarla en sangre
> (And on the instant cut the flower
> Wrung blood from the milk)

A patriarchal order is established and reaffirmed in the father's acceptance of a "fine mare" in exchange for his daughter's violation. The young woman's response to her powerlessness in this patriarchal system is to commit suicide by hanging herself from her father's orange tree.

A sense of futility and inevitability pervades the poem. It is a pessimistic statement about the impossibility of breaking the chains of oppression enslaving women. However, Corpi posits a challenge to the reader to become involved in effecting a change in the current state of affairs where rape is committed with impunity by males and with the tacit approval of other males. The author structures the challenge through the protagonist's final demise, for it is impossible to leave the reader untouched when reading the lines:

> Y Guadalupe . . . Guadalupe colgó
> su vida del naranjo del huerto
> y se quedó muy quieta allí
> con los ojos al río abiertos
> (And Guadalupe . . . Guadalupe hung her life
> from the orange tree in the orchard,
> and stayed there quietly,
> her eyes open to the river.)

Guadalupe's hauntingly opened eyes point to the scene of the crime, to the dastardly deed left unpunished. The young woman's tragic death is a more powerful call to arms than strident rhetoric could ever be: It is very difficult, once having read the poem, to ever forget Guadalupe's accusing dead eyes.

In a recent interview with Mireya Pérez-Erdeli, Lucha Corpi confides her extreme psychological and spiritual need to write poetry. After a two-year hiatus from her creative writing, she declared:

> El silencio poético de dos años casi me mata y despés volvió otra voz muy diferente a la de *Palabras* (la primera colección). Es una voz más sombría. En *Palabras* hay mucha luz y hay mucho color y hay muchos contrastes. Es poesía de sentidos, es sensual. En *Ciudad en la niebla,* que es el siguiente que escribí, son los elementos del invierno, la poesía es sombría. Es dura. Es una voz distante. Es una voz que está activamente participando en lo que ve, y lo que siente y lo que esta a su alrededor.[17]

Indeed, Lucha Corpi's seven new poems included here are evidence of an intellectual abstractness much more pronounced than in her earlier work. Their imagery can be classified as bordering on, if not directly partaking of, the magic realism mode so prevalent in Latin American writers.

Lucha Corpi, a Mexicana/Chicana from Jaltipán, Veracruz, received a solid education in Mexico and thus is perfectly at home in the Spanish language. Corpi, of course, is bilingual and does write some of her creative work in English. One of Corpi's major contributions to Chicana poetry is to insist (by her actions) that Spanish is part of our literary cultural heritage and we should never forget it. This is indeed a strong political stance, since in our English-dominant country it is difficult, if not impossible, to publish in other languages. As a poet wishing to communicate, therefore, she is taking a risk in challenging the English-speaking world with her Spanish-written poetry.

Seen in the above light, Lucha's poetry makes a strong political statement. However Lucha may not even be conscious of the political stance she is assuming by merely writing in Spanish. Her intellectual honesty impels her to write from the heart and, if Spanish is the communicative code that surfaces, so be it. Her internal need to write supersedes all other external factors. Fortunately for the reader, this particular stance has produced some of the most outstanding, beautifully constructed poetry written in Spanish this side of the border. Lucha's grasp and dexterity of the Cervantine tongue equals, if not supersedes, some of the best poets in Latin America.

The collection published in this study is introspective, subjective and impregnated with internal tension. It is the expression of an anguished soul who suffers the pangs of a highly developed intellectual mind in search of answers to an existential angst and, not apprehending them, reverts to a bittersweet melancholy. At the center of Lucha's poetry is the eternal conflict between man versus man and man versus woman. Corpi thematizes the futility of seeking and finding harmony with the Other. With steely implacability the poetic voice dissects relationships only to discover pain and disillusion. Lucha's poems end in despair ("Invernario") or stoic resignation ("Recuerdo íntimo"). Her liberal, progressive concern for the human condition is evident in "Indocumentada angustia" and "Sonata a dos voces." The last two poems in the collection "Canción de invierno" and "Llueve" reflect on the theme of death and its inescapability. The motif of the constantly falling rain is the thread that unites the seven poems.

Corpi's first poem "Invernario" projects a paradoxical universe of abstract images with sensual, down-to-earth elements. The first stanza commences with a set of disembodied eyes reflecting the turbulent discharge of violent natural phenomena — a rain storm approaching. In the mirror-like surface of these cold, surrealistic, penetrating eyes, the cobbled-stone streets as well as the sensual greenery of the wheat fields still humid from the night rain are faithfully reflected. Other elements found in a small rural Mexican town — white-washed houses, an old peasant with violin in hand, etc. — are encompassed in the all-seeing eyes.

The second stanza changes from the third person narrator to the first person, and we find that the poetic persona too is included in the all-powerful reflecting gaze. However, upon perceiving her reflection, the poetic voice is surprised to see that her reflected self is not realistic but has been fragmented into a thousand pieces "como quien mira en el mar / su imagen fragmentada / por la corriente indómita." The poetic voice realizes that seeing herself in the gaze of the Other has been lethal, for she has been transformed from her initial humanity into the natural inanimate world of

en coral

y sombra

y pez

en roca

y mineral fosforescente.

The metaphor "coral" conjures a vision of red, that is, blood—suffering. Coral is an inert element belonging to the natural world. The poetic persona first metamorphosed from human to coral is further decomposed to *sombra* (shadow)—a mere illusion of what she used to be as a human being. Although the third element transforms the poetic persona back to the animate world, fish, this can be perceived as another metaphor for nothingness since the illusiveness of the fish swimming in water renders their corporeality difficult to observe. The next line, nevertheless, retransforms the persona from a live entity back into the mineral world of the rock. The final line completely annihilates even this corporeality by converting her merely into a bright evanescent light: "mineral fosforescente."

The dehumanizing experience leaves the poetic voice and her desire for human contact imprisoned in a world of suffering and silence "entre el demiángulo del ojo / y el origen del cantar." The severity of this suffering and unsatisfied desire is rendered through the shocking and unsettling image of "como un suicida impenitente / me acecha mi deseo / por sus brazos." The bittersweet desire of self-annihilation is perceived through the metaphor of the "suicida impenitente."

If "Invernario" evinces an alienated self whose only escape from this torturous existence is to self-destruct, we encounter a more harmonious self in "Recuerdo íntimo." In this poem the poetic voice narrates in the first person singular an anecdote from the past. In a bittersweet, melancholic tone stimulated into the recall mode by the rainy weather, the poetic "I" reminisces about a similar rainy day in the past. The narrator describes how the three of them—the cat Finnigan, the baby and the poetic persona—immersed themselves in the warm comforting water of the bath tub—an urban Noah's Ark —and waited out the storm, thus escaping annihilation. Unbearable memories creep into the poetic consciousness. The poet, however, refuses to yield and takes comfort in the purring of the cat and the smile of her two-year-old child: "Es todo lo que necesito recordar."

"Fuga" depicts a poetic persona who narrates the process of escaping from an imprisoned state to a more liberated one. The narrating voice describes her lack of freedom, both physical and verbal, through the metaphors "muro"=heavy, thick walls, and "silencio"=silence, voicelessness. Flight is perceived as initiating in her aural sense, the ear (*oído*) since the flutterings of wings—again a metaphor for freedom—and the murmuring of falling rain—a metaphor for "outside"—beacon the protagonist to flee. The transformation of the poetic persona from prisoner to free spirit is phoenix-like, for the flight to freedom is structured through the metaphor of fire:

> me decidí por el fuego
> y en su promesa de agostos oportunos
> mi corazón ardió
> una noche de invierno.[18]

The imprisoned poetic voice fantasizing a future alive with warmth and promise severs the cold shackles that imprison her and flees.

The second stanza introduces an interlocutor "you" to whom the poetic voice directs her ire. The reader now realizes it was a lover who through his caresses imprisoned the protagonist. Stanzas 2–7 incorporate powerful action verbs in the first person preterit to structure the violent action the poetic person had to undertake in order to free herself: "Crucé," "lancé," "caufericé," "borré," "clausuré." These verbs depict actions of leaving and discarding. Included is the verb *caufericé* which is a medical term and has resonances of pain, lacerations and wounds. The finality of the actions are structured through the word *clausuré* (closed): "y clausuré las puertas de la historia / para no recordar más tu nombre ni mi nombre." The stanza conveys the superhuman effort to erase and forever forget the past, the lover's name and even her "self" that was part of that lover.

As the narrator escapes—*afuera*—she finds an unexpected freedom and discovers her poetic voice. The motif of gaining knowledge through suffering is encoded in the lines, "Afuera / en el invierno de los dioses / con mano temblorosa destapé el silencio." The narrator perceives poets as Gods who in their "winter"—winter being a metonym for extreme suffering (as for example winter of our discontent)—create poetry. Here then in the temporal space of the Winter of the Gods the poet discovers her creativity: she dares to "uncover" with "tremulous" hand the "silence" reigning tyrannically over her before her flight. Witchlike, the poetic voice discovers her powers and the seeds of her poetic fire burst out over her body, her temples (mind), her "pechos" (heart=emotions, feelings) and fingers (instruments for structuring the written word).[19] Explosively, poetry bursts forth through the images of "sangre" (blood=life), "trigo"=fertility, "luz de junio" (summer light). The protagonist continues to describe the poetic universe newly found. This vibrant, vital universe is populated with beautifully constructed images garnered from the cosmos (the night, the stars, the evening light), human experience ("dolor / y canto"), biological miracles ("espiga," "pez dorado"), and marine life from whence we all came ("escama," "espuma," "sal").

Closure is achieved through the image of a prehistoric marine animal, the whale, who, impregnated with knowledge due to her longevity, announces —even though with melancholic voice—the beauty of a future harmonious poetic life: "anunciando la amplitud ecuánime / de un equinoccio boreal."

In "Indocumentada angustia" Lucha Corpi denounces the destructiveness and rapacious nature of urban industrialized society and the plight of the undocumented worker exploited by that society. The "rascacielos" (skyscraper) is a metonym for industrialized western civilization. Industrialized society in turn is described as insatiable harpies destroying the cosmos: eating stars, the moon, poisoning the wind. Technological society is a destroyer of dreams, of the imagination, of fantasy. The wind imprisoned in this man-made jail (the skyscrapers) becomes enraged and strikes out at the flowers destroying them, thereby introducing even more violence in the cosmos. The wind's destructive force can only be soothed by the falling rain.

As the falling rain soothes the angry wind, the fog emerges pregnant with life (migratory birds), and through its misty sponginess cushions the pain, the sufferings of the partly hidden (in the fog's mist) undocumented worker. The sad plight of the Mexican migratory worker is rendered in the poem's closure:

> acallando la indocumentada angustia
> del ilegal en su propia tierra,
> hundiendo sus dedos en la luna
> y en la lejanía sin puertos
> ni faros.

The Mexican immigrant, who once owned this land, now can only dream of achieving a better life ("hundiendo sus dedos en la luna," the poetic phrase having a double valence in meaning: through hard work and through his dreams of a better life). There is really no hope for ending the sufferings of the migrant worker. Dispossessed, the migrant is a perpetual pilgrim in search of his own land, set adrift without beacons or ports. Although Corpi has stated in an interview that

> no escribo poesía política y por esa razón siempre estoy al margen y además escribo poesía en español y por esa razón siempre estoy al margen de la literatura chicana. Estoy en las orillas. Es decir si tú le dices a alguien que vas a tener una conferencia y vas a invitar a escritores chicanos, te aseguro que en el 90% de los casos no piensan en mi para invitarme. Piensan en Lorna Dee Cervantes, Alma Villanueva, Bernice Zamora, en otras escritoras. Porque son escritoras que llevan como centro de su trabajo el barrio. Yo no me crié en un barrio—es otra vez falsificar la experiencia, la existencia. Para mí eso sería oportunista, tratar de pasar y de escribir así para poder ser parte de ese mundo. Yo no nací, no crecí en el barrio y si empiezo a falsificar mi experiencia, empiezo a falsificar todo.[20]

"Indocumentada angustia" demonstrates Corpi's sensitivity toward the sufferings of *mexicanos* in the United States. It should be pointed out that the poem, although belonging to the social protest genre, is infused with beauty and poetic sensibility and underscores that politics and poetics are not mutually exclusive but can be profitable partners in beautifully conveying a specific message.

Webster's dictionary describes the sonata as a musical composition "in three or four movements contrasted in rhythm and mood but related in tonality and having unity of sentiment and style." Lucha Corpi in her poem "Sonata a dos voces" utilizes the structure of the sonata to render a poetic composition in two "movements": a "Largo Frenético" and an "Adagio." Part one describes the frantic rush of urban life. Time is dissolved and annihilated in the mad rush to survive the urban jungle.

> Se congregan parvadas de semanas
> domingos llenos de números
> jueves quiméricos
> en los que el tiempo
> se traiciona a sí mismo
> y regresa a la hora cero.

The irony of this mad rush to annihilate time is delineated through the pedestrian tasks the poetic voice is forced to undertake: meetings, messages, groceries, dirty clothes, etc.

The poetic persona continues enumerating the infinite number of everyday tasks demanded in our daily lives. However, she begins with such pedestrian activities as stitching a shirt and slowly enters the poetic world through the metaphor "deshilar ausencias." Here the domestic task of sewing *deshilar,* undoing stitches, is applied to undoing the memory of an absent loved one. The image of the absent loved one is reiterated in the line "y el amigo partió sin decir palabra." The poetic voice becomes progressively more melancholic and closes the first "movement" with a nostalgic bittersweet tone: "cuando hubo que plantar jacintos / en las tumbas de nuestros muertos."

The "Largo Frenético" describes the conditions that have left the poetic persona voiceless, inarticulate, without the ability to write poetry: "y la palabra queda entrelabios / como un débil aroma a jazmines muertos." A linkage is made here between the flowers planted at the tomb of the dead and the dead voice exhaling only the aroma of "jazmines muertos." The poetic persona, however, realizes that life continues, and the image of a young girl, perhaps the poet herself in her father's house, dreams of a future life traveling around the world. The continuation of life, in spite of the violence surrounding it, is rendered in the image of the "limonero" which "ha dado flor y fruto / entre mil balas de lluvia / y la violencia del viento." This stanza foreshadows the closure of the poem and the message of social protest encoded in it. The final stanza delivers the political message that

> en El Salvador los niños mueren de prisa
> y en Africa la sangre se seca lenta
> y no hay palabra que pueda detener
> el largo beso de sombras de la muerte

The only salvation left for humanity, the only solution to the senseless killings in our troubled globe is to love each other.

For the narrator poetic creativity, the poetic voice, is silenced by both the inanities of life (washing dirty clothes, answering memos, attending endless meetings) and the bloody violence raining on all parts of the planet. Both are deadly to the poets desire to create, to sing songs of life.

"Canción de Invierno" is an elegiac poem dedicated to Magdalena Mora, a graduate student at the University of California, Los Angeles. Mora was extremely active in social issues concerning Chicanos. Her premature death

was a blow to the Chicano activist community. Corpi in "Canción de In-
vierno" thematizes the transitoriness of life: here today, gone tomorrow. The
Hispanic model for this poem is the elegy written by Jorge Manrique, El
Marqués de Santillana (1440–1479), in "Coplas por la muerte de su padre."
Analogous to the Marqués de Santillana's poem, Corpi elucidates on the
"fugacidad de la vida":

> En un abrir
> y cerrar de ojos
> lleno
> de magia
> relojes
> y sueños viejos
> llega el invierno:

Life's ultimate destiny is death. The constant transformations of energy
yield the never-ending cycle of life-death-life-death. The thermodynamics of
the universe stimulate continuous chemical reactions and transformations.
The poet intuits this basic law of physics:

> Nada hay fijo ni perenne
> ni la lluvia
> ni la semilla
> ni tú
> ni yo
> ni nuestro dolor
> en este mundo que sangra

The state of continuous flux in the universe, the unfathomable nature of
these mysterious never-ending transformations produces unbounded anxiety
and angst in the poetic voice. And the only weapon the poet has at her dis-
posal to combat complete annihilation is the poem itself: "venciendo la furia
del olvido verso a verso."

Corpi's last poem "Llueve" returns to the motif of the continuously falling winter rains utilized to structure the infinite melancholy and sadness the
poetic voice is experiencing. The uninterrupted falling rain is analogous to
the falling tears the poetic voice seems to be shedding. The sentient world
outside is affected by the incessant rain. A nexus between the poet's past and
the insect world is structured in the fourth stanza:

> Las hormigas
> desterradas de sus nidos
> cargan sus muertos
> hasta que ellas mismas
> caen bajo el peso
> en una tina de baño
> o en la alacena
> llena de miel y de pan

The poet and the ants have been exiled from their homes, from paradise. The flood annihilates many of these ants and their compatriots unselfishly carry the dead ants with them only to perish under the weight of the dead burden.

The poet wishes for a spark of life to interrupt the gray, mist of the falling rain. But the electrical spark fails to materialize and only the rain continues in its endless downpour. The poetic persona intuits that the time is not yet ripe for a transformation:

> mas solo llueve
> Lluvia fina
> Lluvia mansa
> Lluvia infinita
> No es tiempo, no es tiempo

Evangelina Vigil's six poems evince a new introspection and preoccupation with both time and the creative process. Her first poem in this series "the parting" is an elegy; embedded in the poem, however, are two central concerns: the inability to decipher the meaning of life through nature's primal language—"we listened to the cricket's urgent song / a message we tried to decipher / it eluded us"—and the circularity of time.[21] The poem situates the action at wintertime. Summer's bountiful days of fertile sunshine turn to autumn and the harvesting of the fruits of summer. The inception of winter introduces the final falling of the last green leaf, and death and desolation predominate in a winter landscape bereft of green plants and flowers, bereft of life.

The motif of the cricket (which in American popular lore is a lucky omen) will be a constant element reiterated in her other poems. The cricket is presented here as the bearer of nature's special message. The poetic persona, however, is unable to decode this "urgent song." Nevertheless, the messenger is able to plant the seed and induce a state of somnolence, of sleep. And it is in this dream state that the poetic persona and the other mourners become more receptive to nature's specific message; as the mourners sink into a sleep stupor, they are immediately awakened by the fierce wind that insistently encircles the house and demands to be led back to life: "rattling windows / shaking the screens / like spirits, wanting in." Here the connection between the dearly departed, nature and those in mourning is cleverly structured through the linkage between the insistent personified wind rattling and shaking the windows and screens, and the "spirits" who refuse to disappear. They want to join the living inside the house.

The man-made artifacts, the windows, impede the spirits' entrance but nevertheless allow the mourners to decipher, to some extent, nature's encoded message. The branches of the young trees struggling persistently to survive the winter wind outside the grievers' window indicate that springtime will eventually follow. This realization of the circularity of time is expressed in the last two lines of the stanza: "time's simultaneous arrival / and departure."

Having grasped nature's message of time's "eternal return," the mourners' can finally accept the beloved's death and can let go of him/her ("despedir"="soltar").[22] The ritual parting is enacted in the Spanish language with a heartfelt *despedida* ("despedida"="acompañar por cortesía al que se va a marchar.") The Spanish formula of the *despedida*—"adiós, querido amigo"—is augmented with the acknowledgement that this separation is not forever, for we shall all eventually follow those same footsteps into infinity—"nos vemos en el infinito," the poet intones.

The second poem in this series, "in its absence," reiterates the theme of the "eternal return" and time's circularity. Here the two themes of time's circular nature and the creative process are conflated, since the central concern of the poetic voice is structured in the disquieting question of "If nothing new exists under the sun what is left for me [the poet] to create?"

The despair of lacking inspiration to create new "songs" is reiterated in "the giving." "No longer / no longer can I—the poetic voice insists—think it"; the poem is gone, words elude the poet. The vacuum created in the poetic mind is perceived to be related to the demands of every day living.[23] The poet finds this overwhelming, time-consuming, deadening. Those who are different from the mass of humanity are forced to conform. The price the poet pays for fitting in, for conforming, is the loss of poetic inspiration.

Therefore, the frustrated narrator is left with the bitter realization that "it's those who think like most / who excel."

Again in "spillage" the theme of poetic ennui, of the inability to write, is structured through the artifacts utilized in writing. The pen is perceived as static, cold, dead: "pen lies cold." Other writing utensils frustrate the poetic persona: "ink bottle sits" inactive; unenergized, the bottle of ink is personified and depicted as "sitting" unproductively. The next line, however, is even more despairing for the ink that is made to flow through the writers creative hand has spilled stupidly on the waiting blank page. The "indigo blotches" connote painful, purple "moretones" (from *morado*—purple) on the body. The poet suffers from writer's block and lack of inspiration. Time, however, is relentless "and tomorrow arrives / before daybreak / and yesterday's words / can never be retrieved." Time stops for no one and each day of unproductiveness in the artistic realm can never be recuperated. The poetic persona is aware of the terrible loss: "a sigh of realization / is worth an eternity." Paradoxically, it is precisely this writer's block which led to the construction of the poem.

The absence of the creative voice in "spillage" contrasts sharply with the bountiful creativity and communicative skill of the natural kingdom in the poem, "equinox." In this poem we encounter once again the "cicadas" chattering in the month of August. The second stanza directs the reader to another animal domain full of activity and sensual pleasure: the trout in the river jumping and splashing, communicating their sense of being and beauty in their own natural code—body language.

A hint of the circularity of time is injected in the third stanza where the spectra of death and decay is introduced through the metaphor of parched summer grass. The reader recognizes that with "parched summer grass" autumn and winter are just around the corner. Nevertheless this negative desolate image is contrasted with the "tall pecan trees" that gracefully celebrate their being alive and their own creativity through a perfectly choreographed dance. The stately trees do not fear the advancing shadows (of death through winter) but beckon them, gracefully knowing that they (the pecan trees) too will return next spring with bountiful fruit.

The fourth stanza journeys to outer space to the confines of the powerful sun in whose furnace-like center is the source of all creative energy. Thus cicadas, trout and pecan trees are all joined together through the symbol of the archetypal creator, the sun. The fifth stanza introduces the human element in the form of a child—an embryonic adult. The child symbolizes the continuation of creative activity for it gently stirs "in the center of afternoon dreams." [24] The last stanza returns to the cicadas and their lazy chatter; the circle is finally complete.

The preoccupation with the "eternal return" surfaces anew in "hacia un invierno." Nature and time form the central axis structuring Vigil's poetic universe. The winter season is once more utilized as a metaphor for the end of a cycle, for death. The theme of poetic creativity conjoins nature and circular time to weave the triad informing Vigil's six poems.

In "hacia un invierno" the first stanza introduces the creative process of poetry as a painful ordeal that drains the poet emotionally and physically. Poetic creativity is perceived as emanating from internal wounds (both physical and emotional). The words are equated with blood which drips from internal lacerations. A metamorphosis ensues as the words "drip" becoming letters which hurt and wound, letters which cause emotional pain both in the writer and the reader: "ojos llorosos leyéndolas / agua salada borrándolas." The powerful cleansing function of water from the falling teardrops do not alleviate the emotional turmoil of the grieving soul who continues to suffer.

The poetic voice once again seeks to find the answer in nature; in the singing of the "chicharras," cicadas. The poet intuits that nature knows the meaning of life and, furthermore, that structured in the natural world is the encoded message which humans fail to decipher. Yet the singing *chicharras,* analogous to the poet, insist on singing the truth albeit to no avail.

The cosmic forces of nature, too, encode a message. The day bright and resplendent in the morning transmits its message like the *chicharras;* eventually, however, it too hides its face in the arms of the night, the *chicharra* eventually ceases to communicate its "urgent song" and becomes silent. And it is only the "grillo," cricket, whose solitary song accompanies the souls that contemplate the full moon hoping to find the answer beyond its silvery face.

Night-time and the starry sky bring hope to the poetic voice who in the darkness of the night nurtures a new illusion, a new hope. The poetic persona realizes the circularity of the process and wonders what it is that makes "hope spring eternal in the souls of humankind?"

. . . .

Several of Denise Chávez' poems in this collection are structured around the tension elicited by erotic passion and the easing of this tension through the cooling, soothing effect of water, often depicted as falling rain. In the poem "I Am Your Mary Magdalene," the poetic persona addresses an interlocutor who does not share the aroused, sexual desire the narrator is experiencing. The poetic "I" experiences feelings of guilt at her unbound, uncontrolled eroticism and compares herself to the archetypal repentant prostitute, the biblical Mary Magdalene. According to the New Testament, Mary Magdalene is the harlot who wishes to join Jesus' group. She bathes Jesus' feet with precious oils and when the Apostles try to reproach her for her wastefulness and for her pat wicked life, Jesus exonerates her and forgives her sins.[25] The poetic voice, by self-naming herself Mary Magdalene and expressing a desire to wash her beloved's feet, is paralleling the biblical prostitute and her tale of sin, forgiveness and reconciliation. The narrating "I" confesses her "transgressions":

> Often I have had to apologize
> to men
> for passions
> wouldn't know
> it would be this way

Female sexuality in our patriarchal culture has been denied, kept a dark secret up until recent times. It is only with the advent of the feminist movement that both men and women have acknowledged the extent and intensity of female sexuality. Chávez in her poem explores the problematics of female passion: men are often frightened by it; they do not like sexually aggressive women and are repulsed at women's openness of their sexual desires. Just as women have been socialized into hiding their intelligence, they have been equally socialized into repressing their sexual feelings.[26] A sexually active woman outside of marriage was stoned to death in biblical times.[27] During the Victorian period, even married women were supposed to dislike sex and saw the conjugal act merely as another wifely duty to be performed at her husband's request.[28] In our own century in the 1950s the dictum was: "Nice girls don't."

The poetic persona in "I Am Your Mary Magdalene" is punished for her sexuality and ardent passion: "Okay, banishment— / that high tower." In a repentant voice the protagonist seeks forgiveness in the closing stanza: "I am your Mary Magdalene / come let me wash your feet."

The tension between lover and poetic persona is discerned in other poems such as "Tears," "Door," "Chekhov Green Love," and "Two Butterflies." A sense of frustrated passion, unsatisfied or unrequited love permeate these poems. Often the falling rain in Chávez' poetry brings a release from the extreme tension the poetic persona is experiencing. The falling rain is analogous to the act of making love, particularly at the point of orgasm. After the falling rain, the poetic persona experiences calm and relaxation.

• • • • • • • • • •

Naomi Quiñónez's fierce critique of patriarchal culture is constructed through a series of poems that depict the alienated woman: the woman alienated from her body, from herself. Her works point to the construction of female identity from the perspective of the male gaze. The woman, who is not an "authentic" woman, but one defined and molded into a caricature by male dominated Madison Avenue's commercial advertisements. This definition is inscribed in the poem "Ultima II True Blue Eye Shadows of the Past." The poem focuses with hard, unflinching images on the emptiness of a woman's ritual each night as she unmasks, "unmakes" herself. The noun "teatro" (theater) is invoked to describe the falseness, the inauthenticity of her life. The props for making the "feminine" are enumerated in a scathing description of the nightly undressing ritual women undergo: "high heels stranded in the Bali girdle," "terror" at having forgotten one's lipstick at a bar.

The pain of being a woman, a woman jilted, scorned, left by a man is starkly depicted. The attempt to make this pain disappear through alcoholic bouts, the remembrance of unwanted pregnancies aborted but not erased from memory are chronicled in these uncompromising lyrics. The narrator rightly expresses the belief, "Somewhere there is a woman / dying to get out / past a burgundy rinsed head, / dying to leave the black leather / mini skirt at the scene / of someone else's crime." The lyrics hit below the belt and hold up a mirror to the face of a walking-wounded woman who, because of the dictates of a patriarchal culture, is still in the grasp of the woman-as-Barbie-Doll, or woman-as-playmate of the month, syndrome.

The poem "Ultima II True Blue Eye Shadows of the Past" presents a woman whose "authentic" self is "Dying to spread legs wide and leap / past Hanes Opaque pantyhose / and a hundred stumbling men." Somewhere inside this farce, this poor imitation of a woman, lies a poet "who loves passion / more than Ultima II True blue / eye shadows of the past." The narrator's voice seeks liberation for this woman who is imprisoned in the clutches of Madison Avenue's version of womanhood.

In her poem "The Photograph," Quiñónez continues the theme of unauthentic womanhood by presenting the travails of another protagonist,

Adriana, who is likewise trapped in the patriarchal signs of femininity; Adriana of the blustering petticoats, the orange lips, the French-twist, the tiny waist, the spiked heels, and so forth. The reader is again presented with the patriarchally constructed image of the feminine. The fact that Adriana— representative of womanhood—is alienated from herself is clearly stated in the poem: "Adriana of the / absent self / the misplaced alma / the searching wound." The protagonist is portrayed as part of the scenario used to fulfill male egos; as yet another object surrounding the male, who likewise being alienated himself, searches through material objects in order to find himself. The male here is also viewed as a "constructed man." The poetic voice intones: "Diego, the uncertain myth / of constructed men / the navigated ego / of place and placement."

The poem "The Photograph" is placed within the context of the 1950s (1958), a decade that witnessed the construction of womanhood in the image of the Marilyn Monroes, the Sophia Lorens, Jayne Mansfields, and other love goddesses who were unreal, unauthentic representations of womanhood. The construction of the feminine in a certain mold eventually led, through the efforts of feminists, to the scathing critique of this misrepresentation. The French feminist Simone de Bouvoir in her book *The Second Sex,* and later in the 1960s, the American feminist Betty Friedman in her manifesto *The Feminine Mystique* critiqued the false social construction of women.

The reality of women's lives and the fall from goddess to victim of spousal abuse and rape is chronicled in Quiñónez's next poem "Spousal Rape." The poem is structured around the metaphor of a meal—a meal consumed by the male animal (here represented by a lion) and where the main "dish" is the female. The female bears the brunt of male violence and uncontrolled sexual desire. Spousal rape, ignored for many years by the courts and society, nevertheless leaves its indelible mark on the body of the woman, a signature of male violence that is never erased. The poetic voice gives closure to the poem with precisely this knowledge: "How many meals they managed / no one is certain / only the teeth marks on her throat / will ever say."

In her poetry Quiñónez focuses not only on the victimized female but also presents an image of the archetypical strong female in "Ay que María Felix (or María was no Virgin)." In this poem the protagonist is a speaking subject. With a firm and strong sense of self, the poetic voice begins "I am María Felix." María Felix, as almost every Mexican and some Mexican Americans know is the Mexican movie star who represented the quintessential strong woman—the *hembra*—or counterpart to the macho. María Felix defines and represents herself—arrogant, with an attitude, not a victim but instead the victimizer herself since she is always breaking men's hearts. She is a "Mexican to the max / molcajete Mama / calling the shots / shooting from the hips." However this, too, is a *teatro,* as the poetic voice implies; she is an invention of patriarchal cinematic imagination for members of a male audience who like their women strong. "Que teatro / swishing feminine / to the backlash of salvation."

The poetic voice inquires as to the veracity or authenticity of this silver screen invention: "Is she me, or a channel 34 mirage?" Again, the construction of womanhood by patriarchal society is only an "illusion of sexuality." Nevertheless, the image of the strong woman, of one who can spit in a man's eye and leave is alluring to women. Although the poetic voice acknowledges that this representation of women is merely a cruel illusion, she nevertheless finds comfort in the image of a woman who is not a victim: "Ave María, / Y que viva la Mujer!" Long live woman!—woman with a capital M is contrasted with Ave María—the Virgin Mary—she who has been touted as a model of women's submission to a patriarchal order.

Quiñónez seeks to empower women through the poetic voice structured in the poem "La Diosa In Every Woman." This empowerment is sought via the rekindling of our relationship with precolumbian Aztec mother goddesses. The poem is structured through the metaphor of the altar—an altar conceptualized in the female form of an offering of prayer for enlightenment, growth, and personal power and not in the patriarchal conceptualization of the altar as a place to kill, shed blood—a site where sacrificial rites are made to a bloodthirsty male deity. In order to fully comprehend the poem, one has to be knowledgeable of the Aztec pantheon of female goddesses— Coyolxauhqui, Coatilicue, Malinalxochitli and Tonantzin.

Coyolxauhqui is the Goddess of the Moon who, with her four hundred brothers and sisters, the stars, sought to prevent the birth of Huitzilopochtli, God of War, by killing Coatlicue their mother. Coatlicue, on the other hand is the Goddess of Life and Death, representing the duality of life that encompasses both ends of the spectrum. Tonantzin is the nurturing mother earth. She is a protectress and loving mother who looks after her children. Quiñónez's poem then is an altar, a woman's altar where women can find their voice—a voice taken away by patriarchal society. The poetic voice rejects the pedestal where previously women had been enshrined and imprisoned into passivity and inarticulate silence: stone idols don't speak. The shattered woman on the street can identify with Coyolxauhqui, the dismembered

Aztec goddess and as such we, her female descendants, can reconfigure her, can make her whole again. With new knowledge women can seek unity and wholeness with themselves and with each other.

Likewise the women from Guatemala (or other Latin American countries) can identify with Coatlicue—the giver of life and death—for women indeed bring life to this world. Since Coatlicue is that entity in which opposites reside, in which conflict and resolution are encompassed within her nature (i.e. snakes—symbolic of regeneration, of life—and the skulls decorating her attire representing death), she is an excellent model for representing the duality of life. Gloria Anzaldúa, the Chicana feminist theoretician and poet, has found her to be a source of inspiration, of creativity.

Through the figure of Malinalxochitli one can find the power or strength to fight the battles encountered in our daily lives. The poetic voice suggests those downtrodden women oppressed by their daily exploitation in the work-place, for example, the seamstresses, can gain comfort, strength, and con-fidence through identification with the goddess Malinalxochitli. Tonantzin, on the other hand, is perceived as the source of fertility, of giving birth, but a birth not only of babies but of a new consciousness. The poetic voice finds inspiration for both men and women in these ancient goddesses. They represent a new beginning and not an end, for Quiñónez's altar is an altar of empowerment and not one of deadly sacrifice.

Quiñónez's poems chronicle women's daily struggle to give meaning to life. They reflect a search for authenticity, an authenticity that has been lost in the mire of patriarchal society with its emphasis on power over others and on destruction through its fascination with war.

．．．．．．．．．．

The much-touted 1980s christened and enshrined as the decade of the Hispanic proved illusory at best and a cruel hoax on an exploding ethnic population who thought they were at last emerging from the shadows of invisibility. The optimistic hope of acquiring equity in the economic, politi-cal, educational, and social spheres of American society were dashed with the opening of the 1990s decade. This decade is proving to be an era of anti-immigrant backlash with the introduction of Proposition 187 in Cali-fornia in 1994. Proposition 187 seeks to deny an education to undocumented children, non-emergency medical services to undocumented workers, and in general to restrict social services to undocumented workers (who are in fact taxpayers). A new proposition dubbed the Civil Rights Initiative seeks to abolish affirmative action programs in the state of California and is being presented to the voters at the next state election. At the national level Newt Gingrich and his Contract with America followers are seeking to introduce similar bills. A period of increasing mean-spiritedness toward the poor, the "foreign" looking, the Other, and all of those not fitting the conservative ideal of middle- and upper-class America has been unfolding in this decade.

The poets, always attuned to the spirit of the ages, have begun to express through their lyrics a sense of outrage and protest. Gloria Enedina Álvarez's short poems in her collection *La Excusa/The Excuse* explore themes of alienation, of love lost and found, of spiritual despair and philosophical searching. However, her later poems are grounded in the reality of social inequalities and injustices.

Álvarez's poems in *La Excusa/The Excuse* collection written at the inception of the 1990s evidence a preoccupation with language and with the metaphysical as is shown in "Acordeón" [Accordion]:

Estoy atrapada	I am caught
en un mundo de luz	in a world of light
Páginas ilimitadas se abren a mi	Boundless pages open up to me
La palabra escapa	The word escapes
después regresa, salta	then bounces back
Atrás cortinas vagas de pensamiento.	Behind vague curtains of thought

The mystery of language continues to pervade the poet's imagination in "Sin complicaciones" ["Without Complications"]. Here she ponders the paradox of language, which when uttered (in anger, hate, or scorn) can produce "ríos de silencio," rivers of silence.

The unfulfilled promise of language is critiqued in "Vuelvo y no recuerdo" ["I Return and I Don't Remember"]. The poem explores the optimistic seduction of words that promise to open channels of communication only to yield intolerable silences. Silence searches for "the word" to communicate with others. The Lacanian Symbolic Order, which seeks to make present that which is absent, is evident in these poems. The Symbolic Order does not yield that desired connection with the Other, and a sense of loneliness, alienation, of lack pervades the poem. The poet only knows "silence with its need to speak." The world of the Symbolic Order is unacceptable and leads the poetic voice to the imaginary world of dreams. The need to speak, to have a voice, to be able to articulate becomes psychologically unbearable and is somatically transposed to the body, which will experience pain. The knots in the tongue and the vocal cords will evidence themselves as knots in the body. The present is never verbally experienced but only "felt" through extra-linguistic modes such as "visions, dreams, admonitions, games, rites, lost words twisted by the distance and the noise." The poem explores the need to assert oneself and fiercely fights the fear of disappearing into nothingness. Diana Rebolledo in her seminal book *Women Singing in the Snow: A Cultural Analysis of Chicana Literature* (1995) elucidates:

> For many years Chicanas have been unable to write or to publish their writing if they did write. They were also working within a system in which was language denied them. Thus to be able to write meant they had to "seize the language" (Ostriker) and become the subjects of their own narrations, and not the objects. This implies an extraordinary measure of empowerment for those women who were supposed to stay at home, be good wives and mothers, and be caregivers: active within the domestic sphere but not the public one. To find language, then voice, then consciousness of self and to be able to insert themselves as subjects has been very difficult, particularly for minority women writers. (Rebolledo, 1995:x).

Álvarez's preoccupation with woman-as-speaking-subject continues to manifest itself in "Hueso de la noche" ["Bone of Night"]. And the image of being tongue-tied emerges again in "Deaf" in the startling line "Your tongue is tied to the bedpost." The male, too, can be without the Word, inarticulate, as expressed in the poem "De viaje" ["On a Trip"] and in "The Day It Began" ["El día que inició"] where she exhorts her male interlocutor to

> Accept its commitment
> To speak to act
> Take the Word
> Take your Word
> Take it for your own sake.

Álvarez uses more metaphysical terms in her poem "Spark/Chispa." Here the poet explores the meaning of life. She poses a series of beautifully crafted rhetorical questions to an invisible interlocutor regarding the meaning of reality. She does this by juxtaposing spiritual, poetic images against an incredibly beautiful natural landscape. Toward the closure of the poem she contrasts the physical reality of words, i.e. the materiality upon which they are based—the tongue, the lips, the palate, the air, with their spirituality.

The existential and metaphysical preoccupations of the early nineties yield to social concerns by 1993. Here Álvarez's poems evidence a preoccupation with events taking place in Latin America and the slaughter of innocents taking place there through senseless class and racial wars. Her poem "Fallen Comrade, There Is No Mourning You" is a commemorative paean to a Maya-Quiche woman. The poetic voice does not mourn the death of a valiant soldier-woman but intuits that a victory in death for the sacrifice will make "every daybreak fertile, / dressing the morning star with hope." The poet calls for solidarity on the part of Chicanos with the courageous Maya-Quiche Indians against their oppressors.

The desperation and hopelessness of urban life is explored in her poems "Still Dreams" and "Contrastes/Contrasts." The poet zeroes in on the blight of the urban landscape abandoned by the middle-class Euroamerican majority. The poor, the homeless, the addicts, the winos, the dispossessed, the children, the throw-away people contrast sharply with zones of urban development right in the middle of skid row. The poet brays at the injustice of it all.

Álvarez continues her cry against social injustice in her poem "Vende futuro" ["Sells the Future"] where her protest centers on the hardships of immigrant workers. In "Totem/La siempre firme" Álvarez returns to expound on the vicissitudes experienced by women whose lives are filled with pain, racism, sexism, and poverty. The title plays on the stereotype of the super-woman who is all things to all people. Beyond the stereotype, according to Álvarez, is a woman who suffers, who feels pain, who is humiliated beyond belief. The central image of the body beset by life's hard knocks conveys to perfection the pain suffered by Latina women in a world that exploits them unmercifully and takes them for granted.

··········

Alma E. Cervantes's poetry is raw, untamed, speaking from the heart of the barrio. Therein lies its force and red-hot sparks that fly from an "untamed" tongue, as Gloria Anzaldúa would put it, speaking volumes in which jab-like lines describe Chicana life on the other side of the tracks. The poems expound upon the violent "Piquetitos of Love," the jaded, worn-out dreams of jilted Chicanas and of love come and gone ("Had I Ironed Your Shirt"). The lot of the downtrodden Chicana is articulated in "Harta" while another group of downtrodden sisters is delineated in "A Toast." The hard-luck stories of winas (alcoholic women) barely surviving on the edge can be contrasted with those who make it in spite of overwhelming odds ("The Roots of Chicana Urban Planners"). Yet a glimmer of tenderness through the cracks of concrete-hard barrio life can be perceived in the light-hearted "Reflections of 'La Vieja,'" which is a poetic commentary on getting old together.

Cervantes's poetic tone changes in "In My Dreams" once again. Scholarly criticism in the future will divide Chicano/a writers in the 1990s as pre-Proposition 187 and post-Proposition 187. One writer, of course, can belong to both since many have been writing in the past decade. With the new social impetus of Proposition 187 however, they will no doubt address the political issues surrounding this legislation as Chicano/a poets tend to be very committed to issues of social justice and generally express this commitment through the lyrics of their poems.

PROSE

Denise Chávez informs us that the "*Novena Narrativas y Ofrendas Nuevomexicanas* was inspired by cultural traditions of cuentistas (storytellers), *santeros* and *ofrendas* (constructed and assembled collage mementos), especially popular during All Souls Day in the Southwest and in Latin America." Indeed, Chávez is charting new ground in offering this unique conceptualization of theater, folk art (sculpture), folk belief, and folk customs. The author elaborates that "the *Novena Narrativas* are not prayers, but introspective personal thoughts in monologue." Thus we have in this New Mexican writer's work nine characters: Isabel, the artist-narrator; Jesusita, storeowner and spinster; Esperanza, wife of a Vietnam veteran; Minda, foster child; Magdalena, mother of seven children; Tomasa, nursing home resident; Juana, factory employee; Pauline, Chicana teenager; and Corrine, a bag lady.

The first character, Isabel, introduces herself as an artist, a playwright, giving shape to the play which the audience is about to see. As she revises her play, she transforms herself into some of the characters that the artist-actress will portray. She then begins to arrange the props and to set up the altar, the *ofrenda*. Through her own character, Isabel voices the strong connection she feels between herself and other women. Isabel affirms that the lot of women is a hard one. She feels a vital thread running through womankind which helps sustain and nourish them spiritually. Reiterated in the monologue is the close relationship with a grandmother figure, her "gramita," manifesting the importance that the "abuelita" has in Chicana literature.[29]

The monologue concludes with Isabel's rush to get back to work and meet the deadline of the play that is about to be presented. Here Isabel dons the garments, assumes the posture and voice of the character about to be portrayed.

Described as a "mouse-like spinster," speaking with "high reedy voice with a certain lisp," Jesusita brings forth the image of the sad, unmarried small-town aging woman. Jesusita's life is centered around her work and the Church. The "tienda de abarrotes" she runs is as outdated and old as the spinster herself. The spinster's world is crumbling, decaying around her just as her candles are breaking from old age and neglect. A new generation is coming forth and Jesusita's only refuge is the Church. Of course Jesusita did have a suitor in her youth whom she could have married. However she turned him down (his ears were too small!). This is merely an excuse, for during the course of the monologue Jesusita inadvertently betrays her fear of men. The monologue is tinged with the tone of regret for missed opportunities.

Esperanza's monologue consists in praying for the welfare of others. Through the narrative of this, the audience is informed of the life of poor Chicanos in the barrios: the alcoholic sons and husbands, the drug addicts, the Vietnam veterans who returned from war mentally traumatized, the soldiers who go to war and never come back. Humor in the narrative surfaces in Esperanza's irreverent behavior toward the Madonna at the end of her monologue: "So if you'll excuse me, Virgencita, voy a comer. Con su permiso, mi Reina."

Possibly the most tragic of the nine characters depicted in the *Novena Narrativas* is seven-year-old Minda who is being sexually abused by her father. The mentally retarded child tells her story through the game of pretend with her doll, (therapists working with sexually abused children utilize dolls and puppets in order to encourage children to verbalize what has happened to them). Young Minda seeks the make-believe world of pretend in order to escape her oppressive environment and to articulate her terrible secret. The adults surrounding her are of no help since they are much older and are preoccupied with their own problems. The Church seems to be the only refuge for these dispossessed souls but even there institutionalized religion becomes oppressive and hostile. The male God is not a benevolent comforting figure. Instead, it is yet another male, terrifying and oppressing women: "See God on the altar? He's got big black strange eyes and silver lightning coming out of his head. Look the other way!"

The Virgin Mary is a figure with whom the women can identify and receive solace. However, her direct connection with institutionalized religion transforms her into an inaccessible figure. "Mary, if you become my mother, I'll become a nun, and then a saint . . . ," Minda intones. Immediately she is perceived as mumbling and being disrespectful and is pinched for her "transgression": "Ouch! Maybe I won't become a saint," cries Minda.

Contrasting with seven-year-old Minda is seventy-eight-year-old Tomasa. The aged woman represents the tragedy of today's highly urbanized society and the problem of dealing properly with the elderly. Tomasa's daughter has placed her in a rest home and the elderly woman is naturally unhappy; she feels abandoned and discarded like a used object which needs to be trashed. The "viejita" retains some spunk and rails at her situation, although she recognizes the reality of it and grudgingly accepts it. Her only escape is to retreat into senility, into happier times in the past: "(Like a little girl, she sits up with her eyes shining beautifully) 'me acuerdo de mi altarcito. Con la Virgencita tan bella.'" Religion and the Virgin Mary again function somewhat as a palliative. However, this is not enough and Tomasa retreats further to the figure of her own mother whom she imagines has returned to be with her.

In the character of Juana, Denise Chávez presents the figure of the oppressed factory worker. Juana is an Indian woman working in a pantyhose factory. The contrast between the "haves" and "have-nots" is sharply delineated in the worker's comment: "The work starts back there. Little by little it moves to me. I do the inside seams. People don't like you to talk about pantyhose. ¡Yo ni las uso!" The work is spiritually unsatisfying and thus totally interchangeable. It could be a factory making "boots or jeans or moccasins . . . or turquoise jewelry . . . algo pa' los turistas, you know." Again religion is sought as a refuge against the deadening life of the factory. The Virgin Mary provides some solace. In this particular case Mary is augmented with other American Indian deities: the sun, the moon and the wind.

Another character depicted is Magdalena. True to her namesake, she is the sinning woman, the kind-hearted whore with a heart as big as her bed. She is the perpetually abused woman who gives and gives and never receives anything in return. Magdalena is the eternal, nurturing figure whose shoulder and bed are ever ready for any male in trouble. She has opened her house and her legs to Señor Gallegos, to compadre Juanito and Toribio, the pimply-faced poet. We meet Magdalena as she is making one more "sacrifice" for her ex-convict husband who has just returned from prison.

Pauline, on the other hand, is a "don't mess with me," ostensibly tough, fourteen-year-old *pachuca*. Neglected in school by her teachers, she has spent most of her time in class physically separated from her classmates with nothing to do. To pass the time away she paints her body with tattoos. The audience realizes that underneath the tough exterior is a vulnerable little girl who has been ignored in school and not taught to read or write. The audience becomes aware of Pauline's stunted artistic talent through her tattoo drawings on her body. Pauline suffers from an inferiority complex and low self-esteem. Believing herself to be "dumb" and a "freak," she attributes her inability to read to her own shortcomings. Thus, in order not to be hurt, she invents a tough persona who guards her from the taunts and ridicule of others. Pauline is the embodiment of the "pushed out" Chicana student, an example of how the school system has failed one more Hispanic child through ignorance, low expectations and neglect.

A dramatic change is effected at the end of Pauline's monologue. A caring Chicana teacher has taken a special interest in Pauline and opened new horizons in the child's mind. The narrative ends optimistically when the tough *pachuquita* announces: "Pauline. My name is Pauline Mendoza. I do tattoos. And I draw. Next year I'm going to move to a new school. And someday . . . someday . . . I'm going to be an artist!"

Contrasting sharply with the optimism exhibited by Pauline is Corrine's life. Corrine is the aged *pachuca* turned bag lady. Corrine tells her story in a tough manner. Having survived the licks and bumps inflicted by life, we meet her at the end of her journey with nothing to hope or strive for except basic survival—a warm place to spend the night and food for her stomach. The tough bag lady insists this was not the way she had planned it. In another time she cared—cared deeply for her children, for her family. A series of bounced checks (which she wrote to buy food to feed her kids) landed her in jail and it was downhill from then on. Her kids were taken away from her, her husband abandoned her, her family disowned her and the only place left for Corrine were the streets. As time takes its toll, even the streets reject her and, not being able to earn any money from prostitution, she turns into a tough bag lady. Again the image of the Virgin Mary becomes the only consolation she has in her impoverished life. In spite of all her adversity, Corrine hangs tough. She continues to survive: "Jesús y María. I got it covered, ésa!"

The *Novena Narrativas* closes with Corrine shedding her clothes and becoming Isabel, the playwright. She returns to the altar and comments on the eight other women's ability to survive in the face of extreme adversity. The optimistic message rendered is that love can save us all—as long as we continue to love our fellow human beings, there is hope for all of us.

Denise Chávez' contribution to Chicana literature are twofold. First, her conceptualization of a new genre — the *Novena Narrativa* is an important addition to Chicano literature. The *Novena Narrativa* is a series of monologues with the central figure of the deity (in this case the Virgin Mary) serving as the a centerpiece and as the connecting link, the *ofrenda,* between all the characters. It draws inspiration from the religious folklore of Mexican Americans. The genre has many possibilities because the deity as well as the characters can change according to an author's creativity and vision. The *Novena Narrativa* thus provides us with a transformational model which can be changed at will according to the characters, scenery, deity and other "surface" structures. Chávez' second contribution is her skill in the elaboration of well-delineated, believable women characters. The audience meets not only various archetypal women figures that inhabit the barrios of the Southwest but also other character types. Chávez exhibits exceptional skill in sharply delineating with a few bold strokes believable characters that linger in our minds long after reading the *Novena.*

The alienated, oppressed, barrio woman is the predominant theme in Helena María Viramontes' short story "Miss Clairol." Arlene, a Chicana factory worker, is a single mother living with her ten-year-old daughter, Champ, and her son Gregorio. The narrative captures the drab nuances of the hours just before Arlene's "big" Saturday night date.

Viramontes deftly structures the low socioeconomic environment surrounding the protagonist and her family by introducing Arlene and Champ shopping at the local K-Mart department store. The picture is that of a working-class woman pathetically trying to achieve some sort of Madison Avenue glamour. Arlene wears clothes which are a couple of sizes too small and is heavily made up with cheap cosmetics. A working-class dialect sprinkled with profanities here and there skillfully delineate the protagonist's social position. The code-switching practiced by the two bilingual characters places the protagonists within a Chicano cultural context. It also connotes the almost complete extinction of the Spanish language, for the code-switching consists mainly of an "amá," "m'ija" and a "tú sabes." The loss of language provides an important clue as to the degree of assimilation of the two women. Both mother and daughter aspire toward acquiring light-colored hair, the mother having recently transformed herself from "Flame" to "Light Ash" blonde. The short story derives its title precisely from this ritual of hair coloring. The mother has already been completely brainwashed into "If you have one life to live, live it as a blonde" syndrome. Her feeble attempts at living the American Dream through blond hair contrast with the reality of her drab, alienated, empty life. Equally sad is her daughter's almost inevitable fate of following the same route; she collects clippings of honey-colored and blonde Miss Breck (Breck is the name brand of a popular shampoo) pictures of models and saves them in a shoe box.

The short story is a harsh indictment of a consumer-oriented capitalist society that values superficialities such as hair color, nail polish, false eyelashes and trivialities such as *Love Cries* perfume. Obviously, in order to sustain a well stocked toilette, even of the most inexpensive kind, the female factory worker has to spend a substantial amount of her meager income. However, Arlene is completely alienated from her true reality and does not realize or comprehend the extent of her alienation. Lonely and craving a minimum of human contact and eagerly anticipating a Cinderella-like night out on the town, Arlene is oblivious to her situation. A hint of the protagonist's estrangement from reality is rendered in the description of her "one blind nipple with a cigarette burn." The description intimates an abused childhood. Indeed, Arlene's relationship to her daughter Champ leaves much to be desired. Her interest in her child is minimal and tends to translate more in terms of a "girlfriend" or "buddy" then a mother-daughter relationship. We are aware of this through the mother's frequent use of profanity and more specifically at the end of the narrative, when Arlene, thoroughly wrapped up in her dimestore romantic fantasy of a night out on a date, completely ignores Champ who stands by the window waving a lonely good-bye.

• • • • • • • • • •

Roberta Fernández' short story "Andrea" is a polished, well structured narrative. Through the artifact of a family album, the author weaves the story of her cousin Andrea's trajectory into the world of dance and theater. The family's "blue album" and Andrea's extraordinary life serve as the structural axis through which the various woman characters narrate their own vision of a particular individual's history, Andrea, and simultaneously yield an inner vision of themselves, their dreams, their aspirations and their frustrations. The actress-dancer's exciting life provides a point of departure from which the parallel lives of Consuelo, the protagonist's mother, other female family members and the protagonist herself can comment, expand upon, reminisce and finally arrive at some type of understanding and self-knowledge about their own lives.

Of particular interest in the story is the clever interpolation of the history of the Mexican American theater in the United States. As Chicano theater scholars such as Nicolás Kanellos and Jorge Huerta have written, the Mexican American theater tradition can be traced to the nativity plays of the sixteenth century.[30] The *pastorelas,* or shepherds' plays, *posadas,* and *auto sacramentales* (mystery plays) were all part of the religious rituals celebrated at various points in the Christian calendar. Fernández in her short story depicts Andrea as having played an important role in the Christmas drama, "La Aurora del Nuevo Día," which dates back to the colonial period in America.[31] Later we are informed Andrea performed in various plays which were popular during the nineteenth century. Thus the reader is informed about such theatrical activities as *revistas* (reviews), *zarzuelas,* (musical plays), *actos* (skits), vaudeville, dances, *sainetes* (farces) and plays from Spain's Golden Age as well as from popular theater from the nineteenth and early twentieth centuries.

However, the short story is not just a chronology of the history of the Mexican American theater in the Southwest. The characters are well-delineated, the prose is natural and flows easily in an intimate conversational tone employed by the narrator. The short story depicts the lives of Chicanas in a nonstereotypical manner. The narrative provides a glimpse into a different life style: the women portrayed are not *campesinas* (peasant women) or the urban poor but lower middle-class Chicanas leading productive lives. It is yet another view of the Mexican American experience: a view of hardworking, well-educated women with dreams and high expectations.

Sheila Ortiz Taylor maps in her short story "Hearts" the tenuous relationships of a family on an outing around Catalina Island off the coast of southern California. The boat in which the family of four (two girls and the father and mother) is supposedly safely moored begins to pitch and roll as a violent storm hits the coast, and the father realizes he does not have the storm anchors aboard.

The story's storm plot parallels the family's equally tenuous relationships, for the reader is told the parents will eventually separate and the mother will marry a more financially secure man. The father's role is highlighted in the short story and, although the mother is portrayed as the practical one, the father is perceived as a sympathetic figure. This departs from many Chicano/a narrative plots where the father figure is often portrayed as a strong, patriarchal figure such as in Helena María Viramontes's short stories in *The Moths* and in Sandra Cisneros's *The House on Mango Street*. The father/daughter relationship is explored in "Hearts" and a warm, close, loving relationship is rendered. This is important in the sense that, generally, in fiction, Chicanas have tended to be "mother's girls" and not "daddy's girls." Ortiz Taylor provides us with yet another paradigm of family relationships in Chicana literature.

CRITICISM

Chicana literary criticism, still burgeoning, has nevertheless begun to question the direction this criticism should pursue in the future. There are two prevailing currents of thought regarding Chicano/a literary criticism.[32] One perceives European, American and Feminist critical discourses as useful tools in the analysis of Chicana writers. The second mode of thought argues for an emancipation from "white" literary theoreticians in a search for an authentic Chicano critical discourse.

Tey Diana Rebolledo's article "The Politics of Poetics: Or, What Am I, A Critic, Doing in This Text Anyhow?" explores the very process of critical analysis and the critic's pivotal role in this endeavor. She particularly targets those Chicano/a critics who, enamored of European and American male theorists (Derrida, Said, Jameson, Williams, Burke, et al.) privilege these white males' and even white feminists' theoretical constructs over the text itself. Rebolledo avers that, while we may be impressing the Establishment and other academics with our grasp of current intellectual giants, we deprivilege the very text we seek to highlight. This intellectual prostituting on the part of Chicano/a critics does a great disservice to Chicano literature, since the text gets literally lost in the process.

There is a need to refocus on the text itself and return Chicano literature to a privileged position instead of relegating it to a secondary status. Rebolledo argues that it is in ourselves, that is, our own literature, our own writers, our own critics, our own words where our strength, originality and ultimate contribution to world criticism and literature lies, and not in the servile imitation and copying of those we have raised to a privileged position by de-privileging ourselves. Privileging our own voices as Chicano/a critics is of central concern in Rebolledo's essay.

....

Yvonne Yarbro-Bejarano in her article "Chicana Literature From a Chicana Feminist Perspective" reiterates the theme of finding our own voice in Chicano/a criticism. Yarbro-Bejarano, however, focuses exclusively on Chicana literature and from a specific feminist perspective. This critic, furthermore, posits a direct connection between Chicana feminist literary criticism and political practice. The Chicana critic is involved and conscious of the political economic status of Chicanas in the community and is not an isolated entity ensconced in an ivory tower. Yarbro-Bejarano perceives issues of race, culture, class, and sex as fundamental for an authentic Chicana feminist critical perspective which cannot be ignored.

Reiterating Rebolledo, Yarbro-Bejarano insists that any originality and contribution we can offer to world literature depends on our ability to draw from our own specific racial and cultural experience. Indeed those Chicanas that have already made a mark on the literary scene—such as Cherríe Moraga, Sandra Cisneros and Helena María Viramontes—derived their inspiration from their specificity as marginalized Chicanas. Their words as expressed in the literary text were forged in the fire of barrio poverty, racism, economic exploitation and gender marginalization. The fire and magic breathing through their works emanates from the pain and suffering experienced as minority women. Yarbro-Bejarano emphasizes the powerful dialectic between Chicana and community in their writings. In this dialectic the vector of love—love for herself as a Chicana and love for other Chicanos—is the main ingredient structuring Chicana poetics.

....

Norma Alarcón, on the other hand, perceives the works of main-stream and feminist literary theoreticians useful in apprehending the Chicana text. In her study, "Making 'Familia' From Scratch: Split Subjectivities in the Work of Helena María Viramontes and Cherríe Moraga," Alarcón finds particularly illuminating Julia Kristeva's theoretical postulates with regard to women in the symbolic contract. For Alarcón a close analysis of recent—1980's—Chicana writing reflects a preoccupation with their subjectivity and with patriarchal society "engendering" her as "woman." These engenderings imprison Chicanas in a sexual identity which has an "overdetermined signification," that is, they are mainly perceived as "future wives/mothers in relation to the symbolic contract within which women may have a voice on the condition that they speak as mothers." This gender over-determination produces a crisis in those recalcitrant Chicanas who question their overly restricted position in the symbolic contract. It is this crisis which erupts into creative explorations of the self, her sexuality and intra- and intersexual relationships. Alarcón incisively applies Kristeva's theoretical construct elucidated in her work on the place of women in the symbolic contract (see, Kristeva, *Revolution in Poetic Language,* 1984). She effectively demonstrates the usefulness of French feminist theory in the exegesis of Chicana writers.

• • • • • • • • • •

Julián Olivares' essay offers a textual analysis of Sandra Cisneros' *The House in Mango Street* (1984) and posits the disjuncture between a male, upper-middle class, white, literary theoretician Gaston Bachelard and a barrio-raised, marginalized Chicana writer. For Bachelard the house conjures up images of warmth and pleasure while for Cisneros the house is viewed in the more realistic terms of the barrio: poverty, oppression, rats, drudgery and so forth. This particular point tends to substantiate Rebolledo's warning of possible misapplication of European literary theoretical constructs to a specific Chicano phenomenon. Nevertheless, since according to Cisneros herself ("From a Writer's Notebook") Gaston Bachelard's book, *The Poetics of Space,* inspired her to write about *her house,* it seems prudent for Chicano/a critics not to completely reject European literary theoreticians (Derrida, Lacan, et al.) but to use them with caution.

Olivares' analysis of *The House On Mango Street* supports Yarbro-Bejarano's contention that Chicano/a creativity will more likely than not emanate from the specificity of barrio experiences, and sexual and economic oppression. Encoded in Cisneros' word, we encounter a woman's voice protesting the oppression of women in the barrios. This again substantiates Yarbro-Bejarano's corollary that a Chicano's /a's love for other Chicanas will often structure their creative works. Both Lucha Corpi's "Romance Negro" and *The House on Mango Street* utter voices of protest against the subordinate status of Chicanas/Mexicanas in a patriarchal society.

Finally, my article "The Politics of Rape: Sexual Transgression in Chicana Fiction" analyzes various Chicana literary texts (Cherríe Moraga's *Giving Up the Ghost,* 1986, Sylvia Lizárraga's "Silver Lake" and Sandra Cisneros'

"Red Clowns"), focusing on their rape-as-metaphor imagery. The study reiterates and confirms the other critics' position on Chicana creativity, that is, Chicanas create out of their personal environment as marginalized, oppressed women concerned with the pernicious effects of a patriarchal political system.

NOTES

1. See Alma Villanueva, *Bloodroot* (Austin: Place of Herons Press, 1982); Lucha Corpi, *Palabras de Mediodía/Noon Words* (Berkeley: El Fuego de Aztlán Publications, 1980); Bernice Zamora, *Restless Serpents* (Menlo Park, California: Diseños Literarios, 1976); Lorna Dee Cervantes, *Emplumada* (Pittsburgh: University of Pittsburgh Press, 1981).

2. Arte Público Press has published Pat Mora, (*Chants*, 1984, and *Borders*, 1986); Evangelina Vigil (*Thirty n' Seen A Lot*, 1982, and *The Computer Is Down*, 1986); Helen María Viramontes (*Moths and Other Stories*, 1985); Denise Chávez, (*The Last of the Menu Girls*, 1986); Angela de Hoyos (*Woman, Woman*, 1985); Ana Castillo, (*Women Are Not Roses*, 1984); Sandra Cisneros (*The House on Mango Street*, 1983), Mary Helen Ponce (*Taking Control*, 1987). This same Press, in addition, published the anthology *Woman of Her Word: Hispanic Woman Write*, 1983), edited by Evangelina Vigil. The Bilingual Review Press has published Estela Portillo Trambley's *Sor Juana and Other Plays* (1983), and *Trini*, (1986), Trambley's first novel; Beverly Silva's *The Second St. Poems*, (1983) and *The Cat and Other Stories*, (1986), a short story collection; Ana Castillo's best selling work *The Mixquiahuala Letters*, (1986). West End Press, Los Angeles, published Naomi Quiñónez' poetry collection *Sueño de Colibrí: Hummingbird Dream*, (1985); and Cherríe Moraga's *Giving Up the Ghost: Theater in Two Acts*, 1986. Alurista's Maize Press published two Chicana poets: Cordelia Candelaria, *Ojo de la Cueva* (1984), and Gina Valdés, *Comiendo Lumbre/Eating Fire*, (1986). Other small presses publishing Mexican American woman writers include M & A Editions, San Antonio, Texas, which published Carmen Tafolla's *Curandera* (1983); Lalo Press, La Jolla, California, published Yolanda Luera's poetry collection *Solitaria J*, (1986); and Relámpago Books Press, Austin, Texas, printed Margarita Cota-Cárdenas' novel *Puppet*, (1985). See also the bibliography section in this volume for additional Chicana authors and their works.

3. It comes as a surprise to many academics to learn that Chicano/a literature is mostly written in English. Departments of Literature in major universities in the United States are ambivalent as to the placement of Chicano literature within academia. Some departments house it in Spanish departments while others house it in the English departments.

4. See the recent study by Patricia Zavella, *Women's Work and Chicano Families: Cannery Workers of the Santa Clara Valley* (Ithaca, New York: Cornell University Press,

1987). For a view of Mexican women working on the U.S.-Mexican border in assembly plants (*maquiladoras*) since the 1960s, see María Patricia Fernández-Kelly, *For We Are Sold, I and My People: Women and Industry in Mexico's Frontier* (Albany: State University of New York Press, 1983).

5. The farmworker and migrant worker as important protagonists in Chicano literature appear in Tomás Rivera's novel . . . *y no se lo tragó la tierra* / . . . *And The Earth Did Not Part* (Berkeley: Quinto Sol Publications, 1971), 2nd. Ed. Arte Público Press, 1987; and Luis Valdez, *Actos: El Teatro Campesino* (San Juan Bautista, California: MENYAH, 1971).

6. Lorna Dee Cervantes posited this view in an impassioned presentation at the *Chicano Literary Criticism in a Social Context Conference,* Stanford University, May 28–30, 1987.

7. Gaston Bachelard, *The Poetics of Space* (Boston: Beacon Press, 1969).

8. See Alicia Suskin Ostriker, *Stealing the Language: The Emergence of Women's Poetry in America* (Boston: Beacon Press, 1986)

9. *Ibid.*

10. In this decade (1980s), the W.W. Norton Company produced the landmark *The Norton Anthology of Literature by Women: The Tradition in English,* eds. Sandra M. Gilbert and Susan Gubar (New York: W. W. Norton & Company, 1985).

11. See my book *Beyond Stereotypes: The Critical Analysis of Chicana Literature* (Binghamton, New York: Bilingual Review Press, 1985).

12. "Pomp and Circumstance" refers to the musical composition played at traditional graduation ceremonies all over the United States.

13. There are numerous studies detailing the substandard conditions existing in schools teaching Chicanos. See for example Thomas P. Carter, *Mexican Americans in Schools: A History of Educational Neglect* (New York: College Entrance Examination Board, 1970); Manuel Ramírez III and Alfredo Castañeda, *Cultural Democracy, Bicognitive Development and Education* (New York: Harcourt Brace Jovanovich Publishers, 1974); U.S. Commission on Civil Rights, *Teachers and Students: Difference in Teacher Interaction with Mexican American and Anglo Students* (Washington, D.C.: Report V: Mexican American Education Study, 1973).

14. See H. J. Rose, *A Handbook of Greek Mythology* (New York: E. P. Dutton & Co., 1959).

15. A young lady in the audience fainted. I checked with the Director of U.C. Irvine's Rape Center about the emotional effects produced during the reading of my paper "The Politics of Rape" (re: the young woman fainting). The Director of the Rape Center commented that presentations on the topic of rape often produce a crisis in some members of the audience; many women begin to cry uncontrollably, some women experience hyperventilation, others need to talk, etc.

16. See Marta Sánchez' analysis of Corpi's poetry in her book *Contemporary Chicana Poetry* (Berkeley: University of California Press, 1985), 139–213.

17. Forthcoming in *The Americas Review* (1989); I am indebted to Julián Olivares for allowing me to quote from Mireya Pérez-Erdelyi's interview of Lucha Corpi in August, 1986.

18. See Gaston Bachelard's study of the poetic imagination and the phenomenon of fire in *The Psychoanalysis of Fire* (Boston: Beacon Press: 1964), especially chapter 4: "Sexualized Fire."

19. *Ibid.*

20. Pérez-Erdelyi.

21. The philosopher Mircea Eliade has expounded in several studies about the circularity of time and its mythic nature; see *The Myth of the Eternal Return: Or Cosmos and History* (Princeton: Princeton University Press, 1974); and *Myth and Reality* (New York: Harper Colophon Books, Harper & Row, Publishers, 1963).

22. See Mircea Eliade, *The Myth of the Eternal Return.*

23. Lucha Corpi reiterates this theme; see the section on Lucha Corpi in this study.

24. See Gaston Bachelard's *The Poetics of Reverie* (Boston: Beacon Press, 1969).

25. "The Gospel According to Luke," *The Holy Bible* (New York: New American Library, 1974), Book 7.

26. See Simone de Beauvoir, *The Second Sex* (New York: Random House, 1952), and Vern L. Bullough, *The Subordinate Sex: A History of Attitudes Toward Women* (New York: Penguin Books, 1974).

27. Vern L. Bullough, *The Subordinate Sex: A History of Attitudes Toward Women.*

28. *Ibid.*

29. See Diana Rebolledo's study on the figure of the *abuelita* in Chicano literature, "Abuelitas, Mythology and Integration in Chicana Literature," *Woman of Her Word: Hispanic Women Write,* Ed. Evangelina Vigil Revista Chicano-Riqueña II :3–4 (1983), 148–58.

30. See Jorge Huerta, *Chicano Theater: Themes and Forms* (Ypsilanti, MI: Bilingual Press/Editorial Bilingüe, 1982); and Nicolás Kanellos, Ed., *Hispanic Theatre in the United States* (Houston: Arte Público Press, 1984); *Mexican American Theatre: Then and Now* (Houston: Arte Público Press, 1983); *Mexican American Theatre: Legacy and Reality* (Pittsburgh: Latin American Literary Review Press, 1987).

31. See Aurora Lucero-White Lea, *Literary Folklore of the Hispanic Southwest* (San Antonio, TX: Naylor Company, 1953).

32. For an early call to reevaluate Chicano critical discourse, see Joseph Sommers, "From the Critical Premise to the Product: Critical Modes and Their Applications to a Chicano Literary Text," *New Directions in Chicano Scholarship, New Scholar,* Richard Romo and Raymond Paredes, Eds. 6 (1977): 51–80; see also Ramón Saldívar's remarks on this subject in "Dialectic of Difference Toward a Theory of the Chicano Novel," *Contemporary Chicano Fiction: A Critical Survey,* Vernon Latin, Ed. (Binghamton, NY: Bilingual Review Press/Editorial Bilingüe, 1986), 13–31.

1. Poetry

❀ ❀ ❀ ❀

Enedina Cásarez Vásquez *Maricela Dreams*

Enedina Cásarez Vásquez *My Mother's Altar*

LORNA DEE CERVANTES

FIRST BEATING

What a strong little sucker you are!
All my grit and guts rolled up in a fist.
All I ever had was strength: head
strong, heart strong, even my genius,
tempered, impermeable; all my soggy wishes
hard-boiled away early, nothing but blades
of glass in the end, fused to the bottom
of my past, bitter crystals shimmering, and
there for good.
    From these damaged goods,
I pass you the flame, my ware. Alive
in your sea of blood and spit and piss
your ventricles unfurl, hurl into space
like the hands of maize, the thick pricks
of daffodils asserting through the wimpy dirt
You beat a good goddamn through the conjugal
mush, up between the aged cracks in my skin,
through my pores I hear it rapping: first poem,
first flush of wings and separation. You give
me this: a heart like a jack-hammer tearing
up my world. Oh my little secret weapon, self
made slayer, you are mine. My strength. Your own.

(first published in *Many Mountains Moving,* Vol.1, Number 1, Boulder Co.)

ASTRO-NO-MÍA

The closest we ever got
to science was the stars
like the Big Dipper ladling
hundreds of thousands of beans
and diamonds for some Greeks
long ago when law was a story
of chased women set in the sky:
Diana, Juno, Pleiades, las siete
hermanas, daughters, captives
of Zeus, and the children, the children
changed into trees, bears, scared into stars.
We wished ourselves into the sky,
held our breaths and stopped dreaming,
stopped stories, our hearts and elevated
up into that ash-trip to heaven-seven
smoked rings of escape from the chase.
Y nada. Punto. We were never stars.
Our mothers would call, the fathers
of fate, heavy like mercury, would trash
our stomachs into our wombs. Cold.
We'd roller coaster back down to the earth,
to the night before school, before
failed examination y el otro
which is much harder to describe.
Study? Sure. We studied hard.
But all I could remember was that man,
Orion, helplessly shooting his shaft
into my lit house from the bow.
¿Y Yo? Hay bow. Y ya voy.

BANANAS
  for Indrek

I

In Estonia, Indrek is taking his children
to the Dollar Market to look at bananas.
He wants them to know about the presence of fruit,
about globes of light tart to the tongue, about the
twang of tangelos, the cloth of persimmons,
the dull little mons of kiwi. There is not a chance
for a taste. Where rubles are scarce, dollars are harder.
Even beef is doled out welfare-thin on Saturday's platter.
They light the few candles not reserved for the dead,
and try not to think of small bites in the coming winter,
of irradiated fields or the diminished catch in the fisherman's
net. They tell of bananas yellow as daffodils. And mango—
which tastes as if the whole world came out from her womb.

II

Columbia, 1928, bananas rot in the fields.
A strip of lost villages between railyard
and cemetery. The United Fruit Company train,
a yellow painted slug, eats up the swamps and jungle.
Campesinos replace Indians who are a dream
and a rubble of bloody stones hacked into coffins:
malaria, tuberculosis, cholera, machetes of the jefes.
They become like the empty carts that shatter
the landscape. Their hands, no longer pulling the teats
from the trees, now twist into death, into silence
and obedience. They wait in Aracataca, poised as
statues between hemispheres. They would rather be
tilling the plots for black beans. They would rather grow
wings and rise as *pericos—parrots, poets, clowns—*a word
which means all this and whose task is messenger from
Mitla, the underworld where the ancestors of the slain

arise with the vengeance of Tláloc. A stench permeates
the wind as bananas, black on the stumps, char
into odor. The murdered Mestizos have long been cleared
and begin their new duties as fertilizer for the plantations.
Feathers fall over the newly spaded soil: turquoise,
scarlet, azure, quetzál, and yellow litters
the graves like gold claws of bananas.

III

Dear I,

The 3" × 6" boxes in front of the hippie
market in Boulder are radiant with marigolds, some
with heads big as my Indian face. They signify
death to me, as it is Labor Day and already
I am making up the guest list for my *Día de los Muertos*
altar. I'll need *maravillas* so this year I plant *caléndulas*
for blooming through snow that will fall before November.
I am shopping for "no-spray" bananas. I forego
the Dole and *Chiquita,* that name always made me
blush for being christened with that title. But now
I am only a little small, though still brown enough
for the— *Where are you from?* Probably my ancestors
planted a placenta here as well as on my Califas coast
where alien shellfish replaced native mussels,
clams and oysters in 1886. *I'm from the 21st Century,*
I tell them, and feel rude for it—when all I desire
is bananas without pesticides. They're smaller
than plantains which are green outside and firm
and golden when sliced. Fried in butter
they turn yellow as over-ripe fruit. And sweet.
I ask the produce manager how to crate and
pack bananas to Estonia. She glares at me
suspiciously: *You can't do that. I know.*
There must be some law. You might spread
diseases. They would arrive as mush, anyway.

I am thinking of children in Estonia with
no fried *plátanos* to eat with their fish as
the Blond turns away, still without shedding
a smile at me—me, Hija del Sol, Earth's Daughter, lover
of bananas. I buy Baltic wheat. I buy up organic
bananas, butter y canela. I ship banana bread.

I V

At Big Mountain uranium
sings through the dreams of the people.
Women dress in glowing symmetries, sheep
clouds gather below the bluffs, sundown
sandstone blooms in four corners. Smell of sage
penetrates as state tractors with chains trawl the resistant
plants, gouging anew the tribal borders, uprooting
all in their path like Amazonian ants, breaking
the hearts of the widows. Elders and children
cut the fence again and again as wind whips
the waist of ancient rock. Sheep nip across
centuries in the people's blood, and are carried
off by the Federal choppers waiting in the canyon
with orders and slings. A long winter, little wool
to spin, medicine lost in the desecration of the desert.
Old women weep as the camera rolls on the dark
side of conquest. Encounter rerun. Uranium. 1992

V

I worry about winter in a place
I've never been, about exiles in their
homeland gathered around a fire,
about the slavery of substance and
gruel: *Will there be enough to eat?*
Will there be enough to feed? And
they dream of beaches and pies, hemispheres

of soft fruit found only in the heat of the planet.
Sugar canes, like Geiger counters, seek out tropics;
and dictate a Resolution to stun the tongues of those
who can afford to pay: imported plums, bullets,
black caviar large as peas, smoked meats
the color of Southern lynchings, what we don't
discuss in letters.
    You are out of work.
Not many jobs today for high physicists
in Estonia, you say. *Poetry, though, is food*
for the soul. And bread? What is cake before
corn and the potato? Before the encounter
of animals, women and wheat? Stocks high
these days in survival products; 500 years later tomato
size tumors bloom in the necks of the pickers.
On my coast, Diablo dominates the golden hills,
the faultlines. On ancestral land Vandenberg shoots nuclear
payloads to Kwajalein, a Pacific atoll, where 68% of all
infants are born amphibian or anemones. But poetry
is for the soul. I speak of spirit, the yellow seed
in air as life is the seed in water, and the poetry
of Improbability, the magic in the Movement
of quarks and sunlight, the subtle basketry
of hadrons and neutrinos of color, how what you do
is what you get—bananas or worry.
What do you say? Your friend,
    a Chicana poet

BIRD AVE.

life on Bird
was tough
Cat-eyes
me and Mousie
estrolándonos y
marchando
con missions
man I can't get no
satisfaction
in and out las
baby baby baby
oooo OOO oooo
baby baby
hits all summer

we wore tease
tight skirts
tough teased hair
talked tough rhymes
developed una
re-puta-ción
for the toughest burns
on Horseshoe

tough
from Memorial Day
to our Labor Day
weekend
we had the key
to the drug locker
of our own developing
temples
highest kites in the district
favors all over town
and we owed
nobody shit

Cat-eyes was beautiful
Mouse made up wizard holds
nobody over 4'11" could contain her
except me—the connection
we always had it
we scored
when we wanted
plus we were ethical

essssahhh Mouse goes
that first initiation
you gotta understand
about Ethics
she had it then
all total control
banging my head on
the blacktop for effect
you flacafeaface
got Ethics
and she gave me
one of those mouse
grins and made
lemon crap
out of my cheeks
before letting me up
all righteous rage

sin class *ni* pomp
and circumstance
we were better
than military
beauty brains & brass
man
we were the trinity
that invented it
the model rambos
I coulda killed her
easy

she knew it
we'd kill it
in ourselves
eventually

we knew it all
the code and the symbology
the poetics and the order
of place and gesture
we were honed for the killing
primed for the time
our *ganga de* carnelias
y rosarías would burst
we tended that bust
cultivated it
blistered it
hitched ourselves
up to its hearse
and made up Bird
on the reins
of some wild ride
from the tracks to
Willow Glen and back
we were running
our own private
miracle mile

man
it was tough
with Cat-eyes
on the corner
buttering 'em up
all stupid and blind
me and Mouse
always ready
to take advantage
of a relevant situation

Don't Fuck With Us
our motto
We're Here to Serve
the ruse
Listen Watch
Be Silent
was the Conquest's
hidden code

man
it was tough
to know it all
and we haven't
learned anything
since

LUCHA CORPI

Hay sabor de vainilla
en el aire dominical

Melancolía de la naranja
que aún cuelga de la rama,
brillante y seductora
sin esperanza de azahar.

Guadalupe se bañaba en el río
muy de tarde en un domingo.

Promesa de leche en los senos

Vainilla el olor de los cabellos

Canela molida el sabor de los ojos

Flor de cacao entre las piernas
Ah, la embriaguez de la caña
entre los labios.

El se acercó y la miró así
rodeada del agua
inundada de tarde

Y en un instante arrancó la flor
Estrujó la leche hasta cambiarla
en sangre

Desparramó la vainilla por el
silencio de la orilla

Bebiose el candente líquido
de los labios

Y después . . . después desapareció
dejando sólo un rastro de sombra
lánguida al borde del agua.

Su madre la encontró y al verla
sacó de su morral un puño de sal
y se la echó por el hombro.

Y a los pocos días su padre
recibió una yegua fina de regalo.

Y Guadalupe . . . Guadalupe colgó
su vida del naranjo del huerto
y se quedó muy quieta ahí
con los ojos al río abiertos.

Hay sabor de vainilla
en el ambiente de la tarde.

Una nostalgia ancestral
se apodera de la mente.

De la rama cuelga una naranja
todavía sin promesa de azahar.

(from *Palabras de Mediodía*)

INVERNARIO

En los ojos que observaron
la tormenta avecinarse
había calles empedradas
y trigales todavía húmedos
por la lluvia de la noche,
un triángulo de sombra
entre dos casas blancas,
un viejo campesino con su violín
envuelto en periódico
en camino a la feria del pueblo.

Me observé en esos ojos
como quien mira en el mar
su imagen fragmentada,
por la corriente indómita
y la ve convertirse
en coral
y sombra
y pez
en roca
y mineral fosforescente.

Desde entonces
aprisionado
entre el demiángulo del ojo
y el origen del cantar
como un suicida impenitente
me acecha mi deseo
por sus brazos.

RECUERDO ÍNTIMO
para Arturo y Finnigan

No había llovido así
desde aquel día en que los perros
destrozaron los únicos zapatos que tenías
y mi bolsa estaba llena solamente
de papeles y palabras.

Llovía tanto aquella tarde
que Finnigan el gato, tú y yo,
a falta de arca, decidimos meternos
a la tina de baño, por si acaso . . .

Esta tarde llueve igual que entonces
pero mi razón se niega a reandar
aquel infame invierno:
Sólo escucho la lluvia en el tejado,
el ronroneo del gato en la tina de baño,
veo la suave luz de tu sonrisa de dos años.

Es todo lo que necesito recordar.

FUGA

Cansada de llevar en los ojos
resplandor, muro y silencio
y al oído
un rumor de alas y lluvia,
entre adiós y puerta inesperada
me decidí por el fuego
y en su promesa de agostos oportunos
mi corazón ardió
una noche de invierno.

Crucé la insolente geometría
que tus manos construyeran
en las agrestes latitudes de febrero.

Tu milagrería de tigres al acecho lancé
a la insubordinada ecología del viento.

Lavé el sabor temible de tu piel
de mis labios.

Cau13rdicé motivo, causa y sentimiento.

Borré tu mirada de mi cuerpo.

Y clausuré las puertas de la historia
para no recordar más tu nombre ni mi nombre.

Afuera
en el invierno de los dioses
con mano temblorosa destapé el silencio.

Conjuré las semillas del fuego.

Las sentí palpitar en mis sienes, en mis
pechos.

En el espacio abierto de mis dedos eran
sangre

 trigo

  y luz de junio.

Eran la noche y sus mil ojos

crepúsculo

 dolor

  y canto

y la espiga tendida en el campo

acantilado

 delta

  y pez dorado

secretos de estrellas en la arena

escama

 espuma

  y sal
y el lamento melancólico de la ballena

anunciando la amplitud ecuánime
de un equinoccio boreal.

CANCIÓN DE INVIERNO
A Magdalena Mora
(1952–1981)

En un abrir
y cerrar de ojos
lleno de
magia
relojes
y sueños viejos
llega el invierno:

El viento rumora melancólico
como el todoencalma del sereno
que velaba la casa de mis padres
-ahí vuelvo cada invierno
para no olvidar quién soy
ni de dónde vengo.

Cantando baja la lluvia
a su destino de mineral y semilla.
Entre el hueco del ala que se extiende
y el entrecerrar de la mirada que descansa
aprendemos a amar en instantes y entregas
y entre la pregunta íntima de la noche
y la respuesta dulciobscura de la madrugada
gestamos dolorosamente una nueva vida.

Nada hay fijo ni perenne
ni la lluvia
ni la semilla
ni tú
ni yo
ni nuestro dolor
en este mundo que sangra
porque vamos siempre tirando senda,
abriendo brecha por caminos desconocidos,
venciendo la furia del olvido verso a verso.

INDOCUMENTADA ANGUSTIA

Arpas insaciables
   los rascacielos
   consumiendo estrellas,
   hartándose de luna,
   encajonando al viento
   que se venga
   rompiendo flores y paraguas
   y se contenta sólo
   cuando su gran lengua transparente
   conoce una vez más
   la tersa piel del agua.

Llega entonces la niebla
   llena de tantas manos
   y aves peregrinas,
   corre entre las hojas pisoteadas
   amortiguando queja y látigo,
   acallando la indocumentada angustia
   del ilegal en su propia tierra,
   hundiendo sus dedos en la luna
   y en la lejanía sin puertos
   ni faros.

SONATA A DOS VOCES
A Mark Greenside

1. Largo Frenético

Cuesta saberse viva
en la actividad inaudita
de estos días.

Se congregan parvadas de semanas
    domingos llenos de números
    jueves quiméricos
    en los que el tiempo
    se traiciona a sí mismo
    y regresa a la hora cero.

Tanto que combatir:
    mensajes a la puerta
    reuniones
    fechas
    nombres sumergidos
    en un mar de sudor
    mercaderías
    sopa
    habas frescas
    y ropa sucia

Tejemanejes que desenredar,
que remendar camisas,
deshilar ausencias
y neutralizar bichos burócratas
para recobrar aquellos sueños
que quedaron en el empeño
cuando se ajustó el presupuesto
y el amigo partió sin decir palabra,
cuando hubo que plantar jacintos
en las tumbas de nuestros muertos.

2. Adagio

Se me ha clavado un silencio en la garganta
un cúmulo de voz coagulada que tenaz impide
todo deseo de canto.
Los ojos apuran el crepúsculo
en sorbos verdemente lentos
y la palabra queda entrelabios
como un débil aroma a jazmines muertos.
Por la calle
alguien silba una tonada taciturna
se detiene y recoge los últimos tréboles
de la temporada
para la hija pequeña en casa
que gusta todavía
de estos diminutos prodigios
la que comparte el sueño del ciempiés
de recorrer el mundo a pie frenético
algún día.
En el patio
el limonero ha dado flor y fruto
entre mil balas de lluvia
y la violencia del viento.
A lo lejos
el tren zumba rumbo al sur
y a galope tendido la niebla lo acompaña.
Estupefacta
la ciudad contempla su perfil
en el espejo pérfido del agua
mientras
en El Salvador los niños mueren de prisa
y en Africa la sangre se seca lenta
y no hay palabra que pueda detener
el largo beso de sombras de la muerte
si no se extiende la mano amiga
si el corazón permanece ajeno
porque
a fin de cuentas
solamente el amor nos salva.

LLUEVE

Las lluvias han llegado
Lluvias de invierno
Lluvias mansas
Ajenas a todo han llegado
Caen infinitas y grises
sobre los caracoles
que en hordas aquelárreas
se reunen junto al limonero,

las hormigas
desterradas de sus nidos
cargan sus muertos
hasta que ellas mismas
caen bajo el peso
en una tina de baño
o en la alacena
llena de miel y de pan.

Llueve, llueve
Lluvia fina
Lluvia mansa
Lluvia infinita . . .

Si un relámpago surgiera de repente
Si súbitamente cruzara el cielo
    intrépido y veloz
Si su descarga hiciera temblar
    los cimientos empedernidos de la urbe
Si en contrapunto
    con el pulsar obscuro del viento
    creara tríadas perfectas
    juegos de luz
       estruendo
          silencio

Mas sólo llueve
Lluvia fina
Lluvia mansa
Lluvia infinita

No es tiempo, no es tiempo . . .

EVANGELINA VIGIL-PIÑÓN

THE PARTING
to the memory of Chichimeca

winter blew in today
cold, relentless
last night in the eve of dreams
we listened to the cricket's urgent song
a message we tried to decipher
it eluded us
and the seed of thought thus planted
we sank into sleep
only to awaken
to fierce winds encircling the house
rattling windows
shaking the screens
like spirits, wanting in
and through the windows we witnessed
the silhouettes of young tallows
their lithe limbs bending and swaying
their tawny leaves fluttering fiercely
time's simultaneous arrival
and departure
and our hearts whispered
la despedida:
adiós, querido amigo
nos vemos en el infinito*

*a final farewell
Godspeed, dearest friend
wait for us there in eternity

IN ITS ABSENCE

and if time continues to
reveal
our legacy
and that of our fathers'
fathers
and children's
children
and if all has been sung
and nothing new
of universal consequence
nudges
the mind
sparks
the spirit
quickens the heartbeat
to a skip

what shall this next song
be about?

GIVING

longer
no longer can I
think it
a poem
one day reality won
over

it's those who think like most
who excel

SPILLAGE

pen lies cold
on glass tabletop
ink bottle sits
indigo
blotches the blank page
and tomorrow arrives
before daybreak
and yesterday's words
can never be retrieved:

a sight of realization
is worth an eternity

EQUINOX

in the center of August
the cicadas
restively
chitter chatter
lazily
back and forth

somewhere far away
the cotton must be high
nearby
trout jump
their silver bodies
splashing above emerald waters

on the parched summer grass
tall pecan trees
choreograph their poses
graceful inconspicuous persuasion
motioning
advancing shadows

far away
in starlit space
the sun burns fiercely
compelling eyes
east

next, a baby child stirs
in the center of afternoon dreams
that will not be remembered
nor known

and the cicadas
lazily
chitter chatter

back and forth
in the lush green shadows
of pecan trees

HACIA UN INVIERNO

son muchas las palabras que han caído
sangre goteando de heridas
formando letras
que lastiman
ojos llorosos leyéndolas
agua salada borrándolas
y el peso de esa pena en el alma
aun constante sigue

las chicharras sabrán
de esa continuidad
sus voces roncas ya
de tanto gritar la verdad
el canto urgente nunca se acaba
sólo estribillo hay:

el día nuevo cierra sus ojos
cara amplia resplandeciente
poco a poco
ocultándose
volteando hacia lo obscuro
su vista despareciéndose
luz volviéndose
un mundo de sueños

la luz ya apagada
el canto urgente de las chicharras
ya grito no es
sino una silenciosa preocupación
al son solitario de un grillo
que acompaña a esas almas
quienes ven hacia los cielos
contemplando el poder
de una luna llena
y queriendo ver

más allá de las estrellas
en busca de una nueva verdad

y la ilusión de ayer
renace
y el alma se da
a la esperanza
con la misma inocencia de ayer:
 . . . mira, chulita . . .
 si tu te duermes
 en tu cunita . . .
¿dónde?
¿dónde y cuándo
nace
este sentimiento?

❧ DENISE CHÁVEZ

LA PESADEZ

La pesadez
que me dejas
no está clara
ni limpia,
sino suave

Un murmullo
de vello
en tu piel resbaladiza
de sudor que pasa
arrancada
en el punto donde la debilidad
yace

I AM YOUR MARY MAGDALENE

I am your Mary Magdalene
come, let me wash your feet
stroke your brow
can we undo the past
throw it away
knotted chords of fevers, dreams?

Often I have had to apologize
to men
for passions
wouldn't know
it would be this way

So, in high school
Johnny called
to say:
You want too much
aren't you embarrassed, shy?

Discount the young boys
their chained libidos
their fat brothers
and forget those conversations
about how you are oversexed
and please, don't write me anymore

Okay, banishment—
that high tower
I can see all the way into the chambered heart
I am back at that place
overlooking blue land
surrounded by gargoyles
the wind

I am your Mary Magdalene
come let me wash your feet

THIS RIVER'S PRAYING PLACE

This river's praying place
is an inconsequential sandy bar
where a fisherman intones prayers
to the nightless fish.
It is a group of cows
placed above his disappearance in the wind.

The river's praying place
is thread of me:
cactus crossed storm of wandering discontent.

I stretch myself in the sand
amid hair-swirled trees;
my head on these future words:
willow reminders of my seeping cold.

Those black ones prodded me still.
I jumped up, flowing with words,
flung to me from the sideways river
of that other place.

Imagine a curtain of water
seen through valley eyes,
imagine its ceaselessly gentle movement
to retire.
You will see me there,
tangled in her hair
exultant now—
downcast later with her silent words.

TEARS

Tears, wells of love-meshed tresses
fall from me.

My soul bleeds for your touch.

I tell you stories no living man has heard,
stories of locked-in sighs,
wandering stories of other lives,
myself as a young girl.

So you know me now as the one who was,
yes, then.

CLOUD

Cloud: crablike
drags her swollen moonless thighs
across the sky

Her secret tendrils engulf mystery
the light full moon puffed cotton

Jagged breasts of air, not flesh
writhe elongated stars in space

The colloidal blue grease
is beaded, broken

Ice sinkholes the earth
over grave star(s)

Some no longer exist. Can it
be?

I cannot imagine vertically
yet have seen cities of foam
whitened flowing streams
felt the last time
a sifting
cloud white hope
It passed . . .

I could never tell time
a quarter till six
and I was at seven
looking above my head
for faces
Chariots in the sky
God colors of white and gold

The clouds open
crablike
the moon rises

ARTERY OF LAND

Artery of land
the water flecks quench
certain
desert thirsts

Your pore-red valleys
wander
sun-paths
along the vision line
of that New Mexico heat

Small children remember
afternoons pricking them

Feigning sleep
in airless rooms

They recall
tiny beads of sweat:

Home.

SILVER INGOTS OF DESIRE

Silver ingots of desire
fasten themselves about me

weighing me down
in all the familiar spots/slots

Bring me a pillow
a story
upon which to lay my head

THE STUDY

Go off to that tomb
that solitary study
that old and quiet
deadness
that holds us all
in its shelves
books whose cobweb binding
sticks,
not the color, the hue of that room
encarmined stillness
dusty red my dear
and oh so dark,
your pages.

STARFLASH

Starflash
Whiteflash
Blueflash

I can see top to bottom in depth
Thunder: you are making love
quaint phrase, making it
as if it could be
Starflash
the very last (imagine if you can)
time
and only the trees are unafraid

We stood in doorways, thunder,
Starflash
listening
to the corrugated breaks
not even any sign
of a cross to depend on

Rain falls on leaves
the sound of caught moisture
fast and Starflash again

I forgot her stories
between the thunder
and the rain

SAYING "OH NO"

Saying
"Oh no"
in that
supposed calm
lovely and still,
like vapor,
air caught
in gloves, the air in gloves
She moves
beneath covers,
not breathing, and yet
breath comes
from her, softly,

In spaces.

EVERYTHING YOU ARE IS TEETH

Everything you are is teeth
whitened, child,
by the sun
your mouth
purple-red at sunset

CUCKOO DEATH CHIME

This postcard:
we think of you
watching a cuckoo death chime

the apostles are broken
the apostles are broken

life will not come out
life will not come out

of the wall
out of the wall clock

we are cold
so cold

A week before you wrote:
we sat in the sun like lizards
our hands touched sky
our words were fused
in a night-blue room of loving

Later:
soundless cries filled your grey throats
dark noises without light
full of the past
voiceless words from cuckoo death
chimes

The apostles were mute
life was walled up
death came forward
with her crystalline knell

we are so cold
we are so cold
so January cold

German postcard for you, sister

Cuckoo
death
chime

DOOR

evening: the brilliancy of white house against navy sky
afterimaged thunder lay still

A woman stands
her lust
treelike
with spaces.

Uncertain she is
cooled by impending rain
lit by instants
the darkest nights
of her longing.

She rages across the sky
her thunder
a thing diffused
a hidden bruise
beloved one, your touch.

She watches the sky
for traces . . .

Behind a screen
thunder ruminates a shadow
across meshed wire.

Unlock the door.
Feel rain.

Door.
A word like that,
halfclosed.

Bending down she is,
almost there.
She, past fever,
in the land of rain.

CHEKHOV GREEN LOVE

Your Chekhov green face
sings to me
in the silence
of you there, me here
writing a sensitive sore note
of love and prayer
grace and wish.

Chekhov green love.

The rain sprinkles our feet
leaps itself near
to our tension
eases the raging.

Silence pauses.

String of guitar
echoes rain!

Softer, gentler than before

The tuning
fine tuning
of our spirits in the rain.

THE STATE OF MY INQUIETUDE

The state of my inquietude:
27 backboned miles.
Española bound
and lost.

This embryonic embrace
binds my heart to you,
to the sky.

My sorrow sings of traveling mile
of soul
flung to cloud equivalent.

THE FEELING OF GOING ON

The feeling of going on
in chill

A remembered thing
above time or place

Beyond
beyond frame
or light of day

A day as cold
as February 7 in the North

New Mexico

We are taught
by cold
by light

THIS THIN LIGHT

This thin light
that seems to separate us
announces mirrors
in a night dark room.

Do you hear the dogs barking
so far away?

The cat-child keens
a song to the trees.

Dogs vanish into dreams.

TWO BUTTERFLIES

Keep the kites
you said
they were a gift of flight
a memory
of ten to six

I was so tired then
all of you
held me close
I couldn't
there wasn't time
I pressed the wind
between dried sheets

Two butterflies
one red
one gold

NAOMI QUIÑÓNEZ

ULTIMA II TRUE BLUE EYE SHADOWS OF THE PAST

It must be hard doing your teatro everyday
Going to bed with high heels
stranded in the Bali girdle
strapped securely around your head,
gasping in silent horror
in the stark realization
that you forgot your lipstick
at the last bar.
Do ex-Catholic school girls
do penance regularly
on splintered bar stool
luxuriating in the pain
of love gone awry?
Do they rub tequila salt
into old wounds
just to watch the welts grow
and feel the sting
of their last unwanted pregnancy?
Somewhere there is a woman
dying to get out
past a burgundy rinsed head,
dying to leave the black leather
mini skirt at the scene
of someone else's crime.
Dying to spread legs wide and leap
past Hanes Opaque pantyhose
and a hundred stumbling men.
Somewhere a tired poet resides
in a Max-matter-of-factor-face
and refuses the regime of the homeless
to find herself a home inside a poet
who loves passion
more than Ultima II True blue
eye shadows of the past.

THE PHOTOGRAPH

What Adriana said
her blustering petticoats
rushing down red steps.
Adriana of the saints
in her nightmares
the lost soul
in the beautiful face.
Adriana of the orange lips
the french-twist
the tiny waist above full
swirling skirts
poised tentatively
on spiked heels.
Adriana of the
absent self
the misplaced alma
the searching wound.
What Adriana said
as she looped elegantly
into the shimmering
blue-finned chevy
chromed shield of
earth-bound goddess,
what Adriana said to Diego
Diego, the uncertain myth
of constructed men
the navigated ego
of place and placement
Diego of the calloused hands
the restless heart
the palpitating eyes
the caged spirit
that made him swell
each time he looked at Adriana
sweet, chocolate candy
beneath the sugar-starched

stiffness of her musical skirts.
What Adriana said to Diego was:
I will be tus noches de aire
filled with Pérez Prado, the Platters
the eternal strains of cha-cha soul.
I will be your wet dreams and dry eyes
at midnight, your disosa tu cruise
fluorescent calls
the fuscia of noches ansiosas
that will sometimes color your face.
This will be one moment in many
sueños del futuro que nunca
van ser realizados,
initials carved into peeling bark
of swaying eucalyptus trees
sunsets over Chinatown,
hungry kisses in the park.
This is will be August 8, 1958
and I will love you
forever.

SPOUSAL RAPE

She sat coolly
the morning cooking in her lap
short attacks of bay water
filled her eyes.

The lion arrived for lunch
she had just dressed her thigh
for the main dish.
He swaggered sideways against her ear.

They landed, entangled in the cat's milk
and struggled horizontally
on the whiskers of a low growl.

How many meals they managed
no one is certain
only the teeth marks on her throat
will ever say.

AY QUE MARÍA FELIX (OR MARÍA WAS NO VIRGIN)

I am María Felix
done up in black
soft wool clinging
lace collar high
and plunging backline
lower than the San Joaquín Valley.
Attitude all the way
arched eyebrow
arrogant tilt of head.
Men swoon meekly at my feet.
Mexicana to the max
Molcajete Mama
calling the shots
shooting from the hips,
full moon of womanhood
casting shadows over
unsuspecting hearts.
Wide wingspan of spell
over the strongest of men.
Que teatro
swishing feminine
to the backlash of salvation.
Perfúmenes rise
from the thick sensuality
of night's mysterious swell.
Who is this woman
that crosses my path and leads me
to unknown worlds of intrigue?
Is she me, or a channel 34 mirage?
Qué susto to discover
the aching hearts of men
and find the stark
loneliness of their dreams
embedded in the illusion of sexuality.
María would peal that
spit-in-your-eye laughter

y dar la media vuelta
into the obscurity
of her own heart.
Head held high
and high heels digging into the cruelty
of love's passion.
I only laugh into the wine
of a dubious power
and find refuge from passion's
cruel illusion.
Ave María,
Y qué viva la Mujer!

LA DIOSA IN EVERY WOMAN

I

This is an altar of women
a woman's altar
where the shy goddess speaks
in voices more powerful
than the songs of our
mutilated histories.
Where one mind opens
like an eye
against the stares
that have tried to
turn us into stone.
This is an altar
not a high pedestal
or a political platform,
but a foundation
of the universe
a stage for our shadows
to act their own truths.
This is an altar
unaltered by the war cries
that have burdened each century
with our own rude deaths.
We place wreaths of sunflowers
wild poppies and rosaries of corn
upon our lips and kiss away
each wounded moment
that has sliced our heads in half
until we have become twice as beautiful
in both our passion and our rage.

II

Who is that woman on the corner
of Brooklyn and Soto Streets?
Her battered vision
has splintered her
into a hundred pieces.
She is Coyolxauhqui
dismembered goddess
whose shattered parts
once scattered the steps
of the patriarchal pyramid.
We recognize her as a new totality
for our connecting visions.
Gather us in your arms Coyolxauhqui
make us whole again.

III

Coatlicue is the braided hair
that lays upon the head
of a Guatemalan woman
drinking a pepsi in MacArthur Park.
The power of life and death
rests like water in her palms.
The two headed serpent of her soul
holds her in two worlds
that have split her mind
into alternating waves of
conflict and reconciliation.
Heal us Coatlicue
become the bridge between the worlds
that separate us from ourselves.

I V

Who is that woman crossing the border?
She is Malinalxochitli
keeper of the power of nature
Warrior Mother and Warrior Sister
who does battle each day
with the pompous winds
that attack the very breath
that survives inside the dreams
of tired seamstresses.
Gather us in your heart
Malinalxochitli
give us courage for the battles ahead.

V

Is that Tonantzín in stiletto heels
with hips the size of mother earth
shaking to the drums of each
fertile moment that gives birth
to new consciousness?
Dance with us Tonantzín
enfold us in your red and black robes
bless the births we give to ourselves
and each other.

V I

This is an altar of women
a woman's altar
constructed for the goddess
inside the heart
of each woman and man.
Come to us Diosa
work through us Diosa

to heal the wounds of flesh and dreams
to plant the seeds of strength.
This is an altar of women
a woman's altar
and here no woman
will be sacrificed.

GLORIA ENEDINA ÁLVAREZ

AODO   ACRIN
CREN   CODO

Estoy atrapada   I am caught
en un mundo de luz   in a world of light
Páginas ilimitadas   Boundless pages
se abren a mí.   open up to me.
La palabra escapa   The world escapes
después regresa, salta   then bounces back

Atrás cortinas vagas de pensamiento.   Behind vague curtains of thought.

SIN COMPLICACIONS	WITHOUT COMPLICATIONS
Dices.	You say
Y los pliegues	And the unfolding
¿Dime?	Tell me?
Dame	Give me
Y decíamos	We said
las palabras interminables	And the words unending
Y dábamos al decirnos	And we gave as we spoke
esos sonidos	those sounds
indescifrables	undecipherable
agudos, largos	sharp, long
y tan sencillos	and so simple
a volver complicados	to become complicated
ríos de silencio.	rivers of silence.
ríos de silencio.	rivers of silence.

ELEGIR

Yo no quiero promesas
quiero hechos
No quiero palabras
que se dividen
y se multiplican
y rodean la
confianza malmedida en
alambres de deseos
inciertos, distantes y nulos
Quiero ver la palabra en vuelo
en distancia medida
en geografía métrica
no en vendado discurso \ ensayo
o la última novedad
la curiosidad del día
la inmensidad de mañana
o nunca o quién sabe
o tú sabes mejor
Es la sonrisa misma
que actúa y confirma.

CHOICE

I don't want promises
but facts
not words
that divide
and multiply
and surround
unmeasured trust
into wires of wishes
uncertain, distant and null
I want to see the Word in flight
in measured distance
in metric geography
not in bandaged discourse \ essay
the latest novelty or
today's curiosity
the immensity of tomorrow
or never or who knows
or you know best
It's the smile, in and of itself
that acts and confirms it.

EL REGALO Y LA PALABRA

La palabra floreció
afilándose
entre sus dientes agudos
y sus palabras largas.

THE WORD AND THE GIFT

The word blossomed
sharpening
on razor teeth
and long words.

THE WORD Y EL REGALO

The word blossomed
afilándose
on razor teeth
y palabras largas.

VUELVO Y NO RECUERDO

Recuerdo sólo presentir\
   presenciar el olvido,
saber el silencio con su
   necesidad de hablar
sin hacerlo nunca, el pensar
   de vivir la ausencia
de sentir nudos en el cuerpo
   y no desatarlos,
no soltar la cuerda, no poder
   medir el tiempo
y volver, a olvidar días,
   recordar sólo sentimientos,
visiones, sueños, admoniciones,
   juegos, ritos,
perdidas palabras, torcidas por
   la distancia y ruido.
Robo al tiempo su mañana para no
diluirme
en verdades ahumadas o mística
   teñida.

VUELVO Y SUEÑO

I RETURN AND DON'T REMEMBER

I remember only a premonition
   to witness oblivion,
to know silence with its need
   to speak
without ever doing it, to live
   absence,
to feel knots in the body
   without untying them,
to not let go of the rope, not
   be able to measure time
and return, forget days,
   remember only feelings,
visions, dreams, admonitions,
   games, rites,
lost words twisted by the
   distance and the noise.
I steal tomorrow from time as
to not dilute myself
in smoked truths or dyed
   mystique.

I RETURN AND DREAM

HUESO DE LA NOCHE

grey flight
purple stars like wishes
measure the night
sola espalda azul
rayada con deseo
mide el frío lento
de su boca atada
púrpuras estrellas
miden la noche
como anhelos
vuelo gris
lone blue back
striped with desire
measures the slow coldness of her bound mouth

una luna llena de
junio 6/6/93

SORDA

El movimiento estremece
    pétalos de polvo creciendo
amarillo alrededor de tu sabor

tu lengua atada a la cabecera
    ya no puedes hablar
tus sueños prestados a otro
    olvidado en tu búsqueda

DEAF

The movement astounds
    stark petals of dust growing
yellow around your taste buds

your tongue is tied to the bedpost
    you can no longer speak
your dreams borrowed by another
    whom you've forgotten in your search

DE VIAJE

Marido sin mujer
padre sin hijos
ciudadano sin patria
imaginador de lengua atada
sexo agredido
visión nublada
maleta de palabras

es abril
va de viaje

ON A TRIP

Husband without wife
Father without sons
Citizen without country
Dreamer with tongue tied
Bruised sex
Clouded vision
Suitcase of words

It is April
He's taking a trip.

EL DIA QUE INICIÓ

Bórrame de ti si quieres
que otra no lo hará te aseguro
ni ella la otra ni la siguiente
detienen la torrente ciega que te persigue
te niega ser más amor que el amor mismo
y más sincero que el presente

Ilusión distorcionada en agua fría
sobre tus manos las del calor mismo amarillo gris
mirando desde el pasillo mi eco en ti
su ruido busca y su reflejo se extiende
sin seguir su hilo verde en el incio continuo
que te fascina que te mata libertades
que te asegura distancia
libertad la que pides y no tomas
teniéndola sin saber

Acepta su compromiso
a hablar actuar
Toma La Palabra
Toma tu Palabra
Tómala por lo que es por ti.

THE DAY IT BEGAN

Erase me from you
if you wish
someone else will not

I assure you
neither her
nor the next
nor the one after
will stop the blinding
storm that persecutes you
It keeps you from being
more love than love itself
and more sincere than today

Distorted illusion in cold water
over your hands
yellow gray
from the passageway
my echo within you
its noise reaches out
its reflection extends
without following its green thread
in the continuous beginning
which fascinates you
which deprives you of your freedom
which ensures distance
freedom that you ask for

but do not take
having it without knowing it

Accept its commitment
to speak to act
Take the Word
Take your Word
Take it for your own sake

CHISPA

¿Quién dice que la luz
traspasando los árboles
en la selva o en el bosque
es un corazón en fuga
convertida en efímera energía?

¿Quién dice que el agua del arroyo
con su gorgoreo
es sólo el reflejo
de un día con momentos prolongados
del ojo mental
traslucientes, fluidos y fugaces?

¿Quién dice que el rocío de la aurora
es una bella estrella azul gris rebelde
sin descanso
decidida en descender aquí,
absorbiendo el calor
de unas lágrimas destilando esperanzas?

¿Quién dice?
El decir es dicho,
es aire que pasa por la boca,
sonidos resbalando, justamente empujando
la lengua al paladar
tocando levemente los dientes
antes de partir más allá
del horizonte bucal,
decidido al vacio desconocido
otorgado, hacia el destino
o tal vez a la memoria—
la memoria intangible y humana
hasta ser Una.

SPARK/CHISPA

In that moment of hope . . .
Who says that the light
seeping through the trees
in the jungle or forest
is a heart in flight
converted into energy,
ephemeral and pure?
Who says that the water
in the brook with its gurgling
is only the reflection of
prolonged moments in the mind's eye,
flowing, fleeing, translucent?
Who says that the morning mist
is a beautiful blue grey star,
a rebel without rest,
set on descending here,
absorbing the warmth
of tears dripping hope?
Who says? Words are common knowledge,
air passing through the mouth
pushing the tongue towards the palate,
softly touching the teeth,

caressing gently before departing
beyond the oral horizon
certain, towards the unknown void
toward Destiny or
perhaps memory—
the intangible human memory
until being One.

FALLEN COMRADE, THERE IS NO MOURNING YOU

"If one falls it is because
someone must fall, in order that
hope would not fall."
—OTTO RENÉ CASTILLO

Haydee, sister Maya-Quiche woman,
they tried to quelch the splendor of
your valor, your seedlings.
Your children will know the rigor
of your womb.
Your blood spilled,
never your honor—that of your people.
It makes every daybreak fertile,
dressing the morning star with hope
alongside so many horrors in this raped
red-grey jungle.
Like the Quetzal, your spirit continues the flight,
landing to render courage
in returning with your kind,
who dress the morning with color, with corn.
They return the green to the mountain
burned and stained with yesterday.
Sister, this extension is a cry of conscience,
a call to action, the length of a landbridge
Guatemala, Mexico, Los Angeles,
to you Chicana.

STILL DREAMS

Still dreams in silence
fly
surrender
dry
shoreless
fallen
winged clouds
among
fragments of sky
dust veils
upon L.A.

The webbed fingers
of the city
surface
in the trembling hand
of the young girl
that reaches out
to pay
one more whisper
CRACK
the opening
skin the city's walls
blood drawn
to the separation
of hands
veins flow
each
in its direction
towards the heart.

CONTRASTES

Interminables cilindros gris
plata reflejando su cálido brillo
contra los viejos rectángulos porosos de ladrillo café rojo,
enanos anciados en el callejón de mala muerte.
Sus sombras desinfectadas se deslizan,
resbalando sobre los anchos bordes de cartón piedra caído,
como máscaras sobre los olores de vida,
perfume mohoso de ayer,
de vidas momentarias con bocinas rechinando,
botellas rompiéndose en armonía con una moción regada
del tiempo traficante, zombies sexuales, alucinaciones vivas
    procesadas
en la fábrica de sueños del dios Dollar,
el llanto de los niños enredado en las escaleras de los hoteles
enmudeciendo a los residentes anestesiados por la jeringa
ánimas penando alimentos en el basurero de la gran ciudad,
desposeídos de su esencia.
Creyeron enterrar su corazón en Bunker Hill,
los gigantes invasores de vidrio,
barriendo un pedazo de Barrio Diamond
para remplazarlo con sus visitantes
que se confunden a diario por sus casi uniformes tonos
de negro, blanco y gris.
Llegaron dejando sus sombras,
pero siempre llevándoselas al salir.
La venganza del diamante, se dice.
Brillantes vidriales congelan los corazones de sus habitantes.

CONTRASTES/CONTRASTS

Interminables, interminable silver gray cylinders
reflecting their cool glitter
against aging brown and brick red porous rectangles
now dwarfed and anchored on skid row.
Its slick disinfected shadows slip over
the wide matte-finish corners of the collapsed tent city,
as if masking los olores de vida, the smell of life,
perfumed with pungent mustiness of yesterday,
of living for the moment or momentarily living
with horns, screeches, bottles breaking in harmony
with the scattered motion of trafficking time, sex zombies,
living hallucinations manufactured in the dream factory
of the money gods,
children's cries winding up hotel staircases
to numb the heavy whispers of its needled residents,
pained souls begging food from the great city's garbage dump,
robbed of their essence.
The invading glass giants thought their hearts lie buried
under Bunker Hill, while they swept aside part of Varrio Diamond
to be replaced by its daily visitors in confusing tones
of black, white and gray.
They come casting their shadows but always
taking them home at dayend.
The Diamond Curse—Brillantes Vidriales—freezes the hearts
of its inhabitants, it's said.

VENDE FUTURO

Cruzamos "la línea entre las cuatro direcciones,
puntos comunes en caminatas largas.
We cross "the line" between four directions.
common points on long paths,
those same steps in other places.
los mismos pasos en otros lugares.
vivir, amar tan duro, tan abierto.
to live, to love so hard, so open.
Breathless Heart, Corazón Sin Suspiros.
pasos tomados por caminantes distintos
Ayer como Hoy
steps taken by different travelers
Today like Yesterday.
I saw him selling oranges.
Was that you, Earth Star?
Lo vi vendiendo naranjas.
Fuiste tú, Astro Terrenal?
Defying the cops with your presence.
outslicking them while you bury the fruit in the bushes—
The Invisible Man
El Invisible—
desafías a la policia con tu presencia,
ganándole, enterrando la fruta en las matas.
I saw him handcuffed, the Caminante.
el sol amaneciendo en sus ojos cafés,
matizando la sonrisa,
muy esperanzado hace un día,
consiguiendo sólo para otra caja de naranjas a cinco dólares
confiscadas hoy como evidencia
Making only enough for another five dollar box of oranges
today, confiscated as evidence.
Invisible Criminal no name, no data, no land
Criminal Invisible sin nombre, sin datos, sin tierra
Smog naranja gris nubla sus dientes brillantes
hoy desparecido, empacado,
desde la Casa de Vidrio al Centro de Detención con la Migra

pérdida de mayoreo
orange grey smog clouds his shiny teeth,
disappeared today, packed away,
from the Glass House to the INS Detention Center,
wholesale loss
naranjeros color a sol, perfume cítrico ahumado,
naranjeras preñadas con un niño en espera en el carrito de marketa.
a un lado, en la salida del freeway, tu salida, Sr. Cultivador
orange sellers, sun colored, smoked citrus perfumed.
pregnant orange sellers, a child waits in the market cart
by the side, at the freeway exit, your exit, Mr. Grower

TOTEM/LA SIEMPRE FIRME

Tantas como yo
hirviendo, hinchadas
So many like me,
brown faced women
boiling, swollen
bodies/lives
a map bordering madness ·
vidas/cuerpos
un mapa frontera con locura
super señora,
chíngate-loca,
dáselo, hácelo,
super e-x-p-l-o-t-a-b-l-e mujer
cuerpos/vidas y fronteras impuestas,
mezcla económico-concreto
bodies/lives and imposed borders,
economic-concrete mix
So many like me
swollen, boiling women
with brown faces
the Chingada, underlined,
her body, her land, her mind
raped and colonized,
in crazy solitary multiple search,
exploit-all insanity
Tantas como yo
hinchadas, mujeres hirviendo,
caras bronceadas
chingándose
como toda la Chingada,
subrayada,
su cuerpo, su tierra,
su mente colonizada
en búsqueda loca, solitaria, multiple,
locura explota-todo,
la Siempre Firme

bajo crítica pesada,
no importa la llaga supurante,
pasándose con Super Macho inasimilable
Always Solid,
always under heavy criticism,
despite the suppurating wound,
overdosing on Super Macho vitamins, unassimilable
Totem pole women
who wear their colors
bright and bold
Mujeres totémicas
llevan sus colores
brillantes, marcados
holding her/holding him/holding herself out
angles cut away and rounded,
deteniéndola/deteniéndolo/deteniéndose
ángulos cortados, redondos
work-hunt
trabajo-cacería
cuerpos/vidas
bodies/lives
un mapa bordering locura,
roto y encendido
broken, in flames.

ALMA E. CERVANTES

PIQUETITOS OF LOVE

Unos cuantos piquetitos,
sólo unas golpeaditas
y a veces unas gotitas
de sangre;
resultados de tanto ser querida.

Lo hizo porque me ama,
He did it because he loves me . . .

mientras baño tu hijo,
un golpe en la vagina,
expresión de valor?
        poder?

El Doctor responde:
"sólo una golpeadita
señora, vuelve con
tu esposo".

the edge of your Love
against my throat
slides from side to side;
a meticulous motioning
of your ternura.

Clenched fist yearning
my soft spoken lips,

broken arms that
refused to embrace,
bruised eyes
that searched an
escape.

I pray, and I plead
one day you will
fall
out of love
for me.

Until that day,
here I am waiting
for your

piquetitos,
golpeaditas,
and the blood
that streams from
the wounds of your loving.

BORN AGAIN CHRISTIAN

Chela was a white hue
chicana of the chingona kind.
Hard face with cheek bones that
cut if you get too close.

Laugh so mean like her
brother Tuttie who makes fun of
Alicia's drunk dad and Tony's mom
who kicks his ass in front of everyone.

No one knows that Chela and Tuttie's dad
is the loco man that hangs out
by the school gate.
Chela always blocked the door
when we picked her up to
walk around the projects.

One night a guy with shiny
shoes and cool smile made
Chela's face soft.
"He talks right,"
Chela said "and he has
nice friends who have lots of
money."

She stopped hanging out, and
we didn't like her anymore.

Shiny shoes and cool smile
disappeared in his ride one night
and never came back for Chela.

Yesterday we knocked on Chela's
door. She looked out with sad eyes
wrapped in a bathrobe, didn't

want to talk but mumbled
"Jesus loves me now" and then
closed the door on our faces.

HAD I IRONED YOUR SHIRT

Had I ironed your shirt,
maybe you'd still be here by
my side.

Like Zorba the Greek
you christened me;
"Mi mujer".

Your rage won no academy awards
and your performance overall was
distorted by feelings
neither one of us could decipher.

I took silence as my refuge
while the fog grew thicker
and the cold mist cut the weak
clasp of your hand in mine.

Wrapping both my arms
around my shoulders
I stepped back
but the fog approached
with no end.

You came to me with quick
burning candles of passion.
None were made to last.

Desperation wrapped itself
around our heads. Distrust
guided us both to the end
of the night.

I watched you ironing your shirt;
resentful strokes back and forth,
back and forth like our efforts

to beat this test that neither one of us
asked for. With a quick snap, your head
turned to me like a bullet and your
angry glare was enough for me to
understand.

had I ironed your shirt, maybe you'd
still be here by my side
with the blinding fog
the cold severing mist
and both my arms wrapped around my
shoulders.

HARTA

Pinches Viejas,
you must have
heard of us.

We clean your
calzones,
feed your hijos,
and pick up the
welfare check.

I stand in line
listening for
"blue light special"
while, mis hijos
play escondidas
beneath clothes
racks.

When I arrive
there you sit
the paper in one
hand,
a cerveza in the
other.

you reach for
La pinche vieja
as she pulls out
a new box of
cigarrillos.

You call out
her name as
the smell of
sopa y carnitas
reaches your senses,

yet when the aroma
of your hijo's
caca interferes,
you demand la pinche vieja's
presence.

A knock at the door
sends you running
to the escusado.

The bill collector
at the puerta begins:
"escúsame, are you
la pinche vieja?"

surely, you must
recognize me,
I don't think I've
changed,
and alas,
to you, all of us
pinche viejas must look
alike.

A TOAST

Winas don't hang out on
street corners,
they live in a house
like the mouse
nervous with
big eyes
and ready abacks,
listening to drip drip
sinks making clink clink
toilet sounds.

They travel to
lonely lands
so no man
can kick'em
and then tuck them
into bed.

They cry in dark
smokey corners
where wino men
can't fit.

Winas drink then talk
about lost broken babies,
hurtful hands, ugly faces
and dirty smells.
Winas don't lie
in drunken stupor.
They don't hurt,
too weak, too broken,
to lift shaky hands
that protect, defend
happy faces,
they couldn't

preserve innocence
behind prison bars,
nursing unhealing
scars.

THE ROOTS OF CHICANA URBAN PLANNERS
Written for Leo Estrada

Mom took us on walks that moved straight
but turned like spirals.

Our footsteps were like the stitches she sewed,
guiding the tela north, west, south, east,
again and again.

We had to keep moving to new yet familiar
neighborhoods, but as time passed
the new ones felt the same as the old ones.

Her Heart, Gut, Mind united in clamor and motion of
the machine.
Determined were her hands that guided tela forward,
always forward.
Her eyes saw more than stitches,
things I longed to see.

We continued to take walks, but the roads kept turning 'round and
'round no
matter how far we travelled.

"Our walks will change when we earn more money," she
reassured me,
but the spiral roads always turned against us.

She continued to push tela forward, always forward, carefully
watching each stitch
take its place.

One day my spiral walks
Ended.

I kissed her goodbye and walked away.
Still guided by the discipline of her hands and
depth of her visions.

Today I cut through old material,
weave through rigid structures
prepare new patterns;
I am a Chicana urban planner.

REFLECTIONS OF "LA VIEJA"

I woke up in the morning
torn by the arrugas on my
face;
ooo, baby, baby, and look at those thighs!

My Viejo looks at me
and those endearing eyes
reflect surprise.

I look at his panza—
there has been a
compromise.

He watches the tele—
young rucas with red lips
and chichonga
hips
who act like
there ain't
no end.

I comb my hair
that no longer bounces,
my hair
highlighted with canas.

I look at the pelón
sitting with the tele.

I remember his nachas
which stood up so sturdy;
I think the pinche
colchón ate then up.

I remember his masculine jaw,
the Azteca nose job—

What a man, I said
to Chata.

I had a pair of
chichis that would
not quit,but now
they always look down.

His nariz is filled
with pelos that grandchildren say
are asco.

I walk to the marketa
to buy the vegetables
admiring the pepinos,
and, with precision
picking the best
chiles.

As I walk home
swift young steps
leave me behind.

As I stir the sopa,
my Viejo calls,
"Vieja, ven a ver
lo que ganaron
en the Lotería."

I used to be "cheet, cheet,
oyes mija . . ."
In the heat of passion,
I was "Mamacita,"
but one day I became
"Vieja."

At dinner he tells
me about the pinche

jefe . . .
I tell him about
Chata's grandson who
is going to college.

Then he says, "Vieja,
I could have been
a foreman
if I had just gotten
my H.S. diploma."
"Sí pues, hombre,
finish your sopa."

In bed, as I put on my
rejuventud cream,
I feel his callos
scratch my legs.

From the darkness
I hear a tired voice
whisper: "Goodnight, Vieja,
I love you."
"Goodnight, Viejo,
yo también te amo."

IN MY DREAMS

"I'm different, pick me, I
am a new generation the one
all you mexican pickers and
pissed off chicanas dreamed of."

What made you voters think
they would be any different
than their men?

Now its over
no more notions of gringa politicians
concerned with immigrant rights,
forget financial aid and
your jefita can die of cancer
before she gets her federal
health benefits.

I day dream of catching those cabronas
on a lucha libre basis:

"In this corner, The masked Feinstein
and her partner, Qué Barbara Boxer!!

The challengers: Refugia de Tijuana
and her sister Furia de Aguas Calientes."

I could see my mom Juana and I
sitting on front row seats eating
our higado with onion tortas lightly dipped in
Grey poupon, washing it down with té de canela.

Calm and confident we'll watch the
skillful hermanas tire their opponents
Guard techniques, Flag waving, and weak promises
of protecting our humane rights, until finally,

Refugia and her sister Furia
apply their famous Reboso Choke Hold, then
I and my mom will jump over the ropes,
position ourselves over their face
a la rancho style when you got to do caca,
and in unison let out a paralyzing pedo.

The crowd will stand and roar,
it would be another victory for all the
sick and tired abuelas and madres who
bust their ass to get a little
food, respect, and English classes!!

11. Prose

❁ ❁ ❁ ❁

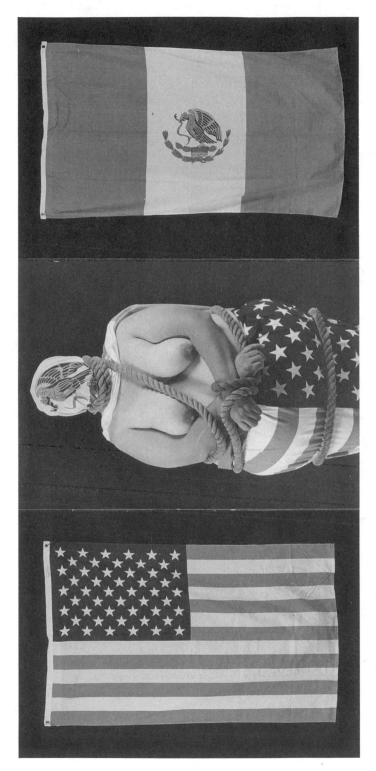

Laura Aguilar *Three Eagles Flying*

Carmen Lomas Garza *Tuna de Nopal/Pedacito de mi Corazón*

❃ Novena Narrativas y Ofrendas Nuevomexicanas

DENISE CHÁVEZ

Novena Narrativas was inspired by cultural traditions of *cuentistas* (storytellers), *santeros* and *ofrendas* (constructed and assembled collage mementos), especially popular during All Souls Day in the Southwest and in Latin America. Inspiration came as well from the *altares* and *nichos* one finds in the family homes.

Novena Narrativas are nine narrations to be performed in monologue by one or more actresses. The characters vary in age—from 7 to 78—and are familiar to those of us who love New Mexico, its traditions, cultures and daily life—full as it is with significant detail. Specifically linked as they are to New Mexico, the women are universal in spirit. They appear one by one, and the great delicate flame of their burning hopes, dreams and devotions rise to the maternal figurehead.

The *Ofrendas Nuevomexicanas* consist of a clay Madonna (in the style of Nuestra Señora de Leche y Buen Parto), which is set on a chest, suggesting an altar in the home. Her garments, corona, and *esplendor* (halo or aura) are constructed of fiber, handwoven and embroidered commercial cloth, ornamental tin and brass work. The setting will include other items, token memorabilia representing parts of the women's lives and culture. The narrator(s) portray(s) the women and assembles the ofrendas as she performs on stage.

Novena Narrativas y Ofrendas Nuevomexicanas was first performed in Taos, New Mexico in February 1986 by Kika Vargas. Since that time, the play has toured throughout the Southwest.

This labor of love began as a collaboration between five women artists: Juanita Jaramillo-Lavadie, a weaver; Sandi Roybal Maestas, a potter; Patricia Vargas-Trujillo, a tinsmith; Denise Chávez, a writer; and Kika Vargas, an actress.

LIST OF CHARACTERS
(In order of appearance)
María Isabel González, the narrator

Jesusita Rael, a storeowner and spinster
Esperanza González, the wife of a Vietnam veteran
Minda Mirabal, a foster child
Magdalena Telles, the mother of seven children
Tomasa Pacheco, a nursing home resident
Juana Martínez, a factory employee
Pauline Mendoza, a Chicana teenager
Corrine, "La Cory" Delgado, a bag lady

The set: *A tall chest, covered by a lace mantel. On it stands a statue of La Virgen de Guadalupe. On either side of the Virgen are two tall candles, and fanning out in front are nine small votive candles, unlit. Nearby is a table and a chair. The space is untidy, scattered with paper; the props, a blanket draped over the chair.*

At rise: *Isabel comes in breathlessly, with a bag of groceries that she sets down on the table. She leaves the food in the bag and organizes the area. The lights come down, and she throws the blanket on the floor, then lays down on it. She is tired and wants to meditate a while. It has been a busy day and she wants to relax. On the floor near her is a large pile of papers, some collated, some not. After a long silence, in the darkness, she turns the lights up slightly and begins to exercise. She does various yoga positions, stretching slowly, first on the floor, then in a seated position. With her back to the audience she begins talking.*

ISABEL
Somebody asked me what I do for a living. I am an artist I said. I write. I am a writer . . . (*Stretching, she grabs a foot, then jumps up, yelling*) Green tennis shoes! That's it, I forgot the shoes! (*Turning up lights, she goes to a pile of papers on the desk and jots down the note*) . . . Jesusita Rael, green tennies . . . (*Back to floor, adjusting self, with Jesusita's voice*) Buenos días le dé Dios, hermana . . . (*Practicing, trying to get voice just right, high, with an S lisp*) Buenos días le dé Dios . . . (*In a shoulder stand, struggling, then falling back and laying there, she turns to one side and begins to collate papers. She talks and collates*) Jesusita, Esperanza, Minda, Madgalena, Tomasa, Juana, Pauline and Corrine; Jesusita, Esperanza, Minda, Magdalena, Tomasa, Juana, Pauline, and La Cory, one, two, three, four, five, six, seven, eight . . .

(*Isabel does this for awhile, then goes to the bag, finds juice, has a sip; she takes out a can of peas and leaves it on the chest, near the altar. On her way back, she picks up a pile of bills, opens them, and then places them face down on the table. She starts to put out the prop pieces; we follow her, as she mumbles and works out the play. She talks as she puts out the props, which include: Jesusita's lace collar, Esperanza's peas, Minda's doll and blanket, Tomasa's wig and cane, Juana's goggles, feathers and cedar, Magdalena's comb, brush, makeup and robe, Pauline's jacket and red headband, and Corrine's bag. She goes into snippets of the characters speech)*

Adrede iba a bailar! (*Dancing around the room singing "El Rancho Grande"*) . . . I didn't care with who! (*Sitting down and hunching over, she becomes Tomasa*) I'm going to live to a ripe old age! (*Then sitting up straight, as herself*) My name is María Isabel González . . . (*Sighing*) When people tell me it's an easy time to be a woman, me río! As far as I'm concerned, when you're a woman, no time is easy. And when you're an artist, it's worse. Those born rich suffer as much as those born poor. But I'm not complaining. I might worry, but then I either sing or pray or laugh. Ríanse, as my gramita used to say. And love! One of the greatest powers we all possess is the ability to love.

(*Getting up and beginning to set the altar*) Just last week I was cleaning up in here, you can imagine what it was like, and I ran across a letter from my mom. She's been dead for years. I sat down and read it, and it was as if she was talking to me. Isabel, Isabel, what are your priorities? Mija, you need some lipstick, you're so pale, are you wearing a bra? It was as though she was right here next to me telling me how much she loved me, how proud of me she was, and to keep on working.

(*Isabel is moved, she pauses in her work. She goes and lights a candle for her mother's spirit*) When I feel alone, I remember behind me stand my grandmother, my mother, all the women who have come before me. Their spirits are always near, watching over me, guiding me, constantly teaching me. Today, when I went out for groceries, I heard one woman telling another, "La vida es una canción." I could have sworn I heard my grama's voice. And then I thought: this woman is a thread that connects me to all women, everywhere. Wherever I go, I *know* the women. I know their deepest joys and pains.

(*Setting things on chest*) Jesusita, Minda, Esperanza, the others . . . They are familiar to me. On the surface, their lives are really different from mine. And yet, when I look at them, I see a light shining from and through them, and in that light I recognize my gramita, my mom, my sister, my friends and myself as well. I understand the passion of their lives. I see that it has made them strong, patient and faithful. They have come full circle to that place of peace we all move toward when we pray or sit in silence.

(*Stretching*) Ay . . . Look, I've really been talking, que habladero! I have to get back to work, I have a deadline, excuse me . . .

(*Becoming Jesusita, she puts on the collar Jesusita wears. Throughout the play, Isabel will become the characters, donning costume pieces and assuming the posture and voice of*

*characters. All is done on stage, without a curtain, in full view of the audience. Each char-
acter should have one or two costume pieces that identify them. A basic black turtle neck
with pants and skirt should serve as the primary costume*)

JESUSITA
(*A mouse-like spinster, she speaks in a high reedy voice, with a certain lisp. She runs a store
of curiosities, sells thread and needles and little yellow candles that are so old that when you
lift them, they break. The store has ceased to really serve the public, but Jesusita would not
dare think of closing it. She wears her funny little hat, green tennies and dusts as she talks*)

Buenos días le dé Dios, Hermana Dioses. Muchísimas gracias por la man-
zanilla que me trajo la última vez. Siéntese, hermana, a platicar. Not too
many customers yet. Todo ha cambiado. ¿Por qué? La gente se levanta tarde,
come demasiado, y nobody va a misa anymore, y por qué? El H-B-O. ¡HBO!
¡La televisión! Pues sí, tengo cable, falta de esa novela desgraciada, *Seduc-
ción.* (*Pause*)

Oh, I been pretty good. I'm not dead yet, gracias a Dios! (*Sighing*) People
don't need different colors of thread anymore, nobody sews. And ahora nadie
usa dedales! My mother always used a thimble. She thought anyone who
didn't was a fool. One time in this very room, Bárbara, she was working on
a dress and she yelled to me, "Jesusita, ven pronto!" She had stabbed herself
with a small needle and it was moving up her arm into the bloodstream. Oh,
yes, she finally got it out. And then she sat down and cried. If she'd lost it, it
would have gone through her blood, gone to her heart, and killed her! Bárbara! Have you heard of anything? That was mamá.

(*Looking around*) Rael's Tienda de Abarrotes. Someday it will just disappear. If I'd gotten married . . . Oh, tuve chansa. His name was Prudencio
Sifuentes. El Ermitaño, they called him, for his role in *Los Pastores*. Oh, I
was too busy with the store. Finally, Prudy moved to Santa Barbara, California. And about a year later, he drowned in the ocean. Bárbaro! No, no, no
tuve ganas de casarme con él. Era muy chapito. His ears were small as well.
I could never marry anyone with ears smaller than my own. ¡Ni lo permita
mi Dios! Oh, I missed having children, but then I started with the Foster Children's Program. They became my kids. Rosella, she lives in Roswell,
Rini's in Tucumcari, and Donacio's a dentist in Downey, California. All the
kids . . . They call me mamá and everything. And they always send me cards
pa' Crismes, you know?

(*Confidentially*) Pero ya me cansé. I'm ready to devote more time to the church. I take communion to the prisoners and up to the Four Directions Nursing Home. Vi a la hermana Tomasa. Bárbara! She don't look too good, that's what I say. Tenía una peluca güera. She was never a blond! but what can you say? (*With resignation*) I'm too busy with God to be worrying about people.

(*Hedging a bit*) ¿La muchachita? She's still with me. Pobrecita Minda. Me da lástima con ella. Es que her father wants her back, ni lo mande Dios. And Magdalena says she'll take her, ni lo mande Dios. And she can't stay here, ni lo mande Dios! (*Crossing herself*) Pobrecita niña, all she really wants is a mother and to be close to God, if God's not a man! (*High, nervous laughter*).

No, I never married . . .

(*Rearranging things on the altar*) ¿No necesita unas velas, hermana? Cera de abeja. They don't make them like they used to, you know?

(*Sighing*) Nobody buys thread anymore. Or buttons. Or needles.

(*Swatting at a fly*) ¡Malditas moscas! Oh, I understand, hermana, you have to go. Lleve esta velita a la hermana Tomasa, if she ain't dead yet, pobrecita. El cancer. I'll see you next week at the Third Order Meeting of Las Franciscanas! Vaya con Dios, Hermana María. ¡Adios!

(*Going back to altar to light a candle and rearrange a little bit more*) Pobrecito Prudy! Como me contaba del amor de California . . . del mar de California. (*She shakes her head as a look of fondness, sadness, almost regret comes to her face*) No era porque era chapito . . . not really . . . eran esas orejitas! Pobrecito Prudy. Que mi madrecita lo tenga descansando en paz . . .

(*Isabel sheds Jesusita and becomes Esperanza*)

ESPERANZA

(*A plain-looking, tired woman; she goes to the altar and lights a candle immediately*)

No tengo mucho tiempo, Madrecita. I have to rush back to work. I just came to check the mail and to eat lunch. (*Making the sign of the cross*) You know my needs better than I do myself. Take care of José, bring him home and help him to stop drinking. Take care of Isabel, ¡ay Isabel, her and her art! She's a wonderful girl, a beautiful woman, Madrecita. Make her strong like all the other women of her family. Take care of everyone else in the family, tía Panchita, Reis and the twins, my ahijado, el Jerry . . .

(*A bit sadder*) Take care of all my hijitos who are already with you in Heaven. El Hector, pobrecito, ni tuvo chansa para vivir. Take care of all the others who were killed in Vietnam, and all the others who suffered from it, like my José, who never got over that terrible war. Take care of todos los alcohólicos y los que sufren de las drogas y mueren de las drogas! Take care of our men and all the women who love them. ¡Cuídalos, Madrecita! Lift them to your loving heart, hold them in the palm of your hand, have mercy on them.

(*Tiredly, to La Virgencita*) Ay, sometimes I'm so tired I can't even pray. All I can do is sit. Sit and be quiet.

(*Getting up and opening a can of peas with a can opener*) I don't have much time, excuse me, Madrecita. Voy a comer mi lonche. Con su permiso, mi Reina.

(*Isabel transforms into the character of Minda, a seven-year-old girl who sits on the floor playing with her doll and blanket*)

MINDA
I have a little friend. Her name is uh. . . uh. . . Jennifer . . . Marie . . . something. Something Anglo. She's seven-years-old, like me. No! She's not fat! She's real pretty. It's not me, I told you, it's my friend, Jennifer Marie. Anyway, it can't be me 'cause she has a mom. And a real father. And she doesn't live where there's garbage and broken beer bottles all over the place! She doesn't have to take short-cuts through Mrs. Ruiz' faded towels and stinky baby diapers or Mr. Ruiz' baggedy-raggedy shorts on the line! (*Giggling hysterically*)

(*Whispering confidentially to the doll and pulling the blanket over her and the door to make a tent*) Now, you can't tell anyone, okay? This is a secret for always and forever. You can't even tell God, understand? Jennifer's father hurts little girls. He beats her and does ugly, dirty things to her. What he does is bad! And he told her if she ever told anybody, he would kill her! (*Crying hysterically*)

(*Dramatic change into the present and herself*) I never even told God. I didn't even know God until Miss Rael took me to church.

(*Does switch-over to Jesusita Rael, with a high voice*) ¡Minda, Minda, Minda, buenos días le dé Dios!

(*Back to herself*) I can't talk to Miss Rael. Her voice is too high and her bones stick out, real sharp! And she never even had a baby! But I can talk to you, mi'jita. You're my best bestest friend! And I can talk to Magdalena, the neighbor. She tells me, "Don't be afraid of your body, Minda. All women are the same that way. It's beautiful! A gift from God the Mother. The female thing won't kill you, or your mother being dead. All things have to die. It's natural."

(*To her doll*) Come on, let's you and me and Miss Rael go to church. (*Pretending to be in church*) Shhh. We have to sit back here with the other old ladies and Miss Rael.

(*Looking around and daydreaming. She then becomes attentive and begins to imitate the way the old ladies sing*) Bendito, bendito, bendito sea Dios. Los ángeles cantan y alaban a Dios. Los ángeles cantan y alaban a Dios . . .

(*Daydreaming again and having a conversation with the doll*) I want a dog. But Miss Rael says, "No. It will only die." Oh, let it! It's natural! Ay, ouch! Don't pinch me. I wasn't daydreaming! I know I have a lot to be grateful for! I'm not fat and ugly! (*To doll*) Miss Rael always pinches me when I talk in church . . .

(*Pointing*) See God on the altar? He's got big black strange eyes and silver lightning coming out of his head. Look the other way!

(*Pointing the other direction*) And that's the God Mother. She's not old and ugly. She's real pretty! I never had a mother, except when I was born and was real sick and almost died. That was when the tubes were in my mouth and nose and the doctors said, "She'll probably die. If she lives, don't expect much."

(*Suddenly changing, becoming violent with the doll*) You're re-tarded, re-tarded! That's what Jennifer's father says to her all the times.

(*Back to earlier conversational tone*) The funny thing is that I lived and my mother died. (*Pause*) Her name was Carmen.

(*Seeing that Rael is after her again, she prays fervently*) Dear Mother of God, save me from the fires of Miss Rael's Hell! I don't want to be afraid of the dark or of God the Man, or spiders, or tunnels that never end, or having babies . . . I want to be a mother someday, when I'm not afraid anymore, okay?

(*As if saying to herself, "Is this a prayer?"*) I wish I had a mother . . .

(*An idea just dawned on her, with a sense of wonder*) Mary, if you become my mother, I'll become a nun, and then a saint . . .

(*Getting pinched again*) Ouch! Maybe I won't become a saint . . . Dear mother God, let me forget everything! Everything! Except love . . . like in a fairy tale . . .

MAGDALENA

(*A youngish-looking woman in her late forties comes out carrying a makeup case, fixing her face and hair as she speaks to someone behind the screen*)

¡Duérmete, mi amor! It's still early, about four. I'm sorry I woke you up. Yes, I'm going. I told you I was. ¿Por qué no vas conmigo? You promised me before Johnny was born that you would climb with me every year as a thank you to la Virgencita. That was seven kids and no marriage license ago!

(*Laughing coyly*) Okay so I'm plenty married now! When you left, I climbed to bring you back. And one year I climbed for el Señor Gallegos, el vecino. It just happened, Mikey, like I told you. Una noche se presentó. His wife, Chila, se estaba muriendo de cancer. He was lonely. Me dio lástima con él. No, I didn't tell him about the baby. He was on the school board, pobrecito. Then there was the climb for el Compadre Juanito. When his wife, Dora, left him with the four kids to run off with his cousin, Humberto, he didn't know what to do. So I told them to move in. There's always room for more. Don't worry about it, Mikey. She missed him and they got back together. They're very happy now. I climbed for them that year. And then one year I climbed for el poeta, Maggie's sobrino, from Portales. Se llamaba Toribio. He was a poet looking for construction work. He didn't have no money and I was getting food stamps, so no problem. But you were the only one I loved, Miguel, you know that!

(*Continuing with conviction*) And then I climbed for all my kids. Yes, and for all their fathers too. They were all good men. And now you've come back. So today I'm climbing for you. And for the baby . . . (*Patting her stomach*)

(*Falling over imaginary shoes*) ¡Ay, Mikey, mi amor, cuidado donde pones los zapatos! It's so good to have you home. Put your shoes under the bed, where you used to keep them? ¡Cómo te extrañé! ¿Por qué no me llamaste? Why didn't you at least write? They don't let you write in prison. Duérmete, mi amor . . . Okay, okay, it's all right.

(*Putting on coat and hat*) There's food in the icebox. Me and the kids will be back tonight after the mass. I have to go, mi amor! Es mi manda. Mikey, mi amor, I love you so much. You don't know. I love life so much! I just want to help people. That's the way it is with me. I see the good in all the men. Me dio lástima con el señor Gallegos. Y también con el compadre Juanito. Y especialmente con el poeta, pobrecito, ni tenía barbas, lleno de espinillas. But you're the only one I've ever loved, mi amor! You gonna stay? I'll get my food stamps any day. When the kids get bigger I'll get a job. The rent is low. We'll get back on our feet, mi amor, you'll see. (*With resignation*) We'll stay together, you and me and the kids.

(*Going to the altar*) Sometimes when I think about you, mi amor, and then I look at you, I love you so much I want to cry. Que la Virgencita me perdone. She understands everything. Everything. And she forgives everything. That's why I have to go on this pilgrimage today, mi amor, that's why . . .

TOMASA

(A 78-year-old woman wearing a tousled blond wig and hospital gown, walking with a cane; she sits)

¡Ay, Esperanza, qué bueno que viniste a visitarme! Take me home, herma-nita, please! *(Starts to cry but quickly snaps out of it)* You never come to see me anymore! Oh, you came last Thursday. We went outside and sat in the sun . . .

(With terror) What's going to happen to me? *(Petulantly)* I want to go home!

(Seriously) Can I walk? What's today? Saturday? Already? Crismes? That's a long time off. I'll be dead by then.

(Angrily) I don't want to go outside! We just came in! ¡Acuéstame, por favor! They never do what I tell them. Where's Ida, she's the one who put me here.

(Crying again) Oh, I'm better. Except for my head. I can't think anymore. *(Patting her hair)* Well, at least I still have all my hair.

(Testily) No, no quiero nada. Today's Monday. That's right. I forgot. What did you say today was? My daughter Ida never comes to see me. She's got her family, I'm in the way. *(Hopelessly)* ¿Qué me va a pasar?

(Planning) Llévame al banco. How much money do I have? It should be enough to get me out of here. I'm moving to San Diego. Ahí tengo unas primitas, Gussie and Tenoria.

(Suddenly deflated, crying) ¿Por qué no me he muerto? Diosito, Diosito, ten misericordia. I know, I know. It's not my time. I'm going to live to a ripe old age. That's what Elena, la flaquita, tells me. I don't feel old. 78? I'm not that old!

(Angry again, hitting the air) ¡Acuéstame! I want to go to sleep and never wake up!

(Suddenly getting a dreamy, faraway look, she softens with wonder) ¿Mamá? ¿Mamá? ¿Cómo está?

(Quietly, sober) Oh, that's right. She's dead. It's my head! What time is it? ¿Ya te vas? ¿Tan pronto? You're the only one who comes to see me. You and la monjita ratoncita Rael. She brings me communion. Antes que te vayas, ¡acuéstame!

(As if grabbing someone's arm) ¿Qué me va a pasar? I'm going to live to a ripe old age. That's what la gordita, Elena, tells me. Dale gracias a la Hermana Rael por las velitas. Vuelve, Esperanza.

(Alone now, she sinks into remembering) Esperanza! Esperanza, I forgot to tell you. ¡Mamá me vino a visitar!

(*Like a little girl, she sits up with her eyes shining beautifully*) Me acuerdo de mi altarcito. Con la Virgencita tan bella. Con su vestido de blanco y su manta de azul. Su carita tan linda, su boca cantando.

(*She gets up, lights a candle and sings*) ¡Oh, María, Madre mía! El consuelo del mortal, ampárame y guíame a la patria celestial.

(*Watching the candle and Virgencita in wonder for a while, she breaks out of her reverie and turns to her mother, who she imagines is next to her*) ¡Mamá! ¡Mire que bonita se ve la Virgen!

JUANA

(*A 56-year-old factory worker, a nativa. She wears goggles, a scarf, apron, and holds a pair of pantyhose in her hands*)

En esta fábrica hay mexicanos, anglos, vietnameses, latinos, and everybody else ain't got a job. Si no fuera pantyhose, it would be boots or jeans or moccasins . . . or turquoise jewelry . . . algo pa' los turistas.

(*Motioning*) The work starts back there. Little by little it moves to me. I do the inside seams. People don't like you to talk about pantyhose. ¡Yo ni las uso!

(*Pausing to place a bingo chip on an imaginary card on a nearby table*) I used to work in the hospital, in the kitchen throwing away the garbage. ¡Ese era trabajo! I had to wear unas botitas verdes, de plástico, como los niños. ¡Todos creían que yo era doctora! When I told them I worked in the kitchen, their faces got sad . . .

(*Suddenly animated as she places a chip on the imaginary bingo card*) Bingo! Bingo! B-12. Over here! Bingo! I just won ten bucks! A month ago I won fifty! See, we have this bingo goes on all the time. "Something for you to think about," nos dice el Señor Wiley, el patrón. No es de estas partes. Ever notice they always bring in the boss from other places? Me conoce. Me dice, "Wuanita, how you doing this fine day?" "Oh, pretty good, pretty good," le digo. "Mucho bueno," me dice. Le gusta hablar español. "Wuanita, you're the best inside seamer I've got. Keep up the good work and one of these days, one of these days, I'm gonna raise you . . . to $3.50!!" "Oh, thank you, Mr. Wiley, thank you!" "Okey, dokey, Wuanita, now git along . . ."

(*Suddenly a change takes place and she becomes quiet, moving in slow motion as she begins to remove her goggles, apron, etc.*) One of these days, the noise gonna stop! It won't be so long. Tengo cincuenta y seis años. 56 years of my hands working. Making tortillas, changing pañales, burning dyes and lyes, boiling water and stabbing needles.

(*Pause*) Mi abuelita me enseñó a trabajar. She taught me the healing life of the herbs, what to do with cota and osha, como sobar con aceite while praying. Cuando se murió, I took her ashes to the pueblo and I scattered them in the wind. She was the only person I had in the world. Estas manos son mi herencia.

(*She has been redressing herself by taking off the scarf and putting on a medicine wheel necklace. Now she lights cedar and picks up macaw feathers*) I remember my abuelita telling me, "Acuérdate que eres india, y que la Virgen María, la mestiza, es tu madre querida. The Mother's Mother is your mother as well. Never forget that. You are a child of many worlds: say your prayers, praise the sun, glorify the moon, and send your spirit in the wind." (*She ends with a chant, singing to the Virgen and the four directions*)

> *Hey oh hey, hey ya no*
> *Hey oh hey, hey ya no*
> *Hey oh hey*
> *Hey oh hey.*

PAULINE
(*Transformation to a 14-year-old girl who sits facing away from the audience responding to an imaginary teacher's questions and demands*)

(*Facing the back wall*) Pauline Mendoza.

(*Turns partly towards the audience*) Pauline Mendoza.

(*Turns full face to the audience*) Pauline Mendoza.

(*Mad*) Pauline Mendoza!

(*Sulkily*) Taos.

(*Told to say everything again loudly, she yells out*) Pauline Mendoza. Taos. 6th Grade. Fourteen years-old.

(*Bitterly*) I'm a freak.

(*Naming things she likes, staccato-like*) Boys. Cars. Makeup. My leather bracelet. My red headband. Black T-shirts. My jean jacket. My hair cut long in back and short on the sides and front. Tattoos. Can I sit down now?

(*In response to a question*) I made all the tattoos. Myself.

(*Withdrawn*) I'm working on one now. No, you can't see. Can I go back to my desk? Okay, okay. So what do you want to know for anyway? I already told you what I liked! I don't want to be nothin'! My teacher, Mrs. Espinoza, makes me sit behind the screen, in the corner, facing the wall. I'm jittery, she says. Hell, so I work on my tattoos. Nothing better to do. I can't barely read or write. I'm dumb. I'm a freak. Don't yell at me!

(*Yelling*) She always yells at me! It's embarrassing!

(*Trying to get back to her seat*) I've got work to do, okay? (*Sits*) 9 × 8? How the hell should I know? Okay, okay. (*Stands*) Yeah, I like my mom. She's pretty young for a mom. I hate school. I hate homework! Thinking? I hate thinking! Maybe I could like it. You want me to read that book? I can't read the whole thing! Don't you understand? I thought substitutes are supposed to know everything! I'm dumb. I'm a freak. I sit in the corner all the time. Can I sit down now? (*Sits*) I been in 6th grade three years. I'm going to move next year. (*Stands*) Okay, okay.

(*Picking up book, trying to read*) Thee . . . his-hist-history of a . . . ah . . . a . . . p-e-o-p-l-e.

(*Angrily*) Yeah, I know the word people! Don't you, or what? The history of people . . . This is boring! People are boring. I don't know. I don't know. I can't read, I told you. I just can't. Can I sit down?

(*Exasperated*) You still want me to talk about myself? Mrs. Espinoza never makes me read out loud. She lets me sit in the corner and be quiet. That's all she wants from me. Yeah! I try to read in church . . . I try to read the prayer books. One . . . one . . . one . . . holy . . . that's as far as I get. I'm a freak even there. So I look at the statues and pictures and I feel better. A freak? What's a freak? A freak is someone who wears a you-know-what in the sixth grade. A freak is someone that has already started their you-know-what in the 6th grade. That's a freak!

(*Off-guard*) That? Oh, that's my tattoo. No. Oh, okay, since you asked. It's Our Lady of Guadalupe. It don't look like a lady on fire; that's rays of gold, stupid! Don't you know nothing? I just started working on it. Yeah, I told you, I go to church. Why do I like tattoos?I don't talk good. I don't think good. It's something cool. A picture like in church, you know, one . . . holy . . . okay . . . the history of a people, okay? Pictures, pictures!

(*Not so harsh now*) I'm working on my tattoos, back there see, where nobody bothers me. It's my art work. I'm working on my tattoos and my drawings. I'm gonna be an artist.

(*More confidentially, but still hard*) My girlfriend, Gloria, she says I'm changing. I don't want to go out and get rowdy and drunk all the time now. Ever since this lady came to our school. She made me stand up and talk. She's an artist. Her name is Isabel Martínez. She's Chicana. I never known anybody . . . a lady and a chicana and an artist . . . It surprised me, you know?

(*Stands up straight and takes a deep breath as she moves to light the candle*) Pauline. My name is Pauline Mendoza. I do tattoos. And I draw. Next year I'm going to move to a new school. And someday . . . someday . . . I'm gonna be an artist!

CORRINE

(*An aging, very tough bag-lady. She drags around a big and colorful bag which she empties on the floor. Throughout the scene she will put on clothing from the bag*)

Antes me importaban las cosas, pero ahora, sss—I take every day as it comes. Some good, some pretty bad! Like the weather. If it looks like rain or snow, I head down to the Holy Bible Rescue Mission para agarrar mi espacio. I stay there or at the Good Faith Shelter, or one of my other spots. Near the Interstate, that overhang with the old colchón . . . that's my bedroom! Or behind Bennie's La Paloma Bar, by the vents. No te apenes! No sweat! Rain or shine, Corrine got it covered, ésa! Ssss.

(*Taking a drink from her wine bottle in the bag*) I don't want your stupid pity, okay? I got enough problems of my own, you start worrying me about your shag rug and your color t.v. . . . I don't need it, okay? I had a family once . . . kids . . . the whole . . . But don't get me wrong, ésa, it's never as good as it looks. I got into writing bad checks. I needed things, you know? I got sent up. That was when they still had the women in the pinta in Santa. Anyway, I was in my 30's ésa, and they took it all away—the kids, the house—and then el tonturio went to live with his novia in Belén. They all disappeared. Yeah, I tried to find them, but my family didn't want to have anything to do with me. So, I did my time. Met me my Sophia. Ay, Sophia, Sophia! ¡Qué corazonada! We wanted to get married. We did, in our hearts. Later we got separated; she started seeing somebody else, you know? So, I said, okay, anyway, I was getting out. The kids in Belén, the jefita in 'Burque, you think she's gonna welcome me back a la vecindad? ¡Tattoos hasta el copete! María and Jesus on my knuckles, my hair dyed blond, my eyebrows shaved and then painted black . . . Una pinta jotita, no less. ¡Niel ésa! Nobody wanted me back the way I was. So I took to the streets. Oh, yeah, I got me a little, here and there, you know, just enough to spend a night, take a shower, get some beer. But didn't last. I was getting old . . . that was over 20 years ago! Pero no te preocupes, ésa, I got it covered!

(*Takes another swig*) Met this lady wanted me to take care of her jefito. Uh-ummmmm! He got this and that wrong with him. Used to be a big man, now look at him. Pobrecito, medio muerto. Anyway, she tried to give me her mother's old clothes to wear. And I said, I don't want them, dammit! You keep your dead woman's things! You think because you're a Mexican with a little bit of money you can treat me like hell? I'm not your slave! Keep your damn job and house and clothes and car and leave me alone. I oughta report you to the authorities—IRA, INS, NBC, CBS—for cruelty to an old woman! I don't need your pity! They think they can give you the slop once they see you in the streets. ¡Qué va! Lo que necesitamos en este estado es una gobernadora como esa Madre Teresa, no? Anyway, I left her holding the clothes and walked over to the Senior Citizens pa' mis enchiladas. It was Friday and I decided to stick around for the baile. Johnny and the Huipiles were playing. Siempre me ha gustado tirar chancla, ¿sabes? Anyway, I went up to this cute viejita to ask her to dance—that's all it was, I swear—y se puso medio weird. So I went up to this dude then, adrede iba a bailar, and I didn't care with who. The dance was over at 5:30 so I walked over to the Holy Bible to see what was happening, you know? It was too late. From there I went over to the Good Faith. ¡Estaba lleno! The mattress was gone and Bennie's was taken. So me fui al bus depot a ver a mi novela, *María de Nadie*. And from there, I came over here. I thought maybe the padrecito would let me sit in the portal . . . (*The actress may name any place she is performing*) ¿Quién sabe?

(*Goes over to the Virgencita to light a candle*) Mi Madrecita sabe, no? Me conoce. She know that when Cory got it, she got it! And when she don't got it . . . ssss . . . it don't matter!

(*Fondly touches the face of the Virgencita*) Te debo, eh, Madrecita? Next time.

(*Opening umbrella as she turns away*) Jesús y María . . . (motioning to the tattoos on her knuckles that spell out these names) I got it covered, ésa!

ISABEL

(*Isabel takes off Corrine's clothes, putting them in the bag. She rearranges herself a bit; as herself, excited*)

All this time I've been thinking about what that lady at the grocery store said, about life being a song. Well, it's true. Life really is a song. ¡La vida es una canción! The song of childhood, the song of love, the song of parting, the song of death . . . Each of our lives is a song, or a prayer, like a novena.

(*Picking up some of the papers*) When life gets to be too much, I simply lift my hands to the Virgencita and the Heavens and I just pray—or sing! Or I sit quietly at my desk thinking about all the lives that pass before me. Sometimes I have to control myself from reaching out and grabbing someone . . .

(*Excited again*) And in total love and acceptance and friendship saying to them, "Sigue adelante, Hermana! Keep going forward! And keep on singing that unending song of love and life — in the fullest, strongest, most beautiful voice you have!"

(*Looking around with joy*) ¡Ay! ¿Qué familia de mujeres, no? What dreams! What hopes! It makes me want to sing!

(*Isabel sings "El Corrido de Las Mujeres." After she finishes singing, she picks a few things and goes out, the pages still on the floor*)

End

✳ Miss Clairol

HELENA MARÍA VIRAMONTES

Arlene and Champ walk to K-Mart. The store is full of bins mounted with bargain buys from T-shirts to rubber sandals. They go to aisle 23, Cosmetics. Arlene, wearing bell bottom jeans two sizes too small, can't bend down to the Miss Clairol boxes, asks Champ.

—Which one amá? asks Champ, chewing her thumb nail.

—Shit, mija, I dunno. Arlene smacks her gum, contemplating the decision. Maybe I need a change, tú sabes. What do you think? She holds up a few blond strands with black roots. Arlene has burned the softness of her hair with peroxide; her hair is stiff, breaks at the ends and she needs plenty of Aqua Net hairspray to tease and tame her ratted hair, then folds it back into a high lump behind her head. For the last few months she has been a platinum "Light Ash" blond, before that a Miss Clairol "Flame" redhead, before that Champ couldn't even identify the color—somewhere between orange and brown, a "Sun Bronze." The only way Champ knows her mother's true hair color is by her roots which, like death, inevitably rise to the truth.

—I hate it, tú sabes, when I can't decide. Arlene is wearing a pink, strapless tube top. Her stomach spills over the hip hugger jeans. Spits the gum onto the floor. Fuck it. And Champ follows her to the rows of nailpolish, next to the Maybelline rack of make-up, across the false eyelashes that look like insects on display in clear, plastic boxes. Arlene pulls out a particular color of nailpolish, looks at the bottom of the bottle for the price, puts it back, gets another. She has a tattoo of purple XXX's on her left finger like a ring. She finally settles for a purple-blackish color, Ripe Plum, that Champ thinks looks like the color of Frankenstein's nails. She looks at her own stubby nails, chewed and gnawed.

Walking over to the eyeshadows, Arlene slowly slinks out another stick of gum from her back pocket, unwraps and crumbles the wrapper into a little ball, lets it drop on the floor. Smacks the gum.

—Grandpa Ham used to make chains with these gum wrappers, she says, toeing the wrapper on the floor with her rubber sandals, her toes dotted with old nailpolish. He started one, tú sabes, that went from room to room. That was before he went nuts, she says, looking at the price of magenta eyeshadow. ¿Sabes qué? What do you think?—lifting the eye shadow to Champ.

—I dunno, responds Champ, shrugging her shoulders the way she always does when she is listening to something else, her own heartbeat, what Gregorio said on the phone yesterday, shrugs her shoulders when Miss Smith says OFELIA, answer my question. She is too busy thinking of things people otherwise dismiss like parentheses, but sticks to her like gum, like a hole on a shirt, like a tattoo, and sometimes she wishes she weren't born with such adhesiveness. The chain went from room to room, round and round like a web, she remembers. That was before he went nuts.

—Champ. You listening? Or in lala land again? Arlene has her arms akimbo on a fold of flesh, pissed.

—I said, I dunno, Champ whines back, still looking at the wrapper on the floor.

—Well you better learn, tú sabes, and fast too. Now think, will this color go good with Pancha's blue dress? Pancha is Arlene's comadre. Since Arlene has a special date tonight, she lent Arlene her royal blue dress that she keeps in a plastic bag at the end of her closet. The dress is made of chiffon, with satin-like material underlining, so that when Arlene first tried it on and strutted about, it crinkled sounds of elegance. The dress fits too tight. Her plump arms squeeze through, her hips breathe in and hold their breath, the seams do all they can to keep the body contained. But Arlene doesn't care as long as it sounds right.

—I think it will, Champ says, and Arlene is very pleased.

—Think so? So do I mija.

They walk out the double doors and Champ never remembers her mother paying.

• • • • • • • • • •

It is four in the afternoon, but already Arlene is preparing for the date. She scrubs the tub, Art Labo on the radio, drops crystals of Jean Nate into the running water, lemon scent rises with the steam. The bathroom door ajar, she removes her top and her breasts flop and sag, pushes her jeans down with some difficulty, kicks them off, and steps in the tub.

—Mija. MIJA—she yells.—Mija, give me a few bobby pins. She is worried about her hair frizzing and so wants to pin it up.

Her mother's voice is faint because Champ is in the closet. There are piles of clothes on the floor, hangers thrown askew and tangled, shoes all piled up or thrown on the top shelf. Champ is looking for her mother's special dress. Pancha says every girl has one at the end of her closet.

—Goddamn it Champ.

Amidst the dirty laundry, the black hole of the closet, she finds nothing.

—NOW

—Alright, ALRIGHT. Cheeze amá, stop yelling, says Champ, and goes in the steamy bathroom, checks the drawers. Hairbrushes jump out, rollers, strands of hair, rummages through bars of soap, combs, eyeshadows, finds nothing; pulls open another drawer, powder, empty bottles of oil, manicure scissors, kotex, dye instructions crinkled and botched, finally, a few bobby pins.

After Arlene pins up her hair, she asks Champ, ¿Sabes qué? Should I wear my hair up? Do I look good with it up? Champ is sitting on the toilet.

—Yea, amá, you look real pretty.

—Thanks mija, says Arlene, ¿Sabes qué? When you get older I'll show you how you can look just as pretty, and she puts her head back, relaxes, like the Calgon commercials.

• • • • • • • • • •

Champ lays on her stomach, T.V. on to some variety show with pogo stick dancers dressed in outfits of stretchy material and glitter. She is wearing one of Gregorio's white T-shirts, the ones he washes and bleaches himself so that the whiteness is impeccable. It drapes over her deflated ten year old body like a dress. She is busy cutting out Miss Breck models from the stacks of old magazines Pancha found in the back of her mother's garage. Champ collects the array of honey colored haired women, puts them in a shoe box with all her other special things.

Arlene is in the bathroom, wrapped in a towel. She has painted her eyebrows so that the two are arched and even, penciled thin and high. The magenta shades her eyelids. The towel slips, reveals one nipple blind from a cigarette burn, a date to forget. She rewraps the towel, likes her reflection, turns to her profile for additional inspection. She feels good, turns up the radio to . . . your love. *For your loveeeee, I will do anything, I will do anything, forrr your love. For your kiss . . .*

Champ looks on. From the open bathroom door, she can see Arlene, anticipation burning like a cigarette from her lips, sliding her shoulders to the ahhhh ahhhhh, and pouting her lips until the song ends. And Champ likes her mother that way.

Arlene carefully stretches black eyeliner, like a fallen question mark, outlines each eye. The work is delicate, her hand trembles cautiously, stops the process to review the face with each line. Arlene the mirror is not Arlene the face who has worn too many relationships, gotten too little sleep. The last touch is the chalky, beige lipstick.

By the time she is finished, her ashtray is full of cigarette butts, Champ's variety show is over, and Jackie Gleason's dancing girls come on to make kaleidoscope patterns with their long legs and arms. Gregorio is still not home, and Champ goes over to the window, checks the houses, the streets, corners, roams the sky with her eyes.

Arlene sits on the toilet, stretches up her nylons, clips them to her girdle. She feels good thinking about the way he will unsnap her nylons, and she will unroll them slowly, point her toes when she does.

Champ opens a can of Campbell soup, finds a perfect pot in the middle of a stack of dishes, pulls it out to the threatening rumbling of the tower. She washes it out, pours the contents of the red can, turns the knob. After it boils, she puts the pot on the sink for it to cool down. She searches for a spoon.

Arlene is a romantic. When Champ begins her period, she will tell her things that only women can know. She will tell her about the first time she made love with a boy, her awkwardness and shyness forcing them to go under the house, where the cool, refined soil made a soft mattress. How she closed her eyes and wondered what to expect, or how the penis was the softest skin she had ever felt against her, how it tickled her, searched for a place to connect. She was eleven and his name was Harry.

She will not tell Champ that her first fuck was a guy named Puppet who ejaculated prematurely, at the sight of her apricot vagina, so plump and fuzzy.—Pendejo—she said—you got it all over me. She rubbed the gooey substance off her legs, her belly in disgust. Ran home to tell Rat and Pancha, her mouth open with laughter.

Arlene powder puffs under her arms, between her breasts, tilts a bottle of *Love Cries* perfume and dabs behind her ears, neck and breasts for those tight caressing songs which permit them to grind their bodies together until she can feel a bulge in his pants and she knows she's in for the night.

Jackie Gleason is a bartender in a saloon. He wears a black bow tie, a white apron, and is polishing a glass. Champ is watching him, sitting in the radius of the gray light, eating her soup from the pot.

Arlene is a romantic. She will dance until Pancha's dress turns a different color, dance until her hair becomes undone, her hips jiggering and quaking beneath a new pair of hosiery, her mascara shadowing under her eyes from the perspiration of the ritual, dance spinning herself into Miss Clairol, and stopping only when it is time to return to the sewing factory, time to wait out the next date, time to change hair color. Time to remember or to forget.

Champ sees Arlene from the window. She can almost hear Arlene's nylons rubbing against one another, hear the crinkling sound of satin when she gets in the blue and white shark-finned Dodge. Champ yells goodbye. It all sounds so right to Arlene who is too busy cranking up the window to hear her daughter.

❈ Andrea

ROBERTA FERNÁNDEZ

> *something about you*
> *all of us*
> *with songs inside*
> *knifing the air of sorrow*
> *with our dance*
> *a carnival of spirits*
> *shredded blossoms*
> *on the water*
> *—Jessica Hagedorn*

The most extraordinary images of Andrea had been neatly mounted inside the black triangular corners in the thick blue album. It had taken my mother almost fifteen years to piece all those pictures together; after that, she had carefully guarded her collection for almost as long as it had taken her to assemble it. Understandably she was so attached to her album that for as long as I could recall, she had been reciting to us all the intricate details behind her cousin Andrea's dramatic adventures. That's how we knew that the backdrop against which Andrea performed had been set a long time ago, even before that memorable day in 1925 when she made her debut at the Teatro Zaragoza in San Antonio.

The photographs were our connection to that past. We were well aware that the oldest photographs on the beige pages had been my grandmother's own mementos of her family back in San Luis Potosí. At first my mother had kept these photos piled in with her own more recent items inside a large hat box but eventually the memorabilia had started to overflow due to the constant arrival of parcels which Andrea kept sending to her. Those bulging packages had been postmarked in San Francisco and Santa Fe, Tucson and Albuquerque, cities which my mother knew only from magazines and the movies. Yet, she'd describe those places so vividly to us that I soon forgot she had not actually been there and began to imagine myself journeying in Andrea's footsteps.

In a sense, my mother had already done this, for by keeping her record of Andrea's career she had relived her cousin's experiences over and over.

Andrea had cooperated in this rerun by jotting down in pencil on the back of each program or photograph the name of the production in which she had appeared, its location and dates, and the role she had played in it. Between the two of them they had constructed a significant record of our family's history.

That material was actually more real to us than the daily lives of the people it depicted, for we all knew Andrea only as the flamboyant actress in the picture book. The last time she had visited us was before my youngest sister Adriana was born when I was so little that the only indication I later had that indeed she had been amongst us was a persistent echo inside my head of a softly melodious voice. Eventually a tangible and exotic personality emerged from those clear-toned chords as I studied the many exciting poses in the photographs and listened to my mother's and my aunts', Griselda and Julieta, rambling stories about this bewitching cousin who for so long had lived in the limelight of make-believe and far-away.

On this particular afternoon in late June we had more reason than usual to leaf through the album. Tía Julieta had just gotten the news that Andrea would finally be visiting us again and as soon as she told us the dates of the visit, I realized that Andrea would be here during the time I would be performing my first solos in Violeta Aguilera's dance recital. The thought of Andrea's presence at my program so moved me that I barely looked at the pictures as Tía Griselda turned the pages of the album. Through the firmness of her voice I sensed that Griselda had already assumed her role of elder sister. I barely listened to her though. Instead, I was caught up with the sounds I was hearing in my head—sounds of castanets and my teacher Violeta's strict counting of the *paso doble*. I, wanting to move to Violeta's directions, tried to drown out Griselda's voice as the music grew more intense inside my head.

I didn't look away from the album though, but closely studied the pictures in the first page. Here was the infant Andrea in a gorgeous baptismal dress. As always I focused on the manner in which her mother—my mother's Tía Florencia—had tilted her to let us have a full view of the tiny smiling baby in her long white batiste gown and ruffled bonnet. Florencia's own proud smile and doting gaze conveyed to the world that this child would be the center of her life. In the background I could hear Griselda telling us that Tía Florencia's parents were sitting on her right. She continued narrating how her great-aunt and uncle had preferred to stay in San Luis Potosí rather than to head north with Florencia and Julián a few months after the photo had been taken in 1910. I felt that I knew all about their journey as I looked at the slender, straight-backed Julián standing on Florencia's left, tucking one arm into his vest, the other around their ten-year old Consuelo's shoulders. As usual little Consuelo's solemn and direct countenance did not fail to draw my attention. Her small face made the music in my head come to a stop as I studied the contrast between her solemnity and the smiling dimpled face of the seven-year old Andrea on the opposite page.

Here Andrea was pictured at Fort McIntosh, in front of one of the big white frame-houses with the screened-in porches which could be found all over the army compound. She had her arms around two of her friends from the fort—Mrs. Anderson, who had been a piano teacher in the local schools while her husband did his military duty, and Mrs. Bristol, a poet of sorts from Connecticut for whom Consuelo at age thirteen had done some housework. My mother had told us that those two women had taken it upon themselves to nurture Andrea's obvious talents by insisting on paying for her training. Andrea had chosen Pepita Montemayor as her teacher, *la gacela de dos países,* whose fame spread all over South Texas and into northern Mexico.

Without listening to what Griselda was saying as she continued to turn the pages, I still knew that she was not particularly fond of either Mrs. Anderson or Mrs. Bristol. So, I tuned her out altogether as the music once again filled my head and I pictured all four of us—Pepita, Andrea, Violeta and me—dancing together to the joyous sounds of the *jota aragonesa* as the steady rhythmic chatter of the eight castanets exploded in a crescendo over and over.

My sisters' gleeful outcry brought the colorful ritual in my head to a stop. As usual they were reacting to a picture of Andrea in a long tunic tied at the waist with a cord. She was surrounded by children and adults, all similarly dressed, each of whom carried a long staff from which flowed crepe paper streamers and flowers. Underneath the picture my mother had written: "*Andrea de pastora en 'La Aurora del Nuevo Día,' Plaza de la Iglesia de San Agustín, 20 de diciembre de 1921.*"

This *pastorela* had been Andrea's initial experience in theater Tía Griselda continued. After that she had appeared in many other local skits mostly featured as a dancer. A photo taken inside the Royal Opera House and dated 1923 showed the thirteen-year-old Andrea dressed as a Spanish Aragonese dancer of one of Pepita's recitals. Although the notations were missing from these early photos we had surmised that Andrea had also been a Tehuana from the Oaxacan Isthmus of Tehuantepec in the same program, for the *aragonesa* and the *tehuana* were placed side by side on the same page.

These photographs were so familiar that I did not think I could be surprised by anything I saw in them but suddenly I became quite taken with Andrea's *tehuana* headpiece. Up to now I knew my own *tehuana* headpiece would be made out of a white starched gauze which would frame my face, then hang down my back; I could not help but notice how it contrasted with Andrea's. Mine now seemed more like a bonnet, for it had a two-inch rim which would lie flat against my face and be pinned to my hair. Its five-inch flounce had tiny vertical tucks; together with the stiff inner lining and the thickness of the starch they would make the flounce stand up, framing my face. Since the whole thing measured at least a yard in length most of the headpiece actually hung down my back. Andrea's, on the other hand, was made of lace and shaped in a complete sphere so that it covered her entire head. Only her face showed through its central opening and she reminded me of a smiling sunflower. I now vaguely recalled Griselda telling me that the *tehuana* headdress had been influenced by the style of the Spanish Renaissance, then adapted to the tropical climate of the Gulf of Mexico. The other possibility for the unusual costume was a story Griselda was not sure was true: that some of the Isthmus Indian women found a trunk full of lace doll dresses which, not knowing what else to do with them, they had put on their heads, thus beginning a new tradition for themselves. How could I have forgotten this story and its accompanying costume I wondered even as I also pondered why mine was now so different.

Suddenly little Adriana broke my concentration. "Can we look at the pictures of Doña Inés? That's my favorite."

"Do you mean this one?" mother asked her as she turned to the back of the album and pointed to a photo of Andrea in a wig with long curls gathered into one big cluster at the back of her head. The hairdo matched her long full-skirted costume with its enormously full sleeves which ended in a tight cuff about six inches long.

"*Sí. Ese es mi favorito,*" Adriana nodded.

"That one was taken at the Teatro Hispano in New York in 1940. Andrea appeared there in *Don Juan Tenorio* on November 2. It was her last performance."

"I like this one," I said, flipping carefully through the pages. "I love the way she is looking at us, her hands crossed at the back of her neck and her arms resting against her head. I've always thought her little heart-shaped mouth was so precious. I also love the dark sequined dress and its long *cola* spread out on the floor."

"Hmmm," began Tía Griselda. "*Me parece muy artificial. Andrea en persona nunca fue así. Acuérdense que han pasado quince años que dejó el teatro.* Fifteen years is a very long time."

"*Tienes razón.* She is another person now," mother agreed. "You can see the contrast in the snapshot she sent us last Christmas. Remember how she and Tony and the kids were all bundled up as they added finishing touches to their giant snowman? He had on a long scarf exactly like the one she had around her neck."

"They looked like they were having a great time," my sister Patricia interjected. I watched her face as she looked in admiration. "I don't understand how you could put so much work into this album. I get bored with scrap books right away, and here you just kept adding to this one throughout all those many years. Didn't you ever get tired of it?"

A wistful expression settled on mother's face. "You can't begin to imagine how much I love handling all the material that kept coming in year after year. On some of my gloomiest days the mailman would arrive with a thick package. When it would come I never knew but I suppose I always anticipated its arrival. As soon as it came I would share the materials with my mother and Griselda and Julieta, and we'd try to guess what the new episode in Andrea's life might mean. There was always such a sparkle in her face. For hours we'd imagine the events in her life which the photo suggested. Much later, when she visited us, we'd listened to her own version of things. Usually I much preferred what we had invented for ourselves since we made those stories so much more complicated than what she'd describe to us. So, by the time I started pasting these black corners into the album placing the pictures inside them, the whole thing had already taken on a life of its own."

She turned to Griselda. "*¿Te acuerdas como nos llegó el primer paquete de recuerdos? ¡Cuánto nos alegró! Llegó en octubre de 1925 cuando yo tenía quince años. Era tan impresionable a esa edad.*"

The recollection of Andrea's first package made mother go over the facts of Andrea's early departure from home. "In 1925 she went to live in San Antonio where she lived for five years. She went there because the year before, in 1924, Consuelo had gotten married to Tomás who a little while later got a job with *La Prensa* in the advertising department. Shortly after Consuelo and Tomás moved to San Antonio, Andrea and Tía Florencia joined them. By then Andrea was fifteen and quite well-known here as a dancer. Pepita Montemayor had seen to it that Andrea would appear as the lead dancer in every program she had. When Andrea was fourteen Pepita selected her as her assistant and even took her to Mexico City for additional training. I felt sorry for Pepita when Andrea decided to go to San Antonio. She had no real contacts in that city, but nonetheless she felt that her chances for being discovered were better there."

"Once she got to San Antonio she sought work in what seemed to her to be the most logical place — the theater. At the Teatro Zaragoza she found herself a job as an usherette after school. This gave her the chance to continue in school while she got acquainted with some of the dance and performing companies that played at the Zaragoza."

Tía Julieta picked up the story. "At the Teatro Zaragoza she found a whole new challenge. Después de que vio 'Los amores de Ramona' se enamoró del teatro. *There she saw for the first time el teatro popular español — los sainetes y las zarzuelas.* The *tiples,* the leading singers in those musical pieces, fascinated her and she often sent us *postalitas* of the *tiples* and the *barítonos.*"

"One day she read an announcement in *La Prensa* about an audition for a *zarzuela* called *La Señora Capitana.*" We could tell that mother enjoyed telling us about this episode. "She auditioned and of course had no trouble getting accepted as a dancer in the chorus. With that bit part she was on her way."

"*Sí, pero lo hizo contra los gustos de Consuelo,*" Griselda interrupted. "'*No te metas más en ese mundo*' Consuelo le seguía diciendo. Al final, sin embargo, Consuelo perdió y Andrea se salió con la suya.*"

As usual, mother quietly came to Andrea's defense. "With her earnings she signed up for voice lessons, and by 1927 she was working in operettas as well as in *zarzuelas.* I'm quite sure that she had a small part in *La viuda alegre* but I don't have a photograph of her in that role. Mostly, though, she performed at the Teatro Hidalgo and at the Zendejas in dramas written by *dramaturgos españoles* and in a few works by some native Tejanos."

"What else did she do after she left San Antonio?" Patricia asked.

"Well, in 1930 when things began to get tough for the theater in San Antonio, Andrea decided to head West with some of her friends since they heard that the Depression was not affecting the theater in Los Angeles in the same way. On the way there she performed in Tucson and in Santa Fe, then she stayed in Los Angeles for quite a while. By 1936, though, she was back in Texas on tour *en los pueblitos de la frontera.* Brownsville, Rio Grande, Laredo, Eagle Pass, El Paso. Before she went to El Paso she ended up in Monterrey and Saltillo but again I don't have any programs from that tour even though she kept saying she was going to send me a package from there. Later, when she finally went to New York she found the *exiliados españoles* who had recently arrived there very excited about the works of a young *español* named Federico García Lorca. I don't think she ever appeared in any of his works though."

Griselda must have decided that it was now time to change the direction of the story. "*Para entonces ya era novia de Tony Carducci. Después de que se casaron en el '41, se fueron a vivir en San Luis, Missouri, donde estaban los padres de Tony. Y allí Andrea le dijo adiós al teatro para siempre.*"

Mother ended the story this time. "*Consuelo perdió a su Tomás* in 1938 in a car accident. Four years later it was her turn to join Andrea and Tony in St. Louis, and they've been together since. But Andrea told me that all these years Consuelo has never asked her about her fifteen years as a performer. Consuelo has simply acted as though all those years just didn't happen."

"*Consuelo siempre ha sido extraña,*" Julieta concluded. "Here the three of us kept such close notice of everything that Andrea did and her own sister pretends that she can just make all those years float down the river without anyone noticing them."

Surprising even myself by changing our cues, I said quite firmly, "I really don't think that Andrea should have given up the theater."

"*Yo creo que Andrea quedó bien satisfecha con su decisión,*" mother replied. "She never seemed to look back. Once she reasoned it out with me. '*La rosa más bella dura poco.*' 'Every rose has its day.' My impression is that she was happy at having spent fifteen good years on a long adventure but that she then wanted a more stable home life, which she really had never experienced, '*No se puede repicar y andar en la procesión*' was how she referred to her decision. 'You can't serve two masters.'

"I'm quite sure that if I had been in Andrea's shoes, I would never, never have given up the theater nor dance," I insisted.

Griselda now seemed intent on putting a stop to the conversation. "*Pues, fíjate que también dicen que cada quien cuenta de la feria según lo que ve en ella.*"

I knew that I did not want to argue with Griselda, so I turned my attention back to the *tehuana de Tehuantepec* who looked so different from the way I would look in a few weeks. As I turned the pages back to the year 1923, I heard the familiar mellifluous voice invite me to share the stage with her. The strains of "Zandunga" sounded faintly in the background and slowly we began to sway to its beat. As the music filled the room though, I could see that Andrea moved so much more lightly than I did, and slowly I faded into the shadowy background so that the thirteen year old Andrea with the lacy white headdress could have center stage by herself, and she took it with full confidence. I closed the book and wondered what it would be like to finally meet this cameleon creature whose many days in the sun my mother had so carefully recorded. I closed my eyes to find that the lights on stage had dimmed but even then Andrea continued gliding, gliding so gently to the song that would sound in my head for a long, long time to come.

II

The 10th of July was circled in red on all the calendars in our home and in that of my Tía Griselda's and Tía Julieta's. On that day Andrea would be arriving, not alone as we had first been told, but accompanied by our cousin Consuelo. Tía Julieta who informed us of the change in plans also said this would be the first time since 1945 that both of them would be visiting us at the same time. On their previous visit the mood had been solemn, for they had come to lay Tía Florencia to rest in the old cemetery next to the tomb of my grandmother, her only sister.

To mark the change in tone for this visit, Tío Memo had gone across the river to purchase Mexican party-favors with which to celebrate the dual homecoming. At the train station he passed out handfuls of multicolored *serpentinas* to both adults and children. For us children he had tiny *remolinos* which would whirl only if we blew since the intense Texas heat was not being relieved by the slightest breeze. Almost as if to avoid any dissatisfaction with the whirligigs, which we really loved, he gave us red and yellow tin noise-makers as well.

In the distance we heard the train announce its arrival and as it rumbled into the Missouri Pacific station the merriment of a few moments before ceased. We waited for a sign to begin our welcome as passenger after passenger disembarked. Finally, Tía Griselda whispered, "*Aquí vienen.*"

Just then an attractive woman with short wavy hair in a white shirt-waist stepped down but instead of coming toward us, she remained next to the train steps looking up into the inner compartment. When a second figure appeared at the door, Tío Memo gave a signal to which we all responded as though we had been practicing for days. We let out a simultaneous loud blaring of the red and yellow *pitos,* a shooting and spiraling of the many-colored paper *serpentinas* and a considerably less successful spinning of the little *remolinos.*

Tío Memo rushed to help Consuelo down the steps and in the seconds it took her to get off the train, the billowing streamers wrapped themselves around her dark print rayon dress and her gray hair tied into a *chongo*. The thin *serpentinas* looked even more dramatic against Andrea's dress and she quickly enhanced the effect by wrapping clusters of them around her neck. "*Bienvenidas*," everyone shouted in unison, followed by one long nasalized greeting from the horns.

The large entourage of well-wishers made the greetings take a long time in that hot summer afternoon but my mother's turn to introduce us to her cousins finally came. I felt uneasy as I faced Andrea in her clean-cut white dress. Her smile did not exude the least bit of the flamboyance I had learned to associate with the figure of the picture book, and as she embraced me and kissed me on the forehead I felt my back stiffen. Consuelo, on the other hand, seemed instantly familiar and in her aging face I immediately recognized the fragile and solemn look of the ten-year-old girl facing the camera of the unknown photographer in San Luis Potosí. I was glad she would be the one riding home in the same car with us, for I felt a great sense of comfort merely in the presence of that familiar somber and ashen face.

Andrea's presence continued to disconcert me when we got home and so instead of participating in the noisy gathering, I merely observed the scene before me. Andrea clearly delighted in the attention and chatted captivatingly about the train ride. She described the many hours it took to cross the Great Plains and her reaction at seeing the oil wells of Oklahoma City. Her description of the whiffs coming from the Dallas-Fort Worth stockyards had us all holding our noses.

"My memory wheels back to my old days on the train and I fell happy moving along those many miles of track," she laughed. Her spontaneity was contagious to everyone except me, and perhaps Consuelo. During a brief lull in the chatter, Griselda turned to Consuelo and asked her "*¿Cómo te pareció el viaje a ti?*"

"It was pretty much like Sis describes it," she answered keeping to the role she must have played all of her life. As I studied her delicate figure I decided to sit next to her on the floor and when I inched myself towards her, she patted my back, then put her arm around my shoulders. For no special reason I decided then and there that I liked her.

"*Cuéntame de ti*," she whispered so that we could carry on our own private conversation in our little corner.

I enjoyed whispering back. "In September I'll be going into the fifth grade but right now I'm mostly a dancer in Violeta Aguilera's class. Next week is my recital. I'm going to do two solos and in two numbers I'm one of three lead dancers." I was surprised at how comfortable I felt with her even as I sensed that she drew back a bit.

"What kind of dancing do you do?" she asked.

"I'll be doing *La boda de Luis Alonso* as a solo, and with Cristina Ruiz and Becky Barrios, two Mexican dances, *Tilingo lingo* and *Zandunga.* My other solo is a *Sevillanas.* It's my favorite number since I get to wear a beautiful white flamenco dress with bright red polka dots."

I heard Consuelo's deep sigh as she turned away. Then she looked at me with her dark eyes. "Dancing may be okay for now but you won't want to keep doing it later. It doesn't lead you anywhere. *Créemelo.*"

"The nuns are always telling me the same thing. They say I spend too much time with my dancing. But I just love it and can't imagine myself doing anything else later," I told her with a smile but as firmly as I could.

Just then Tía Julieta joined us. It seemed that the gathering had started to break up while Consuelo and I had been getting to know each other. Tía Julieta told us that she and Tío Memo were going to take Consuelo with them for now and after a few days we would all trade visitors. Andrea was to stay with us for three or four days first. I felt a little disappointed for I would rather have continued talking with Consuelo. Quickly though I decided that I would help entertain Andrea even though I did think she talked too much.

As soon as we moved to the kitchen to resume our visit, I brought out my mother's blue album and placed it on the table without saying a word.

Andrea reached for it eagerly. "Are these the photographs I sent your mother while I was on the road? *¡Qué gusto verlas!* It's been years since I've seen them. You know that I don't have any of these pictures?"

She smiled as she turned the pages. "Tony's parents would have a fit if they saw them. Like Consuelo they never approved of what I did. I'm really not quite sure just what it is they objected to. I've concluded that they didn't quite like the idea of anyone feeling comfortable and free in front of an audience. For them that is exhibitionism. But then, I don't know if that is truly their objection since they've never wanted to discuss any of it." Her light-hearted laughter reminded me of the voice that had sung around in my head for so long.

"Do you ever feel sorry about giving up the theater?" I asked this cousin who was still a stranger even though she chatted so easily with me.

"Would you believe that I never think about it?" she responded. "I had great fun while I was on stage but once I gave it up to marry Tony I was determined never to go back on my decision." She looked at her photographs at the same time that she continued talking. "When I first met Tony in New York he was very good-looking and very intent on becoming a success. I confess I liked both qualities about him. He was always as extroverted as I was and we had a good time together. Otherwise, we did not have too many things in common then. He had been born in Southern Italy and had come to New York when he was nine. Slowly we realized that we had more similarities than we had first recognized—the Catholic background, our first languages which were so close to each other, a similar type of family interaction. His parents and I get along fairly well in spite of their original objections to me. Consuelo had always been so strict about how we should conduct ourselves as a family and because of this I was able to adapt to their own sense of propriety quite easily. But I must tell you that she gets along with the Carducci's much better than I do. Tony's younger brother and his sisters look upon her as a great-aunt."

"So she does have a good time then. She looks so sad to me," I concluded.

"There is a deep solemnity in Sis," Andrea responded, "but I don't think she is sad. She's had a tough life and she's learned to be very self-contained. She's almost the complete opposite of the way I am. We have so little in common it's almost uncanny. I was brought here as a baby and even as I was growing up I pretty much lived in the present. Consuelo, *al contrario,* had been very close to our grandparents and all the cousins she left behind in San Luis Potosí. As a child she tended to live in her memories, which of course I did not share. Even now she talks about being transplanted and she keeps all the Carducci children entertained for hours with stories about her life as a child. I never had a home to miss so I've pretty much always lived fully in the present."

Andrea paused for a moment, then she turned rather pensive. After a few seconds she continued. "All through my teens I can remember Consuelo comparing everything that she was experiencing to life as she remembered it in her solid city of stone. Once she even went back to live there but by then our grandparents were dead and what she found there no longer corresponded to her memories. That all happened right after Tomás died. Luckily she had had a good life with him. But then in 1937 he died in an awful car accident and Sis went into a deep depression. While in that state she decided to go back to San Luis, and she and Mama set out together to their old home. But after only a year there they came back here. Seven years later when Mama passed away also, Consuelo became quite desolate. Everyone with whom she shared any memories was gone. I certainly was no consolation for her. I'm sure that's why she took to the Carducci's like she did. She has even learned Italian better than I have. Everyone really loves her, especially my Antonietta and my Franco."

Mother, who had kept herself busy preparing dinner as she listened to our conversation, now came to join us. "Andrea, do you realize that you have not even mentioned Consuelo's deepest sorrow as a child? The loss of your father. You were only three when he died and too little to experience serious repercussions. But Consuelo was thirteen at the time and much closer to him than to your mother. For many months after he died she would burst out crying at the most unexpected times. The situation was worsened because we were so poor then. My own father had already died in the revolution and eventually we became a family of women when your father died. Consuelo was forced to seek work when she was only thirteen and the people at the fort took her in as a maid even though they always tried to treat her like a family member. Those efforts never really worked out and she held herself aloof from the Bristols. With you that family had an entirely different relationship. From the moment they met you, they took a strong liking to you. Consuelo inherited their hand-me-downs but they bought you lots of clothes. Later they decided to pay for your dancing classes. You were too little to see what was going on in that situation but Consuelo thought they treated you like a doll. I think that's why she objected so much to your performing. You might say she was jealous but I think it was more complicated than that." Mother paused and sat down next to Andrea, then continued. "Consuelo always had a strong sense of who she was and held her distance from the people she worked for. Yet, they not only doted on you but you obviously cared a lot for them. And they did so much for you. Even after they got transferred, the Bristols and the Andersons continued to pay for your classes. This must have been so terribly hard on Consuelo. You had such a magical childhood while Consuelo had it tough all the way."

Andrea became quiet for the first time since she arrived. "Poor Sis," she finally said. "I do forget just how different our lives have been, and what is so strange about it all is that, except for the twelve years I was on the road, we have lived together under the same roof all of our lives. First here, then in San Antonio and now in St. Louis. The big difference between us lies in Consuelo's early years when I wasn't around yet."

"That's true," mother responded. "*Son las cosas de la vida.*" They both became silent then. Finally, mother said, "Why don't you look at your book? We do that very often here. *Es uno de nuestros pasatiempos favoritos.*"

"No wait," I quickly interjected. "I have something to show you first." Then I ran to my room.

Moments later I glided into the kitchen in my *tehuana* outfit. "Great!" Andrea laughed, clapping as I entered. "So you are wearing a more contemporary headdress. The one I had when I was your age was much more elaborate. But it was so difficult to keep clean and even harder to iron."

"Even so I would have preferred to have an outfit exactly like yours," I murmured.

"What difference does it make?" Andrea retorted. "It's not what you wear that's important. What counts is not the costume but the dance. It's in the movement of your arms, the control of your torso, the limberness of your legs. That's really what counts, just like in life. How easily you can adapt to your surroundings is very important too. *Por desgracia* a part of your outfit comes undone, your best castanets are lost or stolen right before you go on stage. You must adapt to the situation on the spot. That's what makes the difference, not your appearance in itself. Life is changing all the time in spite of the fact that essences remain the same. I think I'm your living proof of that. Even though I've had many dramatic changes in my life, I've petty much remained the same person. *Tú sabes, el hábito no hace el monje.*" Then she reached out for me. "What you are wearing is perfect. Now, tell me, what will your program be like? When is it taking place? Tell me everything. If I am not mistaken I think your teacher studied with Pepita Montemayor, many years after I did of course."

"You know just how well known this are is for its Spanish and Mexican dance teachers," mother reminded Andrea. "Well, most of those presently teaching have had some connection to Pepita."

Sensing the power of continuity in what my mother had just said I suddenly felt better than I had felt in a long time. "The recital is on Wednesday," I told Andrea. "Pretty soon though I'm going to a dress rehearsal. Later, I'll tell you everything you want to know. Right now I'd rather look through this album with you. Then you can tell me everything you remember."

"Or want to remember," she smiled the familiar smile I had learned to admire in the photos. "I haven't seen these pictures in such a long time that even though it may be hard for you to comprehend, I'm really quite removed from them. I guess I always kept a distance from them, which is why I sent them to your mother."

"Mother calls this her *libro de memorias*. We know all of her stories by heart but now you can tell us so much more than what we already know."

"Don't count on it. It sounds as if you all know more than I remember about the Andrea that I once was."

III

On the day of my recital Consuelo came to stay with us. To mark both events my father not only brought Consuelo home but also gave me a present of his own "*Una decoración para esta noche,*" he smiled as I unwrapped the box to find some delicate earrings in the shape of golden rosebuds. Consuelo helped me put them on, then from her purse she pulled a gold chain with a tiny medal of the Virgen de Guadalupe which she slipped on over my head. Enjoying the warmth of being in Consuelo's presence I touched my medal as we moved to the porch while my mother and sisters prepared lunch.

"Andrea said that you speak Italian very well," I told her.

"*Si, mi piace molto parlare con tutta la famiglia di Tony.* It's very much like Spanish and I learned it quite easily. The Carducci's have been very good to me and I felt that learning their language was such a small thing to do for them. Tony's parents remind me of my own relatives in San Luis Potosí, and Grazia, his sister, is my dearest friend. *Mia cara amica. Uno di questi giorni andro in Italia con lei. Capisce?* Did you understand what I said?"

"You said you were going to Italy with someone!" I beamed proudly.

"*Con la sorella di Tony.* With Grazia, Tony's sister. I'd also like to have her visit San Luis Potosí with me."

"What's San Luis Potosí like? So far we haven't gone there even though we're always talking about going."

"Oh, I guess you'd find it a very tranquil place. I was very happy there once with my grandparents and my cousins. They all decided to stay in spite of the revolution when we came here. In those early years I missed them a lot. Then, many years later after Tomás died I went back there with the idea of retracing my steps and recapturing what I left there. But by then Papa Enrique and Mama Hortensia had died, and I had very little in common with my cousins. At that point I felt I had no real family left. So back I went then to St. Louis to live with Andrea and Tony. Once there I became very involved with the Carducci's and their activities. Now I'm even a member of *Gli Figli d'Italia* and through the church I help out a lot in the San Guiseppe festivities. They're my family now. I hardly think about San Luis Potosí anymore although it's a beautiful city with many churches. It's the home I left behind."

"Does Andrea do the same things you do?" I asked.

"Not really. Andrea has many friends all over the city, and she's always going some place with someone or other."

"You sure are different," I commented. "Every time I look at the old photographs of the two of you, I noticed that she was always laughing while you seemed so sad."

I kept looking at her face, paused, then quickly blurted out. "Everyone says that you didn't like for Andrea to be in the theater? Is that true?"

Consuelo's eyes seemed to narrow for an instant, then she became very quiet. After a few seconds she shook her head. "No one has asked me that question before even though I've always known that they all thought I objected to Andrea's performing on stage. But that was never the issue. Do you know that I love the theater? When I was very little, Papa took me with him on the train to Mexico City. We'd go to the *teatro popular,* to the opera, to the variety shows. Right before we came we quit doing that because of the tension of the pending revolution but before that I had associated the lights of the city with the theater. When we first came here everything seemed so dark in comparison. And of course we were so poor we couldn't afford tickets for any program anyway. But nothing of the sort was happening here anyway. Things changed somewhat after the war ended. In fact I remember that Tomás and I shared in the great excitement of having Enrico Carruso stop here at the Royal Opera House in 1921 on his way to Mexico City. That has always been a highlight for me. In St. Louis I used to go to the theater whenever I could. No, no. I never objected to the theater in itself."

Consuelo paused for a moment, then tapped my shoulder. "Before I go on you should know that Andrea and I have gotten along very well ever since she and Tony invited me to live with them. We each know what we can talk about and what is best left unsaid. So what I'm about to tell you has no bearing on our present relationship."

I could tell that she was about to measure her words. Then, inhaling deeply, she went on. "Andrea was spoiled by everyone when she was a child. I think that the woman I worked for, Mrs. Ernestine Bristol, added to the pattern that had already been set. Oh, they all meant well by their actions. Mama felt sorry for Andrea growing up as an orphan and not really knowing Papa like I had. Her teachers made her their pet. And then Mrs. Bristol messed her up even more. I thought that she never treated Andrea like a real person. It seemed to me that she looked upon her as a cute little doll who could do un-usual tricks. Take a bow, twirl to the left, give a good *zapateado*. Andrea loved to perform and she went along with all the requests that were made of her."

"She was only five when she started her classes. Right?"

"Yes, that's true. I knew then it was not her fault that other people took advantage of her eagerness to please. I also knew that all the attention gave her the confidence to continue getting better and better as a performer. But those experiences pushed her farther away from reality. As I've already told you, we were extremely poor after Papa died but Andrea never seemed to connect to our situation because someone was always taking care of her needs, and she seemed to take that for granted. When she came to live with Tomás and me in San Antonio she was obsessed with what she was doing and never contributed to the household. Her money went into voice lessons, clothes, the social life that was more or less expected of young women like her. I soon learned not to expect anything from her, and I suppose I really resented that. But what really bothered me was the way she ignored Mama. Off she went to Los Angeles and all those other places which made her even more absorbed in her career. Months would go by without our hearing from her. I think she was much more in contact with your mother than she was with us, probably because your mother doted on her accomplishments and made her feel important."

"There were so many things I resented in her during those days, but it didn't do me any good to talk about them because she never seemed to be touched by anything that happened to Mama or to me. When Tomás died, she took off some days from work to come to the funeral but then she couldn't stay with me through that trying period because she said she had commit-ments in New York. After all I had done for her, that really hurt me. And throughout all this time I was quite convinced she was telling everyone I dis-approved of her for being an actress and a dancer. And as I've just told you, that in itself was never the real reason I was so disillusioned with her."

"What if you had been in her shoes? Would you have done things differ-ently?" I wondered almost to myself.

"Who knows? Never, by the longest stretch of the imagination would I have gotten myself into the theater. Therefore, it's almost impossible for me to answer that question."

"Golly, Consuelo, you two really had a problem. Mama says that every time we think someone is doing something that may hurt us that we should talk things over as soon as we can. Did you and Andrea ever talk to each other about all this?"

"You tell me what I could possibly have told her. She said she had commitments and it was obvious that she did. One time we had an argument over her lack of interest in the family. She insisted that she had kept us informed about her life. Then she went to the drawer where she knew I kept her few letters and pulled them out as evidence of her communication with us. I became so angry that I tore those letters to shreds. That in turn made her furious, and she picked up the pieces, tore them up into even smaller bits and flushed them down the toilet. Since then, we have never exchanged a word about all those years."

"Consuelo, there's one thing I don't understand," I confessed to her. "On the day of my recital you've just given me this beautiful medal. Isn't it some kind of blessing for tonight? I had the impression you didn't want me to be in the theater either."

She smiled for the first time. "You've got the right idea about the medal. But you jumped to conclusions about the other thing. I'm really not entitled to an opinion on what you do. I don't even truly know what it is. Do you really want to continue dancing for the rest of your life?"

"I only know that I love my dancing so much I can't imagine ever not doing it. Every day I spend hours practicing. It's so much more exciting than just making good grades in school. Oh, I suppose I get good grades too because I work at it. A part of me likes to study real hard but my great love is dancing."

"Well, you must do what is right for you. Tonight I'll be clapping for you as hard as I can. Maybe you can come to dance in St. Louis later if that is what you want. Do you ever think about coming to visit me?"

"Maybe I'll come just before you go to Italy. Then you'll have to take me with you."

"*D'accordo.* We must keep in touch so that this can happen."

As though to seal a pact, she reached out to give me the warmest of hugs, and as before, I felt in the presence of someone I had known forever and ever. While she held me, I imagined the two of us on tour in Rome, chaperoned by Tony Carducci's sister. Everywhere we went I performed my favorite pieces and the face-less Carducci sister-in-law took photographs as fast as she could click the camera. In the distance a tiny figure of Andrea was pasting the pictures in a beautiful silver-covered album.

The image disappeared as my mother came to talk to us. "Lunch is ready. After you eat you'll have to take your nap so that you can be fresh for tonight. We all want you to do very well."

"Guess what, Mama?" I said. "Consuelo has just decided to book me at all the opera houses in Italy and she's going to dance with me at the end of each concert while entire orchestras play 'Malagueña' for us."

"Qué bien," mother laughed. "I better come along to make sure I get lots of material for my second memory book."

IV

That night, euphoric with all the congratulations and the many flowers and chocolates I received after the curtain call, I was convinced that mother would indeed have lots of new material for her next book. Happy with this thought I was running back to the dressing room holding the sweet-smelling red roses which Consuelo had sent when Andrea suddenly appeared in front of me with her camera. "I want this to be a really good picture," she said. "I've used up two rolls of film and now I have only one more picture left. This one is for a close-up. Put your flowers down on the floor. Now pretend you're dancing. Pose."

On cue I started playing the castanets while I danced some steps from "La boda de Luis Alonso." At the moment I held my arms above my head and crossed my wrists, I saw Consuelo among the well-wishers coming toward me. Tears were streaming down her face, and as I looked at her I felt a boundless connection to her. What is she really feeling I wondered. Aware that my smile had faded I suddenly experienced a tremendous tiredness and confusion. Before I had a chance to compose myself, I looked directly into Andrea's camera and at that instant she took the picture.

V

I never saw that picture although I could well imagine what I looked like in it. So much more was left to my imagination as the years passed by quickly without my seeing Andrea and Consuelo again. Life did not turn out to be as predictable as I had imagined it might be during the happy hours we had spent looking at the many dramatic transformations which Andrea had actually experienced against so many odds. As much as I had wanted to follow in her footsteps during the summer of our first and only encounter, I wound up not pursuing a career in dance. Nor did Consuelo make it to Rome as she had hoped. Yet Andrea and Tony did. Over the years I tried to maintain correspondence with both Andrea and Consuelo but it was mostly Consuelo that answered. During each of the next five years following their visit when I continued to get better and better in my dance recitals, I kept them informed of my latest accomplishments by sending them a glossy photo with notations on the date and place of the performance and the numbers I had danced. All of that came to an end in my junior year in high school when I was fifteen and very impressionable. For reasons I have not yet deciphered I allowed myself to be convinced that I should put away my dancing shoes and concentrate on my studies. The nuns, my school counselor and my mother all thought that I needed to be making plans for life after graduation. With various options facing me I did not know anymore if I wanted to be a dancer "for the rest of my life," as they all put it, and I decided that indeed I would pursue other more practical avenues. When I graduated from high school I finished at the top of my class and made it to college just as I and others had expected of me. Every year though I made a point of visiting Violeta's best students to encourage them to stick with their dancing no matter what others might tell them to do.

Off and on I would compare my decision with that of Cristina Ruiz and Becky Barrios. Cristina stayed with Violeta for many years, then opened up her own studio. Becky, on the other hand, went to college and majored in dance, much to her parents' consternation. She made it to New York and occasionally sent me press releases about her work. With those releases and clippings I gathered here and there I tried to keep a scrapbook of sorts about her many successes. But compared to the one my mother had compiled about Andrea's life as an artist, mine seemed rather ordinary and very much in keeping with my own generation's aspirations for fame in the big city, a fact which never seemed to enter into Andrea's fun-filled peregrinations. Becky's hard-won successes seemed meager when compared with what we all now were exposed to through television and there was nothing unique about what she was doing. So my album looked like hundreds of others which friends like me were pasting together for their more adventuresome acquaintances. My mother's album, by contrast, was simply one of a kind, in keeping with Andrea's career which had been bold and extraordinary in its day.

For a short while the blue album was actually mine. My mother made a present of it when I graduated from high school. Although I was very moved that she actually passed it on to me, I also had a slight suspicion that she had given it to me as a token of my having given up, on her strong advice, what had been so precious to me for so long. At the dorm some of the other students occasionally leafed through the album and expressed surprise that I truly had a cousin who was in theater so long ago. No one I knew then could say the same thing. In fact, no one I know now can say it either.

As the years passed I became even more aware of just how special Andrea's early experiences had been, and for her sixtieth birthday I decided she should finally be reunited with the images of her youth. At that time I considered my gesture to be most magnanimous; hence, I was surprised to sense, when she called to acknowledge receipt of the album, that she was not particularly happy that I had given it to her. "It really belongs to your mother," she said.

"You can send it back to her if you'd like," I told her but when the album did not come back I figured she had decided to keep it.

I was quite aware of just how much I missed looking through its pages and recalling my own youthful aspirations. But I also reminded myself that what had been captured in those black and white images were her accomplishments and not mine. I had done the right thing in sending it to her I kept telling myself. Sometimes I wondered why I had not kept at least one of the photographs but again I convinced myself that they belonged, as a unit, with Andrea.

I tried not to have any further remorse, and in fact, for many years I did erase the album's existence altogether from my memory. It all came back in May of last year, however. At that time Becky Barrios called me about an exhibit she was helping with on women in dance. "Do you still have the fantastic album about your cousin which we found so inspiring when we were just starting out in Violeta Aguilera's class?" she inquired.

"I can come up with it," I reassured her.

Thus, I made my call to St. Louis.

Andrea was very happy to hear from me until I mentioned the reason for my call. Without the slightest hesitation she quickly said, "It's gone."

"What do you mean it's gone?"

"It's gone," she repeated. "It's been gone for a long time. About two years after you sent it, Antonietta was looking at it and left it on the kitchen table. Sis found it there and tore up all the pictures. Every one of them. Later, she told me she had shredded them into tiny pieces and put them in a bag. Then, she went to the river's edge and sprinkled them into the water. As Sis described the scene I could see the little pieces of paper floating away like tiny white blossoms bobbing on the water."

"That's terrible," I barely whispered. "How did you feel at the time it happened?"

"I felt bad for your mother. You see, I always considered the album to be her own special way of expressing herself. I just sent her the photographs and other material. But she was the one who put order into it. And she guarded it like a relic. As far as I'm concerned I simply don't think back on the things that are part of my past. For over thirty years I have not been a performer. You, however, acted as though it were only yesterday that I was still dancing and acting in the theater. You refused to accept that I truly had set aside those years. They no longer exist as far as I'm concerned."

"What can I say?" I almost apologized.

"Look, I don't know if this will make you feel better or not but after Sis tore up the pictures, we had our first real conversation about the tensions of those early years. Her resenting my absences and my frustrations with her focus on the past. Her resoluteness. With all the links gone to the part of me that so disturbed her, we both discovered we could now really be as close as we should have been all those years. I simply accept her as she is. Deep inside I suppose I've admired the fact that she had never swerved from her strictly defined value system."

I still could not say anything.

"Look at it this way. Even though Sis had not known I had the album, her finding it served the purpose for which it might have existed in the first place."

"May I speak with Consuelo for a moment?"

Andrea hesitated for a few seconds, then said gently, "She's totally deaf now. Promise me that you won't write to her about this either. She seems quite happy in her own memories. No need to disturb still waters. Let things be. *Agua que no has de beber déjala correr.*"

I paced the floor for quite a while after I hung up. Finally, I picked up the phone and called Becky. I would offer to help her with the exhibit in any way I could. After all, there must be more than one way to put the pieces back together again. Unlike the time I was fifteen, on this occasion I knew what I had to do and I would not allow anyone to dissuade me from it. A clear-toned voice inside my head reminded me that "*De una espina salta una flor.*" Yes, I would reconstruct my own blue album even if those memorable pictures had disappeared long ago, gliding gently down waters I did not yet know. Right before Becky picked up the phone, the strains of *"Zandunga"* once again filled my head. And shadowy figures in lacy white headdresses beckoned me to join them.

GLOSSARY

la gacela de dos países—(literally, the gazelle of two countries)

Andrea de pastora en 'La Aurora del Nuevo Día,' Plaza de la Iglesia de San Agustín, 20 de diciembre de 1921—Andrea as a shepherdess in "La Aurora del Nuevo Día," St. Augustine Church Plaza, December 20, 1921

Pastorela—shepherd play

Sí. Ese es mi favorito.—Yes. That's my favorite.

Me parece muy artificial. Andrea en persona nunca fue así. Acuérdate que han pasado quince años que dejó el teatro.—She looks too artificial. Andrea in person was never like that. Remember that fifteen years have gone by since she left the theater.

Tienes razón.—You're right.

¿Te acuerdas cuando nos llegó el primer paquete de recuerdos? ¡Cuánto nos alegró! Llegó en octubre de 1925 cuando yo tenía quince años. Era tan impresionable a esa edad.—Do you remember when we got our first package full of memories? We were so happy! It first arrived on October, 1925 when I was fifteen. I was so impressionable at that age.

Después de que vio 'Los amores de Ramona' se enamoró del teatro.—After she saw 'The Loves of Ramona' she fell in love with the theater.

el teatro popular español—los sainetes y las zarzuelas—Popular Spanish theater—the short musical pieces

postalitas—little postcards

Sí, pero lo hizo contra los gustos de Consuelo.—Yes, but she did it against Consuelo's wishes.

'No te metas más en ese mundo' Consuelo le seguía diciendo. Al final, sin embargo, Consuelo perdió y Andrea se salió con la suya.—'Don't get further involved in that world,' Consuelo kept telling her. In the end, though, Consuelo lost out and Andrea did what she wanted.

dramaturgos españoles—Spanish dramatists

los pueblitos de la frontera—the little border towns

exiliados españoles—the Spanish exiles

Para entonces ya era novia de Tony Carducci. Después de que se casaron en el '41, se fueron a vivir en San Luis, Missouri, donde ya estaban los padres de Tony. Y allí Andrea le dijo adiós al teatro para siempre.—By then she was already going with Tony Carducci. After they got married in '41 they went to live in St. Louis, Missouri, where Tony's parents lived. And there Andrea said goodby to the theater forever.

Consuelo perdió a su Tomás—Consuelo lost her Tomás

Consuelo siempre ha sido extraña—Consuelo has always been so strange

Yo creo que Andrea quedó bien satisfecha con su decisión.—I think Andrea has always been satisfied with her decision.

Pues, fíjate que también dicen que cada quien cuenta de la feria según lo que ve en ella.—Well, you know what they say. Everyone sees in the fair what it is she wants to see.

Aquí vienen.—Here they come.

¡Bienvenidas!—Welcome!

¿Cómo te pareció el viaje a ti?—What did you think of the trip?

Cuéntame de ti.—Tell me about yourself.

Créemelo—Believe me.

¡Qué gusto verlas!—It's so nice to see them.

al contrario—on the contrary

Son las cosas de la vida—That's life.

Es uno de nuestros pasatiempos favoritos.—It's one of our favorite pastimes.

Por desgracia—Through misfortune

Tú sabes, el hábito no hace al monje.—You know, clothes don't make the man.

libro de memorias—memory book

Si, mi piace molto parlare con tutta la famiglia di Tony.—That's right. I have a good time speaking with Tony's family.

Uno di questi giorni andaro a la Italia con lei. Capisce?—One of these days I want to go to Italy with her. Did you understand what I said?

zapateado—a style of dancing with rapid footsteps that are quite audibly evident

D'accordo.—Okay.

Qué bien—Great.

Agua que no has de beber déjala correr.—Let still waters lie.

De una espina salta una flor.—Something good comes out of every bad turn.

❋ Hearts

SHEILA ORTIZ TAYLOR

I

Under a dome of Catalina stars my father's sailboat dips softly, secured by mooring lines. Below, my father's hands flicker over the breakfast nook table, under the kerosene lamp, until all the cards are dealt. My mother and sister are finishing up the dinner dishes, slowly. My father is impatient to begin the nightly game of Hearts. He snaps on the ship-to-shore. Voices of a woman and a man talking are all but buried in transatlantic static; then suddenly the universe clarifies and the woman is saying how she misses him, how her body craves his, how the clamor in her blood. . . . Then she drowns in an ecstasy of buzzing.

"She didn't *know*," says my mother.

"Didn't know what?" snorts my father.

"Everybody could hear." She takes her place at the table, picks up her cards.

My father looks at my sister to see if she has understood. My sister flicks a membrane over her eyes, arranges her cards into suits.

In a moment my mother will say, "How do you play this game?"

The question will irritate my father less than one might expect. He can afford patience because he is planning how he will, instead of avoiding all hearts, actually garner every single one and thereby not merely avert disaster to himself but bring it down threefold on all our heads.

"How do you play this game?" asks my mother innocently. While my father explains the object of the game and all its rules, I plan my own strategy. I will permit my father to take Dirty Dora, the queen of spades who counts twelve hearts. I will permit him to take every heart, save one. For I have recently learned how to control inanimate objects. From my art teacher.

My father takes the first trick, a heart included. "He's going for them," says my sister sullenly. He keeps the lead. My mother, who has no diamonds, keeps sloughing hearts. My mother is a purely intuitive card player. While my father keeps a running tally of which cards have been played and by whom, my mother plays each round as if it has no history and will have no future. She usually wins.

"I'm hungry," says my sister.

"You just ate," says my mother.

I am watching my father, summoning my powers, waiting for the right moment to stop him with a single heart. I fill the small cabin with my energy, but it is only a prelude to what I can do.

"What's that?" says my father, suddenly alert.

"What's what ?" says my mother, discarding yet another heart onto my father's diamond lead.

"That sound." He slips up the companionway ladder and we listen to his feet clumping overhead. I think perhaps I have overdone it. "Oh my God," he says.

We drop our cards and scamper after him. There is a purple red light in the north and a sudden, heavy chop. The wind keeps changing direction. My father, leaning over the bow talking with a man in a skiff, turns and shouts at us, "Storm coming." He helps the man shove off, then pounds back down the hatchway and turns on the ship-to-shore. We follow, slide back around the table. There is a squealing; the airways are overloaded. Finally the nasal voice of the San Pedro marine operator breaks through in broken dire warnings.

I look with delight at my sister. We relish rough weather and disaster. My mother zips up her Amelia Earhardt jacket and says, "We're leaving."

My father hesitates. He was too old to join the navy in World War II and so has some vague inclination to go down with his ship now. Honor, like the game of hearts, is an alien concept to my mother. She begins to pack a duffel bag.

The boat by now is pitching and rolling. The harbor master, moving among the moored boats in his wallowing launch, is announcing through a bull horn that everybody should set storm anchors and go ashore.

"Where are the storm anchors?" asks my mother.

My father likes always to give the impression that he is the kind of person prepared for any eventuality. There are, for example, two first aid kits on board, as well as a war surplus inflatable life raft that includes K-rations and primitive fishing gear for six people. In the glove compartment of his car, twenty-six miles away on the mainland, is a snakebite kit.

"We have no storm anchors," he says, and whistles into the wind for a shore boat.

But they are overworked. While we wait, he and I double the mooring lines and make everything fast on deck. My mother and sister screw tight the portholes and secure the hatches. At last a single ghostly shore boat wallows toward us, castaways hanging from every line and life rail, and we make our way slowly toward the lights of Avalon.

11

They are lucky to get a room in Island Efficiencies. It is high season, though Island Efficiencies usually has vacancies when places right on the beach or the more elegant hillside hotels with views of the cliffs, the bell tower, the Wrigley mansion have been booked for months. But the storm has blown Island Efficiencies extra trade, people like the family sleeping in Unit 5, who are lucky to have a place at all. Lucky really to be off the beach, where thirty foot waves now engulf the sea wall and even the promenade.

They are safe inside Unit 5, lying on sheets bleached, starched, and ironed by Celeste's Island Laundry, and stretched across and tucked in by Melissa Vargas, who used to work in a hospital on the mainland before she met Ramón near the base in Long Beach, married and moved here after the war.

Ramón, yard man and handyman at Island Efficiencies, had wheeled in the cots, dragging them squeaking and resisting through the rain and wind to Unit 5, where Melissa had made them up for the hollow eyed children while their parents stood, dripping onto the broken linoleum.

It is almost an hour later and everybody has had a hot bath and Melissa Vargas and Ramón are making love in their snug cottage on Clemente Street and the family from the boat are lying in the dark under tight sheets listening to rain drum the roof and wind embrace and release Unit 5 in passionate huffs and impulses.

In her cot by the door the elder daughter is thinking about how she never got a chance to join the Girl Scouts because of her father, who was always about to sail around the world, always putting a For Sale sign in the front yard, and who never let them take a free and easy breath in their lives. If she was a Girl Scout she would survive this storm alone in a cave somewhere and in the morning, when everything had dried up and eased down, she would emerge, new and sure, and eat berries and wild mushrooms without dying, because she would know how.

Her father, on the opposite side of the room is wishing he had bought insurance for his boat and wondering if it is too late now. But if he were to get up, ever so quietly, to make a phone call or two, his wife would wonder where he was going and there is no reason now to let her know that the boat is not insured. She does not understand these things, business, and the importance of insurance and having a plan for everything. Sometimes he worried what she would do without him, although he has stopped smoking, reads Adelle Davis, and drinks Pep-up almost every day. Still a man has to think about these things, about the frail family he holds in the palm of his hand. About the dangers of ordinary living, and the extraordinary living he sometimes finds himself doing, and suddenly he sees his boat dragging free of its mooring lines, drifting directly toward the rocks and he, lying helpless under tight sheets instead of going down with his ship, as was right and honorable. He wrestles his right leg out of the sheet and just as he is about to stand, his wife's cool hand seeks him out and he sits back down on the side of the bed, defeated.

He is restless, she thinks, never able just to turn out the lights in his head and go to sleep. She could dim hers at will, like all her family, could go whole days without thinking of anything at all. Dark and still. She hears him lie down and draw his leg back under the starched sheet. She listens to the rain on the roof and the drumming of her husband's thoughts. Then he says one word: insurance? Ah, she sees now his vision of the boat on the rocks. But what, after all, was insurance? A piece of paper. In nine years she will marry a man who sells insurance for a living. He might as well be a magician.

In the next bed the younger daughter, as if she is watching a platform diver, feels her mother's long stylized drop into a pool of sleep. Forces gathering in the dark now, the girl can hear the laboring engine of her father's heart, can see with him their drifting, blind boat plunging toward rocky cliffs, while below deck unplayed cards lie scattered on the darkened table.

III. Criticism

❀ ❀ ❀ ❀

Carmen Lomas Garza *Curandera Barriendo el Susto*

Yreina Cervántez *Black Legs*

Since I can remember I have always had conflicting feelings about education. Knowledge has been my inspiration, but my experiences as a student of color in the U. S. educational system evoke memories of intimidation, alienation and institutional racism.

As a child growing up in Kansas and later in rural San Diego county, it was obvious that there existed two standards of education within the same classroom —standards applied by mostly white educators. One standard, based upon the precepts of "potential and possibilities," was imparted to the white children, the sons and daughters of ranchers and landowners. Another standard of inferior or lower expectation was inflicted on the Mexican and Indian children, those from families of migrant laborers, workers and the descendants of the original inhabitants of the land.

Sadly, it is no surprise that children internalized either feelings of entitlement and superiority or those of alienation and a profound disappointment in their limited life choices. These extremes reveal the racist structure imposed by the colonizer upon the colonized, the powerful upon the powerless. They are still reflected in the policies of many mainstream institutions, particularly the institutions of higher education.

Black Legs: An Education is based on a sharp recollection that surfaced while I was in graduate school at UCLA. It emerged with the realization that my experiences there echoed the sense of powerlessness and victimization I felt as a child when my enthusiasm to learn and create had been thwarted by racist attitudes.

As an adult, I again confronted institutional racism in the form of indifference within the UCLA Art Department, specifically its resistance to the implementation of a more inclusive curriculum and the very obvious absence of ethnically diverse art faculty and graduate students. Despite the fact that the university is in one of the most "multicultural" of cities, I encountered narrow definition of art/aesthetics or the art of "the Other." These were perceived as outside the accepted mainstream avant garde norms.

Black Legs was my response to the intense frustration I experienced in the institution, my decision not to let it overtake me, and my commitment to creating awareness through my own art work.

I am an artist/activist, and ironically— or fittingly—I am an educator today. This role is still a difficult one for me, given my ambiguous feelings toward education and institutions. But precisely because of my own experiences and my belief in developing alternative systems, I feel that greater representation of people of color in policy-making positions of power will provide the basis for the fundamental changes needed in art and education, to improve the quality of life for our children and for us all.

Black Legs: An Education is a work in progress. Presented are the preliminary sketches for a limited edition handmade book to be printed in either serigraphy or lithography.—Yreina D. Cervántez

1

BLACK LEGS
AN EDUCATION

SCHOOL DAYS 1958-59

2

☑ An Education

I don't know why but I have to go to a new school, I'll miss my cousins. It's far and I HAVE TO WALK ALONE — SCARY. I have butterflies in my stomach.

SCHOOL DAYS 1958-59   SCHOOL DAYS 1958-59

☑ Anticipation
☑ Alone
☑ agüitarse

3

The teacher's name is Miss Kop. She can't say my name right, and when she says it funny everybody laughs. WHAT AM I DOING HERE ?? ENGLISH ONLY... I see the writing on the wall.

☑ Ashamed
☑☑ agüitarse

SCHOOL DAYS 1958-59

I'm the only one. WHY Am I so different ? I want to be friends. They want me to be like them — they like you more if you act like them (and look like them) but I'm me.

☑ Assimilation
☑ agringarse
☑☑ agüitarse

4

The teacher gives me work-sheets with math and cats. I hurry up and finish the math and spend all day drawing and coloring the cats. It makes me feel better, purrr----

☆☆ Artistic
☑ muy de Aquellas

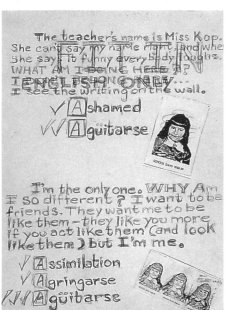

5

6

7

GLOSSARY

Agüitarse -
Low in the dumps, DISPIRITED, to become despondent; to be bothered to make feel low.

AGRINGARSE -
To become anglicized, GRINGOIZED, assimilation.

MUY DE AQUELLAS
Outta site, so fine.

A VOLAR
TO SCRAM, split.

ÁNDALE
GO FOR IT, GO AHEAD ON

AVENTARSE (AVIENTATE)
To give it one's all, to show ones talent

A TODA MADRE (A.T.M.)
The most, the greatest, far out, full force.

PINCHI - DAMNED.

8

✺ The Politics of Poetics:

Or, What Am I, A Critic, Doing

in This Text Anyhow?

TEY DIANA REBOLLEDO

In an essay "Retrieving our Past, Determining our Future" poet Pat Mora chose to begin with a pre-Columbian poem:

> Also they grow cotton
> of many colors:
> red, yellow, pink,
> purple, green, bluish-green,
> blue, light green,
> orange, brown, and dark gold.
> These were the colors of the cotton itself.
> It grew that way from the earth,
> no one colored it.
> And also they raised these
> fowl of rare plumage:
> small birds the color of turquoise,
> some with green feathers,
> with yellow, with flame-colored breasts.
> Every kind of fowl
> that sang beautifully,
> like those that warble in the mountains.[1]

Mora chose this poem because she liked the images of music, color and nature. But then she is a poet. I would like to underscore Mora's choice and begin with some definitions. "*Politics:* intrigue or maneuvering within a group; one's position or attitude on political subjects. *Poetics:* literary criticism dealing with the nature, form and laws of poetry; a study of or treatise on poetry or aesthetics. *Criticism:* the art, skill, or profession of making discriminating judgments, especially of literary or artistic works, detailed investigation of the origin and history of literary documents. *Discourse:* to run about, to speak at length, the process or power of reasoning."[2]

My understanding several months ago was that this symposium "Chicana Creativity and Criticism: Charting New Frontiers in American Literature," would undertake a dialogue between Chicana creative writers and Chicana literary critics with regard to several topics: Are Chicana critics friends or foes to the writers? What function do or can we Chicana critics play in relationship to our literature? And, what the heck are we doing in and to these texts anyway? As Chicanas we are all in this *revoltura* and explosion of literature and poetics together. It is time, perhaps, to take a step back and analyze where we are and where we might be going.

I do not mean the remarks I am about to make to be anti-intellectual, anti-theoretical or anti-aesthetic. Nor do I mean to assume the position of any critic other than myself. Nor am I criticizing the work of any particular literary critic. Nevertheless, I am commenting on what I see as a general phenomena: one that we need to take stock of and one which affects Chicano male critics as well as the females. Juan Bruce-Novoa, in his recent article "Canonical and Noncanonical Texts," thinks there is now a "body of work" which constitutes Chicano literature and which is recognized as such. He recognizes that previously "any mention of canon was clearly understood as a reference to mainstream literature" and, he adds, "to state we were excluded from the canon was to state the obvious. Moreover, there was an ironic sense of worth associated with being outside the canon, almost a sense of purity, because, beyond the exclusionary ethnocentrism implied by the canon, Chicanos infused the term with a criticism of the very existence of a privileged body of texts." [3]

It seems to me that in spite of the explosion of creative and critical activity on the part of both critics and writers, Chicana writers and critics are still within a framework of marginality among Chicano writing as well as in mainstream writing. Some of this may be attributed to time; that is, time for the maturing of our literature as well as of our criticism. In addition to the creation of new insights and perspectives, we are also at a moment of rupture in which we are just beginning to look back to uncover our traditions, whether they be written or oral, and to talk back-to unsay what had been said and frozen in time and place. We are at the moment of questioning everything, even ourselves. Only when it is accomplished can we, with clear conscience, proceed towards some understanding of critical difference.

At the recent Chicano Studies Conference in Salt Lake City (1987), it became clear that for the past several years social scientists and literary critics alike have been engaged in a desperate search for a theoretical/critical discourse in which to situate what is happening to us. There have been discourses and counter-discourses. We talk about historical/materialist perspectives, transformative perspectives, pluralism (which some called a pre-prostituted dominant discourse) and the word hegemony was used in one session alone thirty-two times. Some of the talks began with a few of the questions to be asked, then discussed the methods used to answer those questions, mostly the methods used. I would say a typical talk could be summarized in the following way: the speaker begins, "This paper will focus on the ideology of cultural practice and its modes of signifying." S/he then spends twenty minutes discussing how the works of whatever theoretical greats s/he selects will define, inform and privilege the work s/he is doing. Such names as Jameson, Said, Williams, Hall, Burke and other contemporary *meros, meros* (mostly male) will be invoked over and over. The speaker is then sent a note by the chair of the panel that there is no time left. And whatever the Chicano/a writing or phenomena that was to be discussed is quickly summarized in two minutes. The talk is over. We have talked so much about theory we never get to our conclusion nor focus on the texts. By appropriating mainstream theoreticians and critics we have become so involved in intellectualizing that we lose our sense of our literature and therefore our vitality. This priority of placing our literature in a theoretical framework to "legitimize" it, if the theory overshadows it, in effect undermines our literature or even places it, once again, in a state of oblivion. Privileging the theoretical discourse deprivileges ourselves.

In puzzling over this scenario, which in fact occurred many times in Salt Lake, one could be left with various insights about what is happening to us:

1. We have internalized the dominant ideology so that only by talking theory (construed as a superior form of logic) can our literature and our cultural practices be intellectually viable, that is, acceptable within the traditional academic canon as "legitimate."

2. We are trying to impress ourselves and others with our ability to manipulate theoretical discourse, to use buzz words such as *hegemony, signifying* and even the word *discourse.* Someone once said to me "you are so articulate. You are able to talk in *their* language." I am not sure what this means. On the one hand they may be telling me I am totally assimilated or they may, in reality, be saying that no Chicana can truly be articulate. (I myself often feel that it is only our baroque *conceptismo* that has been transferred into English.)

3. We have entered into the "Age of Criticism" which could be defined as a preoccupation with theoretical structures often not internalized: we feel that theory is power.

4. We have a genuine desire to look beyond the elements (the texts) to the conditions that structured them. We are truly in search of a theoretical framework which yet eludes us or at least some of us (and I count myself among those eludees).

I would like to outline some of the problems that I think we Chicana critics face or that at least I, as a critic in training, think about from time to time. They often as not deal with the question, what am I doing in this text anyhow?

1. First of all I am a reader. But I am not just a reader. My job, as a university professor, is to bring the attention of my students to the text itself. How can I do this if the text is not included in the general course curriculum, in the anthologies or in any way accessible to the student or to the population at large? Perhaps my primary responsibility, therefore, is the promulgation of the works of these writers, to make the writers known. We all know that the material production of Chicana writers is often limited to chapbooks, journals, the few that are accepted by Arte Público Press and Bilingual Press. It is limited even to the Chicano audience and from one region to the next, from one big city to the next, we may not know what is happening. The work being done by Juan Rodríguez, *Third Woman* and the Centro de Escritores de Aztlán, for example, helps but as these texts go out of print, this production becomes more difficult to find. At Salt Lake City a copy of the first printing of Quinto Sol's *El Grito* was proudly held up as the rarity it has become. Of the chapbooks that were and are produced in the 60's, 70's and 80's, many will end up in a rare book room in a library if we are fortunate. Fortunate because it will be preserved as an artifact—the same phenomena which will make the book even more inaccessible.

If this product is inaccessible to those who are its target, in terms of interest, it is virtually unavailable to a larger audience. The role of the Chicana critic then becomes one of facilitator: reproducing and making known the texts of our authors. In itself this may not be an insignificant task since, for example, in a recent struggle with some of my co-authors (not the editors) of a book to be published by Yale University Press, I was told that my method of writing, that is, including entire poems written by Chicanas instead of dissecting them by including between slashes "pertinent" quotes from the text, made my article "hard to read" and "jumpy." While this may be true of my *own* writing, it certainly was not true of those texts of the authors I had included. I was very troubled by the inadequacies of a vision which presumed to have me speak for all Chicanas when they were perfectly able to speak for themselves. My arguments for entire text inclusion were the following: a. These texts were unknown and therefore needed to be reproduced in their entirety; b. These writers were more passionate, forceful and graphic than I; c. I did not want to do to these writers what others have been doing to all of us for centuries, that is, to appropriate their discourse through my discourse. I commented that I had no problem with my strategy and if they were not happy with publishing my chapter as it was, I did not wish it to be included in the volume. Fortunately the article will be published in its jumpy entirety in *The Desert Is No Lady,* title poem by Pat Mora.[4]

2. The second function of a critic may be to analyze the content of the literary production-stepping back from the product in order to see what may be the dominant concerns and themes. I myself have indulged in this type of descriptive thematic analysis (adding, I hope, some analysis in depth as to cultural context and history). One example is a paper I wrote on Abuelitas, noting the scope and complexity of this recurring figure and offering an explanation as to why this figure was approaching what I considered to be mythic proportions.[5] This article has brought mixed reviews. My secretary, who was typing it, asked to take it home to read to her children, and many others have used it in their classrooms for teaching. Recently a contemporary writer remarked to me about critics writing descriptively about things that "everyone already knew about," such as abuelitas. Yet descriptive thematic analysis serves its purpose too, particularly as it grows in sophistication, and as historical and cultural analysis are linked to it. I hope that since my abuelitas article was published and as I have grown as a scholar that my analysis has too.

3. Another important current function for us as critics is to remember our literary history. While contemporary writers may feel that they are seeing the world anew, those of us who are searching out our literary roots are finding women writers who were raising many of the same concerns women voice today—written in a different tone and style and conforming to a different mode; nevertheless, contemporary writers have not arisen from a complete void. If the written word did not survive in enough texts to be known today, nonetheless the oral forms of women's concerns, of women's images have

lived in the tradition from one generation, from one century to another. Thus the critic as literary historian is able to fill in the lacunae and to connect the past and the present.

4. Chicana literary discourse, like most feminist discourse, is a troubled one. It is always searching, questioning and fraught with tensions and contradictions, just as is the creative writing arising from the same creative context. A truly Chicana literary theory would result from the attempt to resolve these things, to mend the rift between doers and thinkers. I think we would all agree that Chicana criticism and theory are still in a state of flux looking for a theoretical, critical framework that is our own, whatever the perspective. I personally find it difficult to have theory (male oriented, French feminist, post structural or whatever is the current fad) be what dictates what we find in our literature. I prefer to have the literature speak for itself and as a critic try to organize and understand it. Perhaps from a more open perspective our own theoretical critical analysis will arise, rather than finding the theory first and imposing it upon the literature.

Recently several Chicana critics have taken up the issue of a theoretical approach to our literature. Norma Cantú in "The Chicana Poet and Her Audience: Notes Towards a Chicana Feminist Aesthetic" acknowledges the lack of a methodological approach in our work but feels that it is a sense of place and world as embedded in particular language use that the Chicana poet communicates to her Chicana audience. For Cantú it is the special relationship between writer and listener, the shared cultural referents that make the poems work.[6] Norma Alarcón, in her perceptive study on the image of La Malinche, reevaluates and reconstructs the symbolic and figurative meaning this figure holds for us as Chicana writers and critics, dealing with the significance of language use and silence within our literature.[7] She also sees significant evolution of the Chicana as "speaking subject" one who brings within herself her race, class and gender, expressing this from a self-conscious point of view. Both of these critics, it seems to me, in addition to being theoretically well grounded, look at the literature from within, in an integrative sense.

5. It is very difficult to work on living authors: authors who read what you write and agree or don't agree. But it is just as difficult to work on authors no longer living. In the practice of literary criticism one (or perhaps I speak for myself only) must practice sound and honorable as well as rigorous criticism. That is, facts must be checked, scholarship must be sound. There is always the danger that the critic, immersed in pursing some essential point, will become overly enthusiastic and confuse the authorial voice with that of

the narrative or poetic voice. If structuralism has taught us anything at all, it is that the Lyric/narrative speaker is just that. As critics we must be careful not to confuse author with speaker.

When dealing with a vigorously living author we must also not be too timid to analyze symbolically what we, as critics, may see in the text—that which the author may not consciously have intended. We know that there are many levels of symbolic discourse that we may not be aware of at any given moment. When the text is published, when the author gives it up to the public domain, it is released and opened up to interpretation by the reader. It exists on its own, separate from the author. The textual interpretation, therefore, is one of integration between the authorial intent, and the text itself, *and* the third (and separate) interpretation or grasping of those two aspects by the reader.

6. We must, as critics, also be careful in our criticism to be honest. I think Chicana critics are often too benign. Our close network between writers and critics makes it difficult to have caustic criticism (which might ruin friendships) but at the same time we may hesitate to be as critical as we should be. One way I know I cope with this, and I imagine others have the same problem, is simply to ignore those texts I don't like, of writers that I do like or to ignore those writers who say nothing to me. This seems to me to be a function of human nature. What is important, however, is that the critic be conscious of her biases. And while we women may be benign to each other, there are still many Chicano critics who refuse to recognize their own biases and misogyny. Raymond Paredes, in a recent review article, is only able to see Chicana literature through a particularly phallocentric focus. If we were to accept his views we would see "if there is one quality that runs consistently through *their* (underlining mine) stories, plays and novels, it is the conviction that men know and care very little about women and that everyone is the worse for it."[8] His review continues with the assumption that men are the focus of Chicana literature, as he assails Beverly Silva, Cherríe Moraga and Ana Castillo as faulted writers, their work, he says, is more interesting "ideologically" than aesthetically. Back to the old notion of "Are They Any Good?" Those writers whose perspectives Paredes does not agree with he considers superficial, and Denise Chávez, with whom he is more in agreement, is merely "flawed."[9]

7. Perhaps more dangerous than ignoring texts we dislike is excluding the works of authors whose perspective we do not share or whose perspective we might feel uncomfortable with. Here I mean specifically the perspective

of sexual preference. There are some fine Lesbian writers such as Cherríe Moraga, Gloria Anzaldúa,—and Veronica Cunningham whose works are often excluded (although less so recently) from our critical thinking. Certainly if critics are serious about historical, cultural and gender context, then all writers need to be included within the general cultural framework. Then too some critics feel more comfortable with socially conscious literature and exclude that coming from the middle class. As the complexities and shades of our literature grows, we must be careful not to canonize a certain few to the exclusion of other equally fine writers.

8. While some scholars see the need for some resolution of dichotomies, for example of Chicana and feminist, Chicana and poet—as if they were mutually exclusive—others examine the relationship between dominant and ethnic communities. The dominant discourse, if we internalize it, would have us believe that we function under such labels, and to some extent we do. I believe, however, as Bernice Zamora so succinctly expressed it, that our complexities are infinite: that we have grown up and survived along the edges, along the borders of so many languages, worlds, cultures and social systems that we constantly fix and focus on the spaces in between, Nepantla as Sor Juana would have seen it. Categories that try to define and limit this incredibly complex process at once become diminished for their inability to capture and contain. Those of us who try to categorize these complexities inevitably fail.

Margarita Cota-Cárdenas in her novel *Puppet* examines the way in which this ideology is imposed. She sees this in part as arising from a single vision of what being Chicana should be.

> Are you Malinche o malinche? Who are you (who am I mal inche)? Seller or buyer? Sold or bought and at what price? What is it to be what so many should say sold-out malinchi who is who are/are we what? At what price without having been there naming putting label tags what who have bought sold malinchismo what other-ismos invented shouted with hate reacting, striking like vipers like snakes THEIR EYES like snakes what who what [10]

Her Malinche breaks the silence of centuries and she does not do so quietly:

> yes yes I went yelling loud too why why and they said tie her up she's too forward too flighty she thinks she's a princess thinks she's her father's daughter thinks she's hot stuff that's it doesn't know her place a real threat

to the tribe take her away haul her off she's a menace to our cause that's it
only learned to say crazy things accuse with HER EYES and they didn't
want them troublemakers in their country. (86)

These labels, specific here to La Malinche but clearly extended to all Chicanas, are of course the very labels culture uses to restrict and limit women's
activity, socially as well as intellectually. Women are so silenced that they are
only left to speak with "their eyes." In a country defined as "their" country,
one that does not belong to her, Cota-Cárdenas makes the connection between Mexico and the United States:

> This country, well I suppose Mexico, Aztlán . . . ? Well, it could have been
> a little more to the north or a little more to the south, it makes no differ-
> ence now, what I was telling you was my version, that's it, my version . . .
> as a woman, that's right, and they can establish the famous dialectic with
> the other versions that you already know very well. (86)

Cota-Cárdenas thus introduces the complexities, the ambiguities in our lives
and, while she does not deny the legitimacy of the other versions (acknowl-
edging them for what they are), overlays another perspective that is hers
alone.

These remarks I have made may seem to be arising from some simplis-
tic assumptions. I myself was trained as a structuralist, semiotic critic. But
increasingly I have become suspicious and yes, even bored, by a criticism
which seems alien to the text about which it purports to talk; by a theoretical basis of patriarchal norms or a theory which does not take the particular
concerns of minority writers and culture into account. I am suspicious of
criticism which ignores the texts of our writers and which turns the vitality
and the passion of those texts of our writers into an empty and meaning-
less set of letters. This sort of criticism, it seems to me, might as well be
analyzing a menu or a telephone directory, and would perhaps be better directed in doing so. As Sor Juana criticized Aristotle—he would have been a
better philosopher had he studied cooking,—I believe that our critical discourse should come from within, within our cultural and historical perspective. This is not to say that I am advocating limited, regional, small-minded
descriptive literary analysis. But I think we should internalize and revolu-
tionize theoretical discourse that comes from outside ourselves, accepting
that which is useful and discarding that which is merely meant to impress.
In the search for our own aesthetic, for our own analytical direction, we

need to look to each other, to recognize that our literature and our cultural production does not need legitimization from the academy, that it already is legitimate in itself. Above all, we must not forget that the most important aspect of our analysis are the texts themselves. As we ask ourselves where are we, what are we doing, we must never appropriate into our own discourse the discourse of the writer herself. If we are to diffuse, support, promote, analyze and understand the work of our writers, we must let them speak for themselves. As a critic I desire the same as poet Pat Mora, I want to see the cotton of many colors, the small birds the color of turquoise, and hear the birds that warble in the mountains.

NOTES

1. In Miguel León-Portilla, *Pre-Columbian Literature of Mexico* (Norman: University of Oklahoma Press, 1969), 41, cited in Mora, "Tradition and Mythology: Signatures of Landscape in Chicana Literature"; in *The Desert is No Lady*, Vera Norwood and Janice Monk, eds. (New Haven: Yale University Press, 1987), pp. 98–124.

2. *Webster's II* (Boston: Houghton Mifflin, 1984).

3. *The Americas Review* 14:3–4 (Fall-Winter, 1986), 119.

4. *The Desert Is No Lady: Southwestern Landscapes in Women's Writing and Art,* Eds. Vera Norwood and Janice Monk (New Haven: Yale University Press, 1987), 96–124.

5. "Abuelitas: Mythology and Integration in Chicana Literature" *Woman of Her Word: Hispanic Women Write,* Ed. Evangelina Vigil, Revista Chicano-Riqueña II :3 4 (1983), 148–58

6. Rebolledo, Ed. *Writing From the Margins* unpublished ms.

7. "Traddutora, Traditora: A Paradigmatic Figure of Chicana Feminism," in *Changing Our Power: An Introduction to Women's Studies,* Jo Whitehorse Cochran, Donna Langston, and Carolyn Woodward, eds. Dubuque, Ia: Kendall-Hunt Publishing Co., 1988.

8. "Review Essay: Recent Chicano Writing," *Rocky Mountain Review* 41:1–2 (1987), 126.

9. Paredes, 128.

10. *Puppet* (Austin, TX: Relámpago Books Press, 1985), p. 85.

❋ Chicana Literature From a
Chicana Feminist Perspective

YVONNE YARBRO-BEJARANO

What are the implications of a Chicana feminist literary criticism?
The existence of a Chicana feminist literary criticism implies the existence,
first of all, of a tradition or body of texts by Chicana writers, which in turn
implies the existence of a community of Chicanas and ideally of a Chicana
feminist political movement. In other words, I do not see the development
and application of a Chicana feminist literary criticism as an academic exercise. Like white feminism, Chicana feminism originates in the community
and on the streets as political activism to end the oppression of women. This
political movement is inseparable from the historical experience of Chicanos
in this country since 1848, an experience marked by economic exploitation
as a class and systematic racial, social and linguistic discrimination designed
to keep Chicanos at the bottom as a reserve pool of cheap labor.

Within this collective experience, the facts and figures concerning Chicanas' education, employment categories and income levels clearly delineate
the major areas of struggle for Chicana feminist movement.[1] There have
always been Chicanas involved in political activism aimed at the specific
situation of Chicanas as working-class women of color, objectified by economic exploitation and discrimination. Lucy González Parsons, the Liga
Femenil Mexicanista, Dolores Hernández, Emma Tenayuca, the miners'
wives in the strike in Santa Rita, New Mexico, in the early 50s, Alicia Esca-
lante and many, many more—these names evoke community, Chicanas who
have laid the groundwork for a contemporary movement.

The Chicana feminist critic, then, does not work in isolation, alone with
her texts and word processor, typewriter or pad and pencil. She is a Chicana—identified critic, alert to the relationships between her work and the
political situation of all Chicanas.[2] The exclusion of Chicanas from literary
authority is intimately linked to the exclusion of Chicanas from other kinds
of power monopolized by privileged white males. Their struggle to appropriate the "I" of literary discourse relates to their struggle for empowerment
in the economic, social and political spheres.

The term "Chicana feminist perspective" also implies certain similarities with and differences from either an exclusively "feminist" or "Chicano" perspective. While sharing with the feminist perspective an analysis of questions of gender and sexuality, there are important differences between a Chicana perspective and the mainstream feminist one with regard to issues of race, culture and class. The Chicano perspective, while incorporating these important facets of race, culture and class, has traditionally neglected issues of gender and sexuality. The Chicana feminist is confronted with a dilemma, caught between two perspectives which appeal strongly to different aspects of her experience. In 1981, the publication of *This Bridge Called My Back* documented the rage and frustration of women of color with the white women's movement, not only for the racism, the tokenism, the exclusion and invisibility of women of color, but also for ignoring the issues of working-class women of color (such as forced sterilization).[3] The creative way out of this dilemma is the development of a Chicana feminism in coalition with other women of color dedicated to the definition of a feminism which would address the specific situation of working-class women of color who do not belong to the dominant culture. While recognizing her Chicana cultural identity and affirming her solidarity with all Chicanos and other Third World men and women to combat racial and economic oppression, the Chicana feminist also spearheads a critique of the destructive aspects of her culture's definition of gender roles. This critique targets heterosexist as well as patriarchal prejudice. Above all, Chicana feminism as a political movement depends on the love of Chicanas for themselves and each other as Chicanas.

Perhaps the most important principle of Chicana feminist criticism is the realization that the Chicana's experience as a woman is inextricable from her experience as a member of an oppressed working-class racial minority and a culture which is not the dominant culture. Her task is to show how in works by Chicanas, elements of gender, race, culture and class coalesce. The very term "Chicana" or "mestiza" communicates the multiple connotations of color and femaleness, as well as historical adumbrations of class and cultural membership within the economic structure and dominant culture of the United States. While this may seem painfully obvious, the assertion of this project in Chicana writing is crucial in combatting the tendency in both white feminist and Chicano discourse to see these elements as mutually exclusive. By asserting herself as Chicana or *mestiza,* the Chicana confronts the damaging fragmentation of her identity into component parts at war with each other. In their critique of the "woman's voice" of white feminist theory, María C. Lugones and Elizabeth V. Spelman suggest that being invited "to speak about being 'women' . . . in distinction from speaking about being Hispana, Black, Jewish, working-class, etc." is an invitation to silence.[4] The Chicana-identified critic also focuses on texts by Chicanas that involve a dual process of self-definition and building community with other Chicanas. In these works, Chicanas are the subjects of the representations, and often relationships between women form their crucial axes. In the 70s and especially the 80s, their works explore the full spectrum of Chicanas' bonds with Chicanas, including lesbianism. The process of self-definition involves what Black critic bell hooks calls moving from the margin to the center.[5] White male writers take for granted the assumption of the subject role to explore and understand self. The fact that Chicanas may tell stories about themselves and other Chicanas challenges the dominant male concepts of cultural ownership and literary authority. In telling these stories, Chicanas reject the dominant culture's definition of what a Chicana is. In writing, they refuse the objectification imposed by gender roles and racial and economic exploitation.

Chicana writers must overcome external, material obstacles to writing, such as limited access to literacy and the means of literary production, and finding time and leisure to write, given the battle for economic survival. But they must also overcome the internalization of the dominant society's definition of women of color. As Black writer Hattie Gossett phrases it, "who told you anybody wants to hear from you? you ain't nothing but a black woman!"[6] In her essay "Speaking in Tongues: A Letter to Third World Women Writers," Gloria Anzaldúa affirms that they must draw power from the very conditions that excluded them from writing in the first place, and write from what she calls the deep core of their identity as working-class women of color who belong to a culture other than the dominant one.[7]

By delving into this deep core, the Chicana writer finds that the self she seeks to define and love is not merely an individual self, but a collective one. In other words, the power, the permission, the authority to tell stories about herself and other Chicanas comes from her cultural, racial/ethnic and linguistic community. This community includes the historical experience of oppression as well as literary tradition. In spite of their material conditions, Chicanas have been writing and telling their stories for over a century. The Chicana writer derives literary authority from the oral tradition of her community, which in turn empowers her to commit her stories to writing.

Since this specific experience has been traditionally excluded from literary representation, it is not surprising that writing that explores the Chicana-as-subject is often accompanied by formal and linguistic innovation. In her essay "Speaking in Tongues," Anzaldúa stresses the need for women of color writers to find their authentic voice, to resist "making it" by becoming less different, to cultivate their differences and their tongues of fire to write about their personal and collective experience as Chicanas (166). The search is for a language that consciously opposes the dominant culture. Poet Cherríe Moraga has written: "I lack language. / The language to clarify / my resistance to the literate. / Words are a war to me. / They threaten my family." This search for an authentic language may include the fear of incomprehensibility, as the poem goes on to articulate: "To gain the word / to describe the loss / I risk losing everything. / I may create a monster . . ./ her voice in the distance / unintelligible illiterate. / These are the monster's words."[8] "Visions of Mexico . . ," by poet Lorna Dee Cervantes, also speaks of the urgent need to dominate the written word in order to smash stereotypes and rewrite history from the perspective of the oppressed:

> "there are songs in my head I could sing to you
> songs that could drone away
> all the mariachi bands you thought you ever heard
> songs that could tell you what I know
> or have learned from my people
> but for that I need words
> simple black nymphs between white sheets of paper
> obedient words obligatory words words I steal
> in the dark when no one can hear me."[9]

As evidenced by the poems quoted above by Moraga and Cervantes, the theme of writing itself may appear as mediator between individual and collective identity in works by Chicanas.

Writing is central in Sandra Cisneros' work of fiction *The House on Mango Street*.[10] *Mango St.* and Helena María Viramontes' collection of stories *Moths*,[11] are innovative in opposite directions—*Moths* characterized by formal experimentation, *Mango St.* by a deceptively simple, accessible style and structure. The short sections that make up this slim novel, *Mango St.*, are marvels of poetic language that capture a young girl's vision of herself and the world she lives in. Though young, Esperanza is painfully aware of the racial and economic oppression her community suffers, but it is the fate of the women in her *barrio* that has the most profound impact on her, especially as she begins to develop sexually and learns that the same fate might be hers. Esperanza gathers strength from the experiences of these women to reject the imposition of rigid gender roles predetermined for her by her culture. Her escape is linked in the text to education and above all to writing. Besides finding her path to self-definition through the women she sees victimized, Esperanza also has positive models who encourage her interest in studying and writing. At the end of the book, Esperanza's journey towards independence merges two central themes, that of writing and a house of her own: "a house as quiet as snow, a space for myself to go, clean as paper before the poem" (100).[12]

Esperanza's rejection of woman's place in the culture involves not only writing but leaving the barrio, raising problematic issues of changing class:

> I put it down on paper and then the ghost does not ache so much. I write it down and Mango says goodbye sometimes. She does not hold me with both arms. She sets me free. One day I will pack my bags of books and paper. One day I will say goodbye to Mango. I am too strong for her to keep me here forever. One day I will go away. Friends and neighbors will say, what happened to Esperanza? Where did she go with all those books and paper? Why did she march so far away? (101–02)

But Esperanza ends the book with the promise to return: "They will not know I have gone away to come back. For the ones I left behind. For the ones who cannot get out" (102).

The House on Mango St. captures the dialectic between self and community in Chicana writing. Esperanza finds her literary voice through her own cultural experience and that of other Chicanas. She seeks self-empowerment through writing, while recognizing her commitment to a community of Chicanas. Writing has been essential in connecting her with the power of women and her promise to pass down that power to other women is fulfilled by the writing and publication of the text itself.

Mango St. is not an isolated example of the importance of writing in Chicana literature. The *teatropoesía* piece *Tongues of Fire,* scripted by Barbara Brinson-Pineda in collaboration with Antonio Curiel (1981), broke new ground in focusing on the Chicana subject as writer, drawing from Anzaldúa's essay which gave the play its title. The text did not privilege one Chicana voice, but created a collective subject through the inclusion of many individual voices speaking to multiple facets of what it means to be Chicana. The tongues of fire of the Chicana writers in the play exposed oppression from without as well as from within the culture, denouncing exploitation and racism but also the subordination of Chicanas through their culture's rigid gender roles and negative attitudes towards female sexuality. Writing emerged as the medium for the definition of the individual subjectivity of the Chicana writer through the articulation of collective experience and identity.

In *The Mixquiahuala Letters*,[13] Ana Castillo plays with the conventions of the epistolary novel, undermining those conventions by inviting the reader to combine and recombine the individual letters in Cortázar fashion. At the same time, the epistolary form calls attention to the role of writing in sifting through and making sense of experience. The narrative voice not only engages in a process of self-exploration through writing, but the form of the writing-letters-foregrounds an explicit exchange with a reader to whom the writing is directed. The novel defines subjectivity in relation to another woman, and the bond between the two women further cemented by the epistolary examination of their relationship is as important as the exploration of self through writing.

In *Giving Up the Ghost,* Cherríe Moraga broke a twenty-year silence in the Chicano theater movement by placing Chicana lesbian sexuality center stage. The text explores the ways in which both lesbian and heterosexual Chicanas' sense of self as sexual beings has been affected by their culture's definitions of masculinity and femininity. The theme of writing emerges at the end of the play. Marisa's writing is both provoked and interrupted by her memories of Amalia and sexual desire, just as the text itself. Marisa's secular "confession" to the audience is the product of her need to exhume and examine her love for this woman and all women. The text presents both the failures and the promises of building community. Just before Marisa speaks of her "daydream[s] with pencil in . . . mouth," she articulates the need for "familia," redefined as women's community: "It's like making familia from scratch / each time all over again . . . with strangers / if I must. / If I must, I will."[14]

The love of Chicanas for themselves and each other is at the heart of Chicana writing, for without this love they could never make the courageous move to place Chicana subjectivity in the center of literary representation, or depict pivotal relationships among women past and present, or even obey the first audacious impulse to put pen to paper. Even as that act of necessity distances the Chicana writer from her oral tradition and not so literate sisters, the continuing commitment to the political situation of all Chicanas creates a community in which readers, critics and writers alike participate.[15]

NOTES

1. Elizabeth Waldman, "Profile of the Chicana: A Statistical Fact Sheet," in *Mexican Women in the United States,* Eds. Adelaida del Castillo & Magdalena Mora (Los Angeles: Chicano Studies, U.C.L.A., 1980), 195–204.

2. My understanding of the similarities and differences between Black and Chicana feminist criticism is indebted to Barbara Smith's "Towards Black Feminist Criticism" (1977), reprinted in *The New Feminist Criticism,* Ed. Elaine Showalter (N.Y.: Pantheon, 1985), 168–85.

3. *This Bridge Called My Back. Writings by Radical Women of Color,* Eds. Cherríe Moraga & Gloria Anzaldúa (Watertown, Ma.: Persephone Press, 1981).

4. "Have We Got a Theory for You! Feminist Theory, Cultural Imperialism and the Demand for 'the Woman's Voice,' " *Women's Studies International Forum,* 6:6 (1983), 574.

5. *Feminist Theory: From Margin to Center* (Boston: South End Press, 1984).

6. *This Bridge Called My Back,* 175–76.

7. *In This Bridge,* 165–74.

8. "It's the Poverty," in Anzaldúa, *This Bridge,* 166.

9. *Emplumada* (Pittsburgh: University of Pittsburgh Press, 1981), 45–46.

10. *The House on Mango Street* (Houston: Arte Público Press, 1985).

11. *The Moths and Other Stories* (Houston: Arte Público Press, 1985).

12. Sonia Saldívar-Hull includes a discussion of *Mango St.* in "Shattering Silences: The Contemporary Chicana Writer," forthcoming in *Women and Words: Female Voices of Power and Poetry,* Ed. Beverly Stoelbe (University of Illinois Press).

13. (Binghamton, N.Y.: Bilingual Press, 1986).

14. (Los Angeles: West End Press, 1986), 58.

15. The concept of a "Black writing community" is developed by Hortense J. Spillers in "Cross-Currents, Discontinuities: Black Women's Fiction," in *Conjuring. Black Women, Fiction and Literary Tradition,* Eds. Marjorie Pryse and Hortense J. Spillers (Bloomington: Indiana University Press, 1985).

❊ Making *Familia* From Scratch: Split Subjectivities in the Work of Helena María Viramontes and Cherríe Moraga

NORMA ALARCÓN

What can be our place in the symbolic contract? If the social contract, far from being that of equal men, is based on an essentially sacrificial relationship of separation and articulation of differences which in this way produces communicable meaning, what is our place in this order of sacrifice and/or of language? No longer wishing to be excluded or no longer content with the function which has always been demanded of us (to maintain, arrange, and perpetuate this sociosymbolic contract as mothers, wives, nurses, doctors, teachers), how can we reveal our place, first as it is bequeathed to us by tradition, and then as we want to transform it?
—*Julia Kristeva*

*"I carried out my role as a priest always feeling as though I was a woman,"
Father Paolo told La Stampa. "Now I want to be a woman and still feel like
a priest. I was looking for the woman inside myself, but trying not to renounce
the priest that I was. Then I realized the rules would not permit this and I
had to leave." She now is living in a small northern Italian village working as a
baby sitter, the newspaper said, and her legal status has been altered from male
to female, though her canonical status remains unclear.*
—*Des Moines Register*

Chicana writers are increasingly employing female-speaking subjects who hark back to explore the subjectivity of women. Often in their writings this subjectivity takes as its point of departure "woman's" over-determined signification as future wives/mothers in relation to the "symbolic contract" within which women may have a voice on the condition that they speak as mothers.[1] The female-speaking subject that would want to speak from a different position than that of a mother, or a future wife/mother, is thrown into a crisis of meaning that begins with her own gendered personal identity and its relational position with others. Paradoxically, as we shall see, a crisis of meaning can ensue even in the case of a female who may have never aspired to speak from a different position than that of a wife/mother.

First, to start the exploration of the question of "woman," I want to discuss Helena M. Viramontes' story "Growing." What young girl can fight a father (and an assenting mother) when he roars "Tú eres mujer"?[2] As Naomi, the protagonist notes, the phrase is uttered as a verdict. It is a judgment meant to ensure the paternal law and view of woman's cultural significance. Within this symbolic structure, Naomi is not supposed to counterspeak her sense of herself as different from what her father says it is. In his view her subjectivity has been decided *a priori* by what is perceived as the body of a woman. The fact that she is compelled to report the phrase in Spanish only points to a particular Chicano/Mexicano rigidity with respect to the signifying system that holds the dyad woman-man in place, and which provides her father with his authority. By switching codes to "mujer," he knows more precisely what his judgment of Naomi ought to signify. If he said "woman," he would be on precarious ground. He is not quite sure what it may mean in Anglo culture, a culture within which he may well feel that he has no authority. Thus, though we may conjecture that Naomi's family transacts some of its communication in English, Spanish is employed in this sentence to guarantee parental authority. Naomi, on the other hand, has learned that "woman" is different from "mujer." As a result, she attempts to assert her difference from what is expected of Mexican/Chicana girls by appealing to the Anglo code. Thus Naomi notes that for the girls "in the United States" experience is different (31).

Though Naomi is correct in her perception of the difference in social experience between girls due to the relatively different cultural/racial codes (perhaps class-rooted codes as well), she is also too young to apprehend that in the "symbolic contract" virtually all women will sooner or later reach a limit with regard to the speaking position that they may take up as "woman." How rapidly that limit is reached and how she may speak thereafter will vary in accordance with the specific "semantic charters" that her cultural linguistic ground offers her.[3] Often that limit is set by how her father (and assenting mother) perceive her body which is always that of a "woman" and underpinned by what her father perceives as her sexual/maternal function. As a result, Naomi feels increasingly imprisoned by the concept "mujer," which her father wields as a weapon against her. Yet, she is hard put to fight him because his evidence for her meaning as "woman" is her own changing body, that is, menarche and breasts. In a sense, then, her very physical experience is used to press her to live out concepts such as "woman" and make Naomi become *"the practical realization of the metaphysical* . . . operating in such a way, moreover, that subjects themselves, being implicated through and through, being produced in it as concepts would lack the means to analyze it. Except in an after-the-fact way whose delays are yet to be fully measured . . ."[4] Within such a "semantic charter" Naomi is too young to understand what is happening to her. She views her sexuality as a very confused mass. Though it may take her the rest of her life to apprehend what may have taken place as a result of the verdict "Tú eres mujer," the narrator of Naomi's circumstance is not too young to conclude as follows: "Now that she was older, her obligations became heavier both at home and at school. There were too many expectations . . . She could no longer be herself and her father no longer trusted her, because she was a woman" (38). All manner of things that she is obliged and expected to do are derived from the "fact" that she is a "woman." Her body is enlisted in a stream of sociosymbolic activities which she also experiences as a splitting her from herself. As Irigaray comments,

> Participation in society requires that [her] body submit itself to a specularization, a speculation, that transforms it into a value-bearing object, a standardized sign, an exchangeable signifier, a 'likeness' with reference to an authoritative model. *A commodity—a woman—is divided into two irreconcilable 'bodies':* her 'natural' body and her socially valued, exchangeable body, which is a particular mimetic expression of masculine values. (180)

Within Mexican/Chicano culture the authoritative model, however unconscious, to which fathers (masculine values) have recourse is the Catholic Holy Family and its assumed social authority. Viramontes, the constructor of this narrative world, is quite aware of that since many of her stories allude to religious expectations and dogma. Given that Naomi feels split from herself when she is pressed to become a "woman" for social and symbolic purposes, who is that self? If *it* could speak what would it say? It is at this point that many a woman of letters of Hispanic origin, in her quest for her subjectivity has turned to mysticism. Santa Teresa is our paradigm in that instance. Others, and here Sor Juana Inés de la Cruz is our paradigm, have opted for the convent (a retreat) so that no one could verify she was a "woman": "Yo no entiendo de esas cosas; / sólo sé que aquí me vine / porque, si es que soy mujer, / ninguno lo verifique."[5] In order to avoid these resolutions which are no solution at all for the contemporary Chicana critic and writer as speaking subjects, I want to pursue an alternate course with reference to two very different female-speaking subjects: Viramontes' own Olga Ruiz in "Snapshots" and Cherríe Moraga's Marisa in *Giving Up The Ghost*.[6] I choose these because, unlike Naomi of "Growing," they speak their subjectivity directly, without the intervention of a narrator who has greater "knowledge." Moreover, in assessing their crisis of meaning with regard to their own gendered personal identity, they have to look back as older women. Naomi is too young to have much to look back to except those moments of play when she experienced herself as forgetting that she was a "woman," though, as we shall see, that in itself can be significant. Both Marisa, who is in her late 20's, and Olga Ruiz, who is past 50, have had an opportunity that Naomi has yet to go through, that is, the increasing pressure to become that "woman" in the sociosymbolic contract. In looking back (and so many Chicana writers have their speaking subjects look back—Sandra Cisneros in *The House on Mango Street,* Ana Castillo in *The Mixquiahuala Letters* and Denise Chávez in *The Last of the Menu Girls* to name a few), Marisa and Olga Ruiz enact, as Irigaray asserts, an analysis "after-the-fact" of the treacherous route on the way to becoming a "woman" or not becoming a "woman."

Virtually all the readers I have talked with are put off by the story "Snapshots." Since there is nothing wrong with the story *qua* story, I ask why? Neither older women nor young women students like Olga Ruiz. Since Olga is the sole speaking subject in the story, as readers we are called upon to enter her world, and her view of it. Only one reader has admitted to me that she feels like Olga Ruiz and she said it with a sigh. Hardly anyone can, or wants to, recognize their subjectivity in Olga Ruiz. Olga Ruiz holds up a deadly mirror for women. If, as Pierre Maranda states, "the text is the light on my face that enables me to see myself in the one-way mirror that I hold in front of it; the text allows me, Narcissus, to marvel at my mind, to believe in myself and, consequently, to have the impression that I live more competently" (191), then Olga Ruiz holds up to us the potential psychosis that awaits us if we live a life like hers. As readers we refuse to take up her "I" as our own, to fuse our "I" with hers. Female readers could come away feeling that they live "more competently," but they are not sure. Olga Ruiz may well remind us of our mothers, or we may even recognize ourselves in Olga's own daughter Marge, whose only advice to her mother is to keep busy. Marge has brought

Olga enough skeins of wool to stock a retail shelf. Even the daughter, that is, younger readers, are caught speechless as to what they may say to help Olga Ruiz out of her crisis of meaning. In short, Olga Ruiz has lived the life of a "woman." How can we help a woman who according to cultural models has lived her life "correctly" and who is now cynical and embittered?

Olga Ruiz has been *framed* by cultural expectations and is now so removed from her sensibility, her contact with her own body and its reality that she states, "I don't know if I should be hungry or not" (98). Was her grandmother right? Did her grandfather's camera, which split the sexes into men who mill "around him expressing their limited knowledge of the invention" (98), and women whose pictures are taken, cut her from her soul? Given her desperate situation, Olga Ruiz appeals to folk beliefs in order to give closure to her crisis of meaning as wife/mother. If she can accept that she was "killed" since infancy, then maybe she can stop her obsessive-compulsive desire to find clues for meaning in the family album. Yet she will be left to wonder if her grandmother's antidote worked to save her, "My grandmother was very upset and cut a piece of my hair, probably to save me from a bad omen" (99). The grandmother's effort to counter the camera's evil work may have worked, in which case Olga Ruiz may be forced to conclude that she did not save herself, that she colluded with society and thus is responsible for her situation. Obviously, she stops short of completely blaming herself, and leaves a seed of doubt, a very small one, since not to doubt that indeed that is the meaning could throw her over the edge into total psychosis.

According to her own account, Olga stands on the threshold of psychosis after thirty years of marriage. However, as Olga remembers it, she had an earlier crisis of meaning as a "woman" after the birth of her daughter, Marge. The discomforts of pregnancy send her into her first quest for self-meaning in the family album as if it were a bible: "I began flipping through my family's photo albums . . . to pass the time and the pain away" (94). She labels her compulsive behavior an "addiction" to "nostalgia." Giving birth becomes for Olga the first occasion in which she feels split from herself. Julia Kristeva has suggested that for many women,

Pregnancy seems to be experienced as the radical ordeal of the splitting of the subject: redoubling up of the body, separating and coexistence of the self and of an other, of nature and of consciousness, of physiology and speech. This fundamental challenge to identity is then accompanied by a fantasy of totality—narcissistic completeness—a sort of instituted, socialized, natural psychosis.[7]

According to sociosymbolic "semantic charters," Olga Ruiz should have found her gendered meaning and should surrender herself to a "narcissistic completeness" in the child, which she subsequently does. However, at that moment Olga found herself divided between the past as the moment of separateness from the child and the future which will demand an uneasy and continued coexistence. Though nothing comes of this critical moment, the sense that she should be separate is signalled by the nostalgic neurosis. By contemplating the family photo album, Olga hopes "some old dream will come into my blank mind" (94). She is depressed "because every detail, as minute as it might seem, made me feel that so much had passed unnoticed" (94). What dream or desire should make itself evident in the photographs? Whatever "had passed unnoticed" is not accompanied by any speech that would help Olga grasp the difference between what she wanted and what she got. Her mind is blank with regard to that self who may have dreamed of another life. She already knows that she has been very capable of devoting herself to the details of homemaking. She is so much the automaton that she cannot stop, though it is no longer necessary that she continue homemaking for others. The only words she can come up with, that can describe what might have been different from the muteness that enveloped her life, are nostalgia, indulgence, anticipation. She cannot come to terms with the separate self that could articulate an alternate past, present or future than what she has had.

Her solution to this particular blankness is brilliant given its truth currency: "Both woman and child are clones: same bathing suit, same pony tails, same ribbons" (97). However, truth does not necessarily grant one a new purchase on life. The snapshot of Olga, Marge and Dave is uncannily like the one of Olga with her parents. In a sense it is like that of the Holy Family triad—father, mother and child—except that the child is a girl, and indeed that is what problematizes the "snapshot." The girl-child does not have a sublime transcendent story. Her story according to that "semantic charter" is to duplicate the wife/maternal tale. How can any meaningful memory stand out in the redoubling of this snapshot? Certainly Olga could not get close to her passionless mother, just as Marge cannot get close to Olga, nor does she appear to want to. They are as distanced from feeling as they are from their core responsive sensibility/sexuality, not only from men but from each other. Mother and daughter are so much alike one would think they could comfort each other, but they cannot. To do so Olga or Marge would have to take up a different speaking position with respect to each other. Before they can see themselves as more than a relational unit of mother-daughter, Olga or Marge would have to take up a different speaking position in their bodies. This position would entail entering into their emotional lives in ways that would strengthen and renew the bond differently, which may shut men out (temporarily?). (Let us remember that the Holy Family is the family of the son not the daughter.) Thus, to contemporanize the situation Marge would have to be capable of speaking to Olga, who is on the verge of madness, in the words of Luce Irigaray, as follows:

> And here you are, this very evening, facing a mourning with no re-membrance. Invested with an emptiness that evokes no memories. That screams at its own rebounding echo. A materiality occupying a void that escapes its grasp. A block sealing the wall of your prison. A buttress to a possible future which, taken away, lets everything crumble indefinitely:
>
> Where are you? Where am I? Where to find the traces of our passage? From the one to the other? From the one into the other? (. . .)
>
> No one to mark the time of your existence, to evoke in you the rise of a passage out of yourself, to tell you: Come here, stay here. No one to tell you: Don't remain caught up between the mirror and this endless loss of yourself. A self separated from another self. A self missing some other self. Two dead selves distanced from each other, with no ties bind-ing them. The self that you see in the mirror severed from the self that nurtures. And, as I've gone, I've lost the place where proof of your sub-sistence once appeared to you.[8]

Olga's middle-of-the-night phone call to Marge is her cry to have Marge reunite her with herself, "I don't know if I should be hungry." To start from the beginning as if she were a baby, so they can "make *familia* from scratch." Since Marge may not possess the wherewithal to respond, the call is ren-dered irrelevant. Before a crisis of meaning can be effected in the relationship between Olga and Marge as mother-daughter-mother, the husbands inter-fere. It is clearly not in their interest to have these two women renegotiate the sociosymbolic contract by effecting a different dialogue between them-selves. If we go on the report that Olga gives us of Marge, Marge herself cannot even begin to grasp that she, too, is abducted from herself, "Immo-bilized in the reflection he expects of [her]. Reduced to the face he fashions for [her] in which to look at himself. Traveling at the whim of his dreams and mirages. Trapped in a single function—mothering."⁹ In short Marge is already also *framed* in her great grandfather's camera-eye which he passed on to the sons. It will be some years before Marge arrives at the speaking position her mother presently holds, by which time it may be too late. For indeed, grasping one's gendered meaning "after-the-fact" entails the removal of the buttress (that is, Mother) which "lets everything crumble indefinitely." In the crumbling may be the speaking position from which to transform the sociosymbolic contract.

In *Giving Up The Ghost,* Cherríe Moraga offers us a heroine who has refused to become a "woman," who has refused to be framed by the camera's eye, "immobilized in the reflection he expects of [her]." On the contrary Marisa desires to take up his "camera's eye," his gaze. In short, Marisa wanted to be a "man" when she was a child. Uncannily, as if the lines of communication between Olga Ruiz and Marisa had been inverted, Marisa implicitly uses the metaphor of the camera except, like a "man," she uses it to frame or trap women. Through Corky, her younger "male" self, Marisa "after-the-fact" reports:

> when I was a little kid I useta love the movies
> every saturday you could find me there
> my eyeballs glued to the screen
> then during the week my friend Tudy and me
> we'd make up our own movies
> one of our favorites was this cowboy one
> where we'd be out in the desert
> 'n' we'd capture these chicks 'n' hold 'em up
> for ransom we'd string 'em up 'n'
> make 'em take their clothes off
> jus' pretending a'course but it useta make me feel
> real tough
> strip we'd say to the wall
> all cool-like. . . .
> I was a big 'n' tough 'n' a dude (5)

Corky's imaginary play, however, the fact that in her mind she was a "dude," is put into action one day. Corky and her friend Tudy (a boy), strip Chrissy down completely, and Corky reports that "after that I was like a maniac all summer" (12). In stripping Chrissy down, Corky looks into the vaginal mirror which makes her a little crazy as she also remembers that "deep down inside / no matter / how / I tried to pull the other / off" (6), she always knew she was a girl. As in Naomi's case, Corky is reminded that she is a girl, and consequently a "woman-to-be" through the body, except that Corky refuses to enter the "semantic charter." We are not sure what will come to Naomi, though she did report that she experienced sexual neutrality during childhood play. There is no neutrality for Corky ever, and even as she puts into play the dyad man-woman, it is in some sense unacceptable. However, she first internalizes the dyad in such a way that, though her body always reminds her that she is a girl/woman, her imaginary desire, the site of her subjectivity, is experienced as that of a "man."

Marisa, the adult Corky, is catapulted into a dance of "symbolic iden- tifications" with the concepts of "man" and "woman" that is always too close for any female's comfort, because they constantly run the risk of being socialized into poses. Because Marisa is a lesbian, one of these is the famous lesbian dyad of the "butch-femme" split. In some sense, Marisa is split asun- der between her male-like subjectivity and behavior, and her literal female body. For Marisa neither alternative "butch" (man) nor "femme" (woman) is acceptable. At this point, one can say that Marisa, out of necessity, either conjures Amalia into her life or that Amalia appears out of nowhere to save her. Both Marisa and Amalia speak their subjectivity "after-the-fact" of the relationship and hold a conversation that hardly ever is enacted face-to-face. It is as if Moraga knows that in "real" life these two women may not be able to speak to each other directly in any effective way, thus we must enter their sociosymbolic lives, in a dialogue that is always a near miss. Thus Moraga effects a process of potential transformations between two women as unlike each other as we could ask for—the lesbian with the subjectivity of a "man" and the traditional heterosexual "woman," who may also be our mother.

There are ways in which one can see the ghostly face of Olga Ruiz in Amalia, except that given the sexual interchange between Marisa and Amalia, Amalia is less repressed than Olga. Yet Amalia is in some ways a stereotypic heterosexual Mexican "woman." Amalia is framed by the eye of her male lovers, the ones for whom she wanted to be an object of desire. Amalia cannot bring herself to desire Marisa until her ideal male lover dies, and his ghost reenters her body so that she may feel enough a "man" to desire Marisa (28). In this fashion we are cued from a different angle, that active sexual desire has been marked masculine. By the end of this "after-the-fact" indirect dialogue both Amalia and Marisa have learned as much about themselves as we have about the variety of gendered crises of meaning.

The subjective agency of desire, the ineffable energy that may help us transform our world has heretofore been the province of whoever "man" is. As a lesbian-identified woman, Marisa does not want just a "woman" (a "femme"), that is a muted object of desire, but as she says: "It's not that you don't want a man, / you don't want a man in a man. / You want a man in a woman. / The woman-part goes without saying. / That's what you always learn to want first" (29). The implication that a girl learns to want a woman first through her relationship to her mother, and places the girl-child in competition with the boy-child for the body of the mother is very suggestive. It brings us face to face with the fantastic cultural silence, religious or Freudian, with regard to what the girl's position is in the Holy Family or Oedipal triad. This lays bare the fact that in that sociosymbolic contract a girl-child may not speak except as would-be mother or mother. In taking refuge in a male identity, Corky/Marisa acquire a speech that is at odds with the body, thus in a different way they are forced into two irreconcilable selves. Amalia, however, thinks that Marisa wanted her so that Marisa could feel (be) the woman in her: "Sometimes I think, with me / that she only wanted to feel herself / so much a woman / that she would no longer be hungry for one" (53). If this is so, then Marisa goes to Amalia, the maternal/heterosexual, for the reconciliation with her female body. As bereft daughter, Marisa reverses the "narcissistic completeness" that Kristeva suggests mothers are expected to attain through the child: "But then was the beautiful woman / in the mirror of the water / you or me?" (27). Moraga here suggests the daughter's quest to unite with the mother in ways that only sons get to do within a too rigid patriarchy. It is clear at the end of the dramatic monologues, that Marisa's severed pieces have come together to enable her creativity, "so I cling to her in my heart, / my daydream with pencil in my mouth, / when I put my fingers / to my own forgotten places" (58).

In my view, in *Giving Up The Ghost,* Moraga puts into play the concepts "man" and "woman" (and the parodic "butch/femme"), with the intuitive knowledge that they operate in our subjectivities, so that it is difficult to analyze them, except in the way she has done. Women speaking with each other in a spiralling way, not quite face-to-face, but with the recollection that at least once they were so close to each other that they could effect a transfusion so as to avoid the extremes—that is a muted "woman's" speaking position, and a male-identified subjectivity. It is to Moraga's credit that she puts the dyad man-woman into play in such a way that she brings into view three re-lational trajectories — the lesbian butch who is killing herself by the implied rejection of her literal body, the mother-daughter relation where the daugh-ter may be forced to take the son (or father's) position so as to get close to her mother, and the hope that the heterosexual woman will not be put off by the lesbian due to homophobia.

For young Chicana writers (and critics) the crisis of meaning as women has increasingly led to a measuring "after-the-fact" of the speaking subject's meanings. The most exciting explorations are those that "measure" the in-tricacies of relationship between and among women. Yet if actual social ex-periences have the potential of effecting a complex and heterogeneous sub-jectivity, the symbolic contract within which "woman" is the repository of meaning and not the agent, constantly presses her to align herself with the symbolic; in this way she is forced to live the life of a "woman/mother." To refuse to live the life of a "woman," which is both literal (body) and sym-bolic (iconic/linguistic configurations), throws her into a crisis of meaning. As young Corky makes clear, if you don't want to be a girl, society as well as she then take it that you want to be a boy. Corky's "error" is that she does not refuse both. How could she? Perhaps, as the older and wiser Marisa suggests, we must make *familia* from scratch" (58). Marisa, who wanted to save her own mother (14) and later Amalia, by having them remember their own "for-gotten places" beyond womanly duty, would, unlike Marge, be capable of saying to Olga Ruiz: "Where are you? Where am I? Where to find the traces of your passage? From the one to the other? From the one into the other?"

In my view, Julia Kristeva goes a long way towards charting a course for the dissident (female) speaking subject. The speaking subject today has to position herself at the margins of the "symbolic contract" and refuse to ac-cept definitions of "woman" and "man" in order to transform the contract. However, as Kristeva's critics have pointed out, a female-speaking subject today has to walk with one foot inside and another outside the interstice that would stake the boundary of what a "woman" may speak. Toril Moi's critique reads as follows: "political reality (the fact that patriarchy defines women and oppresses them accordingly) still makes it necessary to campaign in the name of women, it is important to recognize that in this struggle a woman can-not *be:* she can only exist negatively, as it were, through the refusal of that which is given."[10] Moi adds that as a result Kristeva can state "I therefore understand by "woman," that which cannot be represented, that which is not spoken, that which remains outside naming and ideologies"(163). Thus, it is that both Naomi and Marisa leave their futures open-ended, and Naomi in her way too can challenge her father, for to believe that one "is a woman" is as absurd and obscurantist as to believe that one "is a man" (163).

As Chicana writers explore the subjectivity of their speaking subjects, they are bound, as most of us are, to explore sexual identities as they have been bequeathed. However, as I hope I have made clear, each speaking subject takes positions that vary according to her self-conscious grasp of the engendering process which constantly throws girls/women into a crisis of meaning as women. That self-conscious grasp will be very much dependent on age, cultural ground, and on how she understands herself in relation to others, after the fact. The task before us is to continue to measure the delay and its painful implications.

NOTES

1. "Symbolic contract" is the term Julia Kristeva sometimes employs to refer to the Patriarchal Law and/or linguistic domain. In her work the subject, who is almost always male, is conjectured as one who finds "his identity in the symbolic, [and] *separates* from his fusion with the mother"; in "Revolution in Poetic Language," *The Julia Kristeva Reader,* Ed. Toril Moi (New York: Columbia University Press, 1986), 101. In Kristeva's theoretical perspective the Mother is posited, for the male subject, as an almost inarticulable site (i.e. a site of the Freudian/Lacanian unconscious). I do not take up that line of inquiry in this essay because in asking what our place as female subjects may be within the symbolic contract, the Mother is more than a theoretical site. We are asked to fill the site symbolically and socially. In "Women's Time" from which my epigraph is taken (23–24), Kristeva suggests that women speaking subjects may want to adopt an attitude where "the very dichotomy man/woman as an opposition between two rival entities may be understood as belonging to *metaphysics*" (33). That attitude is the one I have attempted to take vis-a-vis the writers discussed in my essay. See *Signs: Journal of Women in Culture and Society,* 7:1 (Autumn 1981), 13–35.

The second epigraph was written by Bruce Buursma in the *Chicago Tribune* and subsequently reprinted in the *Des Moines Register,* Sunday, October 17, 1987, n.p.

2. *The Moths and Other Stories* (Houston: Arte Publico Press, 1985), 32. All subsequent citations for both "Growing" and "Snapshots," will be noted in the text.

3. Pierre Maranda suggests that "Semantic charters condition our thoughts and emotions. They are culture specific networks that we internalize as we undergo the process of socialization" (185). Moreover these charters or signifying systems "have an inertia and a momentum of their own. There are semantic domains whose inertia

is high: kinship terminologies, the dogmas of authoritarian churches, the conception of sex roles" (184–85). See his essay "The Dialectic of Metaphor: An Anthropological Essay on Hermeneutics," in *The Reader in the Text: Essays on Audience and Interpretation,* Eds. Susan R. Suleiman and Inge Crosman (Princeton: Princeton University Press, 1980), 183–204.

4. Luce Irigaray, *This Sex Which Is Not One,* Trans. Catherine Porter (Ithaca, NY: Cornell University Press, 1985), 189. The ellipsis occurs in the original as if calling for the measurement itself which is what our research is about. In the chapter "Women on the Market" (170–91), from which I cite Irigaray, she also argues that this process turns women qua woman/mother into commodities so as to sustain economic systems and infrastructures that exploit women. Further citations to this work will be noted in the text.

5. For a discussion of Sor Juana's passage from "woman" to "non-woman," see Octavio Paz, *Sor Juana Inés de la Cruz o Las Trampas de la Fé* (México: Fondo de Cultura Económica, 1982), 291.

6. *Giving Up The Ghost* (Los Angeles: West End Press, 1986). References to this work will be cited in the text.

7. "Women's Time," *Signs,* 31.

8. Luce Irigaray, "And The One Doesn't Stir Without the Other," Trans. Helene Vivienne Wenzel, *Signs: Journal of Women in Culture and Society,* 7:1 (Autumn 1981), 64–65.

9. Irigaray, "And the One Doesn't Stir Without the Other," 66.

10. *Sexual/Textual Politics: Feminist Literary Theory* (New York: Methuen, 1986), 163.

Sandra Cisneros' *The House on Mango Street,* and the Poetics of Space

JULIÁN OLIVARES

In some recent essays collectively titled "From a Writer's Note-book,"[1] Sandra Cisneros talks about her development as a writer, making particular references to her award-winning book, *The House on Mango Street.*[2] She states that the nostalgia for the perfect house was impressed on her at an early age from reading many times Virginia Lee Burton's *The Little House.* It was not until her tenure at the Iowa Writers Workshop, however, that it dawned on her that a house, her childhood home, could be the subject of a book. In a class discussion of Gaston Bachelard's *The Poetics of Space,* she came to this realization: "the metaphor of a house, *a house, a house,* it hit me. What did I know except third-floor flats. Surely my classmates knew nothing about that" ("Ghosts and Voices," 72–3). Yet Cisneros' reverie and depiction of house differ markedly from Bachelard's poetic space of house. With Bachelard we note a house conceived in terms of a male-centered ideology. A man born in the upper crust family house, probably never having to do "female" housework and probably never having been confined to the house for reason of his sex, can easily contrive states of reverie and images of a house that a woman might not have, especially an impoverished woman raised in a ghetto. Thus, for Bachelard the house is an image of "felicitous space (. . .) the house shelters daydreaming, the house protects the dreamer, the house allows one to dream in peace (. . .) A house constitutes a body of images that give mankind proofs or illusions of stability."[3] Cisneros inverts Bachelard's nostalgic and privileged utopia, for her's is a different reality: "That's precisely what I chose to write: about third-floor flats, and fear of rats, and drunk husbands sending rocks through windows, anything as far from the poetic as possible. And this is when I discovered the voice I'd been suppressing all along without realizing it."[4]

The determination of genre for *Mango Street* has posed a problem for some critics.[5] Is *Mango Street* a novel, short stories, prose poems, vignettes? Cisneros herself states:

> I recall I wanted to write stories that were a cross between poetry and fiction. I was greatly impressed by Jorge Luis Borges' *Dream Tigers* stories for

their form. I liked how he could fit so much into a page and that the last line of each story was important to the whole in much the same way that the final lines in poems resonate. Except I wanted to write a collection which could be read at any random point without having any knowledge of what came before or after. Or that could be read in a series to tell one big story. I wanted stories like poems, compact and lyrical and ending with a reverberation. ("Do You Know Me?" 78)

She adds that if some of the stories read like poems, it is because some had been poems redone as stories or constructed from the debris of unfinished poems.[6] The focus, then, on compression and lyricism contributes to the brevity of the narratives. With regard to this generic classification, Cisneros states:

I said once that I wrote *Mango Street* naively, that they were "lazy poems." In other words, for me each of the stories could've developed into poems, but they were not poems. They were stories, albeit hovering in that grey area between two genres. My newer work is still exploring this terrain. ("Do You Know Me?" 79)

On a different occasion, Cisneros has called the stories "vignettes."[7] I would affirm that, although some of the narratives of *Mango Street* are "short stories," most are vignettes, that is, literary sketches, like small illustrations nonetheless "hovering in that grey area between two genres."

I should like to discuss some of these stories and vignettes in order to demonstrate the manner in which Cisneros employs her imagery as a poetics of space and, while treating an "unpoetic" subject—as she says, expresses it poetically so that she conveys another element that Bachelard notes inherent to this space, the dialectic of inside and outside, that is, *here* and *there,* integration and alienation, comfort and anxiety (211–12). However, Cisneros again inverts Bachelard's pronouncement on the poetics of space; for Cisneros the inside, the *here,* can be confinement and a source of anguish and alienation. In this discussion we will note examples of (1) how Cisneros expresses an ideological perspective of the downtrodden but, primarily, the condition of the Hispanic woman; (2) the process of a girl's growing up; and (3) the formation of the writer who contrives a special house of her own.

This book begins with the story of the same title: "The House on Mango Street":

We didn't always live on Mango Street. Before that we lived on Loomis on the third floor, and before that we lived on Keeler. Before Keeler it was Pauline, and before that I can't remember. But what I remember most is moving a lot. Each time it seemed there'd be one more of us. By the time we got to Mango Street we were six—Mama, Papa, Carlos, Kiki, my sister Nenny and me. (. . .)

They always told us that one day we would move into a house, a real house that would be ours for always so we wouldn't have to move each year. (. . .)

But the house on Mango Street is not the way they told it at all. It's small and red with tight little steps in front and windows so small you'd think they were holding their breath. Bricks are crumbling in places, and the front door is so swollen you have to push hard to get in. There is no front yard, only four little elms the city planted by the curb. Out back is a small garage for the car we don't own yet and a small yard that looks smaller between the two buildings on either side. There are stairs in our house, but they're ordinary hallway stairs, and the house has only one washroom, very small. Everybody has to share a bedroom—Mama and Papa, Carlos and Kiki, me and Nenny.

Once when we were living on Loomis, a nun from my school passed by and saw me playing out front. The laundromat downstairs had been boarded up because it had been robbed two days before and the owner had painted on the wood *YES WE'RE OPEN* so as not to lose business.

Where do you live? she asked.

There, I said, pointing up to the third floor. You live *there?*

There. I had to look to where she pointed—the third floor, the paint peeling, wooden bars Papa had nailed on the windows so we wouldn't fall out. You live *there?* The way she said it made me feel like nothing. *There.* I lived *there.* I nodded.

I knew then I had to have a house. A real house. One I could point to. But this isn't it. The house on Mango Street isn't it. For the time being, Mama said. Temporary, said Papa. But I know how those things go. (7–9)

Mango Street is a street sign, a marker, that circumscribes the neighborhood to its Latino population of Puerto Ricans, Chicanos and Mexican immigrants. This house is not the young protagonist's dream house; it is only a temporary house. The semes that we ordinarily perceive in house, and the ones that Bachelard assumes—such as comfort, security, tranquility, esteem—are lacking. This is a house that constrains, one that she wants to leave; consequently, the house sets up a dialectic of inside and outside: of living *here* and wishing to leave for *there*.

The house becomes, essentially, the narrator's first universe. She begins here because it is the beginning of her conscious narrative reflection. She describes the house from the outside; this external depiction is a metonymical description and presentation of self: "I knew then I had to have a house. A real house. One I could point to." By pointing to this dilapidated house, she points to herself. House and narrator become identified as one, thereby revealing an ideological perspective of poverty and shame. Consequently, she wants to point to another house and to point to another self. And as she longs for this other house and self, she also longs for another name. But she will find that in growing up and writing, she will come to inhabit a special house and to fit into, find comfort, in her name.

In "My Name" the protagonist says: "In English my name means hope. In Spanish it means too many letters. It means sadness, it means waiting . . . It is the Mexican records my father plays on Sunday mornings when he is shaving, songs like sobbing" (12). In this vignette Esperanza traces the reason for the discomfiture with her name to cultural oppression, the Mexican males' suppression of their women. Esperanza was named after her Mexican great-grandmother who was wild but tamed by her husband, so that: "She looked out the window all her life, the way so many women sit their sadness on an elbow . . . Esperanza, I have inherited her name, but I don't want to inherit her place by the window" (12). Here we have not the space of contentment but of sadness, and a dialectic of inside/outside. The woman's place is one of domestic confinement, not one of liberation and choice. Thus, Esperanza would like to baptize herself "under a new name, a name more like the real me, the one nobody sees. Esperanza as Lisandra or Maritza or Zeze the X. Yes. Something like Zeze the X will do" (13). That is, Esperanza prefers a name not culturally embedded in a dominating, male-centered ideology.

Such a dialectic of inside/outside, of confinement and desire for the freedom of the outside world is expressed in various stories. Marin, from the story of the same name, who is too beautiful for her own good and will be sent back to Puerto Rico to her mother, who wants to work downtown because "you . . . can meet someone in the subway who might marry and take you to live in a big house far away," never comes out of the house "until her aunt comes home from work, and even then she can only stay out in front. She is there every night with the radio . . . Marin, under the streetlight, dancing by herself, is singing the same song somewhere. I know. Is waiting for a car to stop, a star to fall. Someone to change her life. Anybody" (27–8). And then there is Rafaela, too beautiful for her own good:

> On Tuesdays Rafaela's husband comes home late because that's the night he plays dominoes. And then Rafaela, who is still young, gets locked indoors because her husband is afraid Rafaela will run away since she is too beautiful to look at. ("Rafaela Who Drinks Coconut and Papaya Juice on Tuesdays," 76)

One way to leave house and barrio is to acquire an education. In "Alicia Who Sees Mice" (32), a vignette both lyrical and hauntingly realistic, the narrator describes her friend's life. Alicia, whose mother has died so she has inherited her "mama's rolling pin and sleepiness," must arise early to make her father's lunchbox tortillas:

> Close your eyes and they'll go away her father says, or you're just imagining. And anyway, a woman's place is sleeping so she can wake up early with the tortilla star, the one that appears early just in time to rise and catch the hind legs hidden behind the sink, beneath the four-clawed tub, under the swollen floorboards nobody fixes in the corner of your eyes.

Here we note a space of misery and subjugation, a dialectic of inside/outside, a Latina's perception of life—all magnificently crystallized in the image of the "tortilla star." To Alicia Venus, the morning star, does not mean wishing upon or waiting for a star to fall down—as it does for Rafaela, nor romance nor the freedom of the outside world; instead, it means having to get up early, a rolling pin and tortillas. Here we do not see the tortilla as a symbol of cultural identity but as a symbol of a subjugating ideology, of sexual domination, of the imposition of a role that the young woman must assume. Here Venus—and the implication of sex and marriage as escape—is deromanticized, is eclipsed by a cultural reality that points to the drudgery of the inside. Alicia "studies for the first time at the university. Two trains and a bus, because she doesn't want to spend her whole life in a factory or behind a rolling pin . . . Is afraid of nothing except four-legged fur and fathers."

There are two types of girls in *Mango Street*. There are those few who strive for an education, like Alicia and the narrator, but most want to grow up fast, get married and get out.[8] But these, like Minerva, usually have to get married, and they leave a father for a domineering husband. Such is the fate of Sally in "Linoleum Roses":

> Sally got married like we knew she would, young and not ready but married just the same. She met a marshmallow salesman at a school bazaar and she married him in another state where it's legal to get married before eighth grade . . . She says she is in love, but I think she did it to escape. (. . .)
>
> [Her husband] wont let her talk on the telephone. And he doesn't let her look out the window. And he doesn't like her friends, so nobody gets to visit her unless he is working.
>
> She sits at home because she is afraid to go outside without his permission. She looks at all the things they own: the towels and the toaster, the alarm clock and the drapes. She likes looking at the walls, at how neatly their corners meet, the linoleum roses on the floor, the ceiling smooth as wedding cake. (95)

The title is an oxymoron expressing an inversion of the positive semes of house and revealing a dialectic of inside/outside. "Linoleum roses" is a trope for household confinement and drudgery, in which the semes of rose—beauty, femininity, garden (the outside)—and rose as a metaphor for woman are ironically treated. The roses decorate the linoleum floor that Sally will have to scrub. This is an image of her future. The image of the final line, the "ceiling smooth as wedding cake," resonates through the story in an ironical twist, a wedding picture of despair.

Such images as "tortilla star" and "linoleum roses" are the type of imagery that perhaps only a woman could create, because they are derived from a woman's perception of reality; that is to say, that this imagery is not biologically determined but that it is culturally inscribed. A woman's place may be in the home but it is a patriarchal domain.

With regard to the poetics of space and the dialectic of inside/outside and as these apply to the process of growing up, I shall give only one example, but one that also touches on the formation of the writer.[9] It is taken from the story "Hips," in which the process of a girl's growing up is initially described as a physical change, the widening of the hips:

> One day you wake up and they are there. Ready and waiting like a new Buick with the keys in the ignition. Ready to take you where?

They're good for holding a baby when you're cooking, Rachel says turning the jump rope a little quicker. She has no imagination. (. . .)

They bloom like roses, I continue because it's obvious I'm the only one that can speak with any authority; I have science on my side. The bones just one day open. Just like that. (47)

Here, then, Esperanza, Lucy and Rachel are discussing hips while jumping rope with little Nenny. At this point the kids' game turns into a creative exercise as the older girls take turns *improvising* rhymes about hips as they jump to the rhythm of the jump rope. Esperanza sings:

> *Some are skinny like chicken lips.*
> *Some are baggy like soggy band-aids*
> *after you get out of the bathtub.*
> *I don't care what kind I get.*
> *Just as long as I get hips.* (49)

Then little Nenny jumps inside but can only sing the usual kids' rhymes: "Engine, engine, number nine." Suddenly, the awareness of time passing and of growing up is given a spatial dimension. Esperanza, on the outside, is looking at Nenny inside the arc of the swinging rope that now separates Nenny's childhood dimension from her present awareness of just having left behind that very same childhood: "Nenny, I say, but she doesn't hear me. She is too many light years away. She is in a world we don't belong to anymore Nenny. Going. Going" (50). Yet Esperanza has not totally grown out of her childhood. She is still tied to that dimension. Although we perceive a change in voice at the end of the story, she is still swinging the rope.

Indications of Esperanza's formation as a writer and predictions of her eventual move from home and Mango Street are given in two stories related to death, suggesting perhaps that creativity is not only a means of escape from the confines of Mango Street but also an affirmation of life and a rebirth. The first story is "Born Bad," in which Esperanza reads her poetry to her aunt who appears to be dying from polio. The aunt replies:

That's nice. That's very good, she said in her tired voice. You must remember to keep writing, Esperanza. You must keep writing. It will help keep you free, and I said yes, but at that time I didn't know what she meant. (56)

In "The Three Sisters" three mysterious women appear at the funeral of a neighbor's child. Here Esperanza begins to fit into the cultural space of her name. These women seek out Esperanza for special attention:

What's your name, the cat-eyed one asked.

Esperanza, I said.

Esperanza, the old blue-veined one repeated in a high thin voice. Esperanza . . . a good name. (. . .)

Look at her hands, cat-eyed said.

And they turned them over and over as if they were looking for something.

She's special.

Yes, she'll go very far . . .

Make a wish.

A wish?

Yes, make a wish. What do you want?

Anything? I said.

Well, why not?

I closed my eyes.

Did you wish already?

Yes, I said.

Well, that's all there is to it. It'll come true.

How do you know? I asked.

We know, we know.

Esperanza. The one with marble hands called aside. Esperanza. She held my face with her blue-veined hands and looked and looked at me. A long silence. When you leave you must remember always to come back, she said.

What?

When you leave you must remember to come back for the others. A circle, understand? You will always be Esperanza. You will always be Mango Street. You can't erase what you know. You can't forget who you are.

Then I didn't know what to say. It was as if she could read my mind, as if she knew what I had wished for, and I felt ashamed for having made such a selfish wish.

You must remember to come back. For the ones who cannot leave as easily as you. You will remember? She asked as if she was telling me. Yes, yes, I said a little confused. (97–8)

In this paradigm of the fairy godmother, Esperanza receives a wish that she does not understand. How can she leave from *here* to *there* and still be

Mango Street? How can she come back for the others? What is the meaning of the circle? Esperanza thought that by leaving Mango Street and living in another house, one that she could point to with pride, she would leave behind forever an environment she believed to be only temporary. A mysterious woman embeds in Esperanza's psyche a cultural and political determination which will find expression in her vocation as a writer. Esperanza will move away from the confining space of house and barrio, but paradoxically within them she has encountered a different sort of space, the space of writing. Through her creativity, she comes to inhabit the house of story-telling. Although she longs for "A House of My Own" (100)—

> Not a flat. Not an apartment in back. Not a man's house. Not a daddy's. A house all my own. With my porch and my pillow, my pretty purple petunias. My books and my stories. My two shoes waiting beside the bed. Nobody to shake a stick at. Nobody's garbage to pick up after.

—it is clear, nonetheless, that a magical house is had though the creative imagination: "Only a house quiet as snow, a space for myself to go, clean as paper before the poem."

The realization of the possibility of escape through the space of writing, as well as the determination to move away from Mango Street, are expressed in "Mango Says Goodbye Sometimes" (101–02):

> I like to tell stories. I am going to tell you a story about a girl who didn't want to belong.
>
> We didn't always live on Mango Street. Before that we lived on Loomis on the third floor, and before that we lived on Keeler. Before Keeler it was Pauline, but what I remember most is Mango Street, sad red house, the house I belong but do not belong to.
>
> I put it down on paper and then the ghost does not ache so much. I write it down and Mango says goodbye sometimes. She does not hold me with both arms. She sets me free.
>
> One day I will pack my bags of books and paper. One day I will say goodbye to Mango. I am too strong for her to keep me here forever. One day I will go away.
>
> Friends and neighbors will say, What happened to that Esperanza? Where did she go with all those books and paper? Why did she march so far away?
>
> They will not know I have gone away to come back. For the ones I left behind. For the ones who cannot get out.

I do not hold with Juan Rodríguez that Cisneros' book ultimately sets forth the traditional ideology that happiness, for example, comes with the realization of the "American Dream," a house of one's own. In his review of *Mango Street,* Rodríguez states:

> That Esperanza chooses to leave Mango St., chooses to move away from her social/cultural base to become more "Anglicized," more individualistic; that she chooses to move from the real to the fantasy plane of the world as the only means of accepting and surviving the limited and limiting social conditions of her barrio becomes problematic to the more serious reader.[10]

This insistence on the preference for a comforting and materialistic life ignores the ideology of a social class' liberation, particularly that of its women, to whom the book is dedicated. The house the protagonist longs for, certainly, is a house where she can have her own room[11] and one that she can point to in pride, but, as noted through this discussion of the poetics of space, it is fundamentally a metaphor for the house of story-telling. Neither here in the house on Mango Street nor in the "fantasy plane of the world"— as Rodríguez states, does the protagonist indulge in escapism. Esperanza wants to leave but is unable, so she attains release from her confinement through her writing. Yet even here she never leaves Mango Street; because, instead of fantasizing, she writes of her reality.[12] Erlinda Gonzales and Diana Rebolledo confirm that the house is symbolic of consciousness and collective memory, and is a nourishing structure so that "the narrator comes to understand that, despite her need for a space of her own, Mango Street *is* really a part of her—an essential creative part she will never be able to leave"; consequently, she searches in (as narrator) and will return to (as author) her neighborhood "for the human and historical materials of which [her] stories will be made."[13] On the higher plane of art, then, Esperanza transcends her condition, finding another house which is the space of literature. Yet what she writes about—"third-floor flats, and fear of rats, and drunk husbands sending rocks through windows, anything as far from the poetic as possible"— reinforces her solidarity with the people, the women, of Mango Street.

We can agree, and probably Cisneros on this occasion does, with Bachelard's observation on the house as the space of daydreaming: "the places in which we have experienced daydreaming reconstitute themselves in a new daydream, and it is because our memories of former dwelling places are relived as daydreams that these dwelling places of the past remain in us for all time" (6). The house that Esperanza lives and lived in will always be associated with the house of story-telling — "What I remember most is Mango Street"; because of it she became a writer. Esperanza will leave Mango Street but take it with her for always, for it is inscribed within her.

NOTES

1. "From a Writer's Notebook": "Ghosts and Voices: Writing from Obsession," "Do You Know Me? I Wrote *The House on Mango Street*," *The Americas Review* 15:1 (1987), 69–73, 77–79.

2. *The House on Mango Street* (Houston: Arte Público Press, 1984).

3. *The Poetics of Space,* Trans. María Jolas (Boston: Beacon Press, 1969²).

4. Although Cisneros echoes the strong family bonds that Tomás Rivera speaks of with regard to the *casa,* home, theme, her criticism of patriarchal domination offers a challenging perspective. See Rivera for his discussion of the themes of *casa, barrio* and *lucha* in Chicano literature, in "Chicano Literature: Fiesta of the Living," *Books Abroad* 49:3 (1975), 439–52.

5. See, Pedro Gutiérrez-Revuelta, "Género e ideología en el libro de Sandra Cisneros: *The House on Mango Street*," *Crítica* 1:3 (1986), 48–59.

6. Eg., "The Three Sisters," "Beautiful and Cruel," "A House of My Own," in "Do You Know Me?" 79.

7. "The softly insistent voice of a poet," *Austin American Statesman* (March 11, 1986), 14–15.

8. The dialectic of inside/outside also is manifested in the personae some of the characters assume. For example, there is Sally who, outside the house, "is the girl with eyes like Egypt and nylons the color of smoke. The boys at school think she's beautiful (. . .) Her father says to be this beautiful is trouble (. . .) And why do you always have to go straight home after school? You become a different Sally. You pull your skirt straight, you rub the blue paint off your eyelids. You don't laugh, Sally. You look at your feet and walk fast to the house you can't come out from. Sally, do you sometimes wish you didn't have to go home?" ("Sally," 77–8).

9. Another example is "The Monkey Garden," 87–91.

10. "*The House on Mango Street,* by Sandra Cisneros," *Austin Chronicle* (August 10, 1984), cited in Gutiérrez-Revuelta, 52.

11. Cf., Virginia Woolf, "A Room of One's Own."

12. Even were she to move away from the barrio and have her own house, Esperanza states her conviction not to forget who she is nor where she came from:

One day I'll own my own house, but I won't forget who I am or where I came from. Passing bums will ask, Can I come in? I'll offer them the attic, ask them to stay, because I know how it is to be without a house.

Some days after dinner, guests and I will sit in front of a fire. Floorboards will squeak upstairs. The attic grumble.
Rats? they'll ask.
Bums, I'll say, and I'll be happy.
— "Bums in the Attic," 81.

13. "Growing Up Chicano: Tomás Rivera and Sandra Cisneros," *International Studies in Honor of Tomás Rivera,* Ed. Julián Olivares (Houston: Arte Público Press, 1985), 109–20.

The Politics of Rape:

Sexual Transgression in Chicana Fiction

MARÍA HERRERA-SOBEK

Men rape because they own (have) the law.
They rape because they are the law.
They rape because they make the law.
They rape because they are the
guardians of the peace, of law and order.
They rape because they have the power,
the language, the money, the knowledge,
the strength, a penis, a phallus.

Men say that:
-in any case we're asking for it,
-that we are not careful enough,
-that we shouldn't follow strangers,
-but that you can't say no to your father,
-that we provoke it,
-that we are accomplices,
-that we should learn a good lesson from it,
-that we shouldn't go out without a protector,
-Bodily rape is merely the acting out of a daily ideological reality.[1]

Feminist critics view rape in patriarchal societies as a metaphorical construct skillfully designed to insure the continuation of phallocratic rule.[2] Chicana writers, as expressed through their creative works, seem to concur with this position and have utilized the rape-as-metaphor construct to critique the patriarchal system that oppresses them. It is my position that as members of an ethnic minority, and thus doubly marginalized, Chicana authors are vitally concerned with the inferior status they have been relegated. The Chicana writer has therefore taken the concept of rape and has successfully elaborated it in her writings as a literary motif in order to engage the reader in a reconstruction of the experience from the victim's perspective and from a feminist point of view.

In this study I focus on the structurization of the rape scene in Mexican American women literary works, particularly in short stories and plays and its utilization as metaphor encoding a denunciation of the subordinate status of these women at various levels: societal, individual and familial. Thus, in formulating a theoretical framework for the reading and interpretation of Chicana works, the social context and pragmatic function will be of primary importance. This veers from established literary canons which supposedly privilege the aesthetic function but which in fact are permeated with ideological content.

Rape as a literary motif is not necessarily a new construct; it is vividly illustrated in Greek mythology where male gods routinely and wantonly rape female divinities. Examples abound; some of the most commonly known include Zeus's rapings of Leda, Cyble, Europa, Hera and Nemesis, to name a few. Apollo's rape of Daphne, Hades' rape of Persephone and King Tereus' rape of Philomena have often served as structural frameworks for many artists in various fields of creative endeavor such as painting and literature.[3] Many scholars have interpreted the above mythical rape constructs depicting violent acts against Goddesses as denoting in metaphorical terms the political takeover and supplanting of matriarchal society by a patriarchal one.

Recent Chicana fictional works, although not necessarily inspired by Greek myths, incorporate the theme of rape within their texts. Exegesis of these works yield significant information with regard to Chicana male-female relations as well as women's artistic techniques in the elaboration of a specific human phenomenon, that is, sexual assault that involves a subject and an object in ideological and physical combat and that is necessarily experienced from two totally different perspectives.

Cherríe Moraga, for example, structures the metaphoric construct of rape in her two-act play *Giving Up the Ghost* to articulate its function as a political signifier of women's inferior status with regard to men. In a monologue directed at the audience and utilizing tough street jargon she confides:

> Got raped once. When I was a kid. Taken me a long time to say that was exactly what happened, but that was exactly what happened. Makes you more aware than ever that you are one hunerd percent female, just in case you had any doubts one hunerd percent female whether you act it or like it or not[4]

Moraga encodes in her play, through the construct inherent in the act of raping, the consequence and process of making, engendering, a group of humans—women. In this process of engendering, fabricating, that is, making a gender, the end result is a hole and absence: women as invisible, voiceless, worthless, devalued objects. They are silent entities dominated by ingrained patriarchal vectors where the Name of The Father is Law, and years of socialization to obey the Father's Law transforms the female subject into a quavering accomplice in her own rape. That is to say, women are socialized into being participants in their own oppression.

The rape scene in Moraga's play occurs in a catholic school, the geographic space of the deflowering denoting both the ritual aspect of raping by situating it in a sacred space, and the total encompassing nature of patriarchal rule, since the catholic church is ruled by a patriarchal system par excellence. The twelve-year-old protagonist "Corky" is waiting for her friend Rosie. A Mexican Spanish-speaking male posing as a janitor and who resembles her uncle approaches her, asking for assistance in repairing her teacher's desk drawer. He directs her to stand in front of the desk with both hands supporting the supposedly broken drawer:

> It turns out he wants me to stand in front of the drawer with my hands holding each up 'n' my legs apart, así. (she demonstrates) 'n' believe it or not, I do 'n' believe it or not, this hijo de la chingada madre sits behind me on the floor 'n' reaches his arm up between my legs that I'm straining to keep closed even though he keeps saying all business-like "Abrete más, por favor, las piernas. Abrete poco más, señorita. "Still all polite 'n' like a pendeja . . .I do. Little by little, he gets my legs open. (39)

Intuitively sensing that what is happening to her is not right but meekly obeying the authoritative man's command, she continues to hope her friend Rosie will show up to save her from the uncomfortable and dangerous situation. But Rosie does not appear and the events leading to the inevitable rape continue.

As the attempted rape proceeds Moraga structures a shift from Spanish to English in the interlocutor's voice:

> "Don't move," he tells me. In English. His accent gone. 'n' I don.'

Total confusion invades the twelve year old girl's mind. The screwdriver which the "custodian" is holding next to her genitals "feels like ice" and simultaneously provokes a rush of memories related to her father. Father and rapist begin to merge in a vertigo of flashing images transversing through the child's mind:

From then on all I see in my mind's eye . . . were my eyes shut?
Is this screwdriver he's got in his sweaty palm
yellow glass handle
shiny metal
the kind my father useta use to fix things around the house
remembered how I'd help him
how he'd take me on his jobs with him
'n' I kept getting him confused in my mind this man 'n' his arm
with my father kept imagining him my father returned come back

The multivalent symbolism associated with the screwdriver adds to the metaphoric structurization of the rape scene, for the vocable "screw" is associated with sexual intercourse of the hostile, hurting kind: to screw someone is to inflict some kind of violence on them either metaphorically or literally. Thus the screwdriver, a phallocratic symbol, serves to link father and rapist into one unbroken chain of patriarchal "screwers."

The young girl, afraid the screwdriver is going to be shoved up her body, begins to sob. Complete confusion invades her mind, and rapist and father merge into one:

"¿Dónde 'stas papá?" I keep running through my mind.
"¿dónde 'stás?"
'n' finally I imagine the man answering
"aquí estoy. Soy tu papá."
'n' this gives me permission to go 'head
to not hafta fight. (41)

The poetic persona yields with the resignation of a young girl socialized into obeying the Voice of the Father. Blocking the consequences and criminality of the violent act visited upon her, her mind disengages from any sensation and identity of self and her only concern is to hurry up and get it over with "So I can go back to being myself 'n' a kid again (42)."
However, because the young girl is a virgin, penetration is not easily accomplished. The poetic voice recounts:

Then he hit me with it
into what was supposed to be a hole (. . .)
But with this one
there was no hole
he had to make it

'n' I see myself down there like a face
with no opening
a face with no features
no eyes no nose no mouth
only little lines where they shoulda been
so I dint cry.
I never cried as he shoved the thing
into what was supposed to be a mouth
with no teeth
with no hate
with no voice
only a hole. A HOLE!
(gritando)
HE MADE ME A HOLE! (42–3)

The protagonist experiences a process of dismemberment: she first loses sensation around her kneecaps; furthermore, her genitals assume a life of their own—they flap "in the wind like a bird / a wounded bird" (41). As she slowly looses her identity as a human being, her face merges into a mass of flesh without any of the distinctive features that normally serve to highlight and express her individuality. She is transformed into what street jargon expresses as "a piece of meat": "a face with no features / no eyes no nose no mouth."

The violent act visited upon the young woman on the verge of adolescence produces a *hole,* a nothingness, an empty space. The female child is obliterated at the precise temporal juncture of becoming a woman. The artistic recreation of the rape scene encodes a political metaphor for society's marginalization of women. It traces, in a few powerful lines, the socialization process visited upon the female sex which indoctrinates them into accepting a subordinate position in the socio-political landscape of a system. The violation itself symbolizes the final act which obliterates women from the system. The process of raping, "making an absence," transforms women into silent, invisible, non-existent entities—as holes to be filled by males.

If Moraga's rape scene symbolizes the social and political marginalization of women to the extent that they become a "hole," a "nothing," Sylvia Lizárraga's structurization of the rape scene in "Silver Lake Road"[5] confirms the consequences articulated in Moraga's play: women's marginality leads to economic and social dependence on the male. Oppression in this narrative is transcribed as economic dependency for the protagonist of the story, a single mother whose employment possibilities are limited and whose meager salary allows barely enough for survival. The only alternative possible for the main character is marriage to a Mr. Álvarez whom she does not love nor feel any type of attraction. He symbolically represents the male world of self-sufficiency through his professional training in the sphere of finance.

Using a stream-of-consciousness technique, Lizarraga introduces the protagonist in the mundane but necessary task of grocery shopping. We enter her mind as she busily tries to juggle her responsibilities as a single mother: car payments, increasing babysitting costs, grocery bills, etc. A rain storm is rapidly approaching and a sixteen-year-old hitchhiker approaches her in the parking lot of the grocery story and asks her for a ride. She hesitates and then, feeling sorry for the young man, relents. However, just as she is about to drop him off a short distance later, he flashes out a knife and forces her to drive to an isolated area. There he orders her to get out of the car and walk toward the nearby woods where he proceeds to sexually assault her. The omniscient narrator describes the scene:

> He threw himself on top of her. The knife now at her throat left her without movement. Fear paralyzed her, impeding her resistance. With his body on top of her, he pressed down more and more, compelling her to do his will. Impotent and defenseless against that inescapable act, she closed her eyes. Frustration filled her mouth with a bitter flavor. She felt as if her integrity, her pride, her life itself were being crushed in that brambly ground as she lay trampled and dragged down by that violating force. Suddenly it was over.
>
> The icy wind howled, pushing and swaying her body, but she no longer heard it or felt it. Dumfounded, she began to walk back towards town. Far away, very far away were the worries of an hour ago, the groceries, tía Maclovia, Mr. Álvarez. Oh, yes, Mr. Álvarez. (121–22)

The theme of the disembodied feeling after a sexual violation is reiterated in Lizárraga's short story. As previously discussed in Moraga's play, the victim of sexual assault loses her identity as a human being and is transformed into a formless entity devoid of feeling and bodily sensations. The natural elements, "icy wind" and "brambly ground," buffet the nameless victim's body, paralleling the "buffeting" received at the hands of the rapist. Both nature and patriarchal society conspire to oppress women and the only solution left to the anonymous protagonist is to marry Mr. Álvarez and seek refuge under male protection. The representation of women without a voice, without a language are structured within the narrative through the adjectives, verbs, and adverbs utilized in the description of the rape scene. The knife at the throat conveying silence, the words and phrase "paralyzed" and "without movement," connoting women's passivity, the "pressing down" and "compelling her to do his will"—all parallel the status of women in society. Furthermore the juxtaposition of the nameless woman contrasts sharply with the named and titled Mr. Álvarez. By the opposition named/nameless the author conveys the precarious existence of women: an invisible, powerless minority within a minority, since Mr. Álvarez by his surname is situated within the parameters of the Hispanic community. The rape in the narrative can be construed as a political statement underscoring women's vulnerability both economically and physically.

Noteworthy is that the age of the assailant in Lizárraga's story (he is only sixteen) further captures the vulnerability of even adult women. Other minority authors have incorporated this incongruent dyad older woman/young man "full of [their] power" in their literary structures. Ntozake Shange in her *for colored girls who have considered suicide/when the rainbow is enuf* portrays the sexual advances of a twelve year old. The protagonist trapped in the subway responds:

No man ya cant go wit me/1 dont even
Know you/No/I dont wanna kiss you/
You aint but 12 yrs old/No man/Please
Please Leave me alone/Tomorrow/Yeah[6]

Carolyn Mitchell comments in her analysis of the above scene:

Her hysterical response and the exhorted promise of a meeting tomorrow captures the fear women in the city have for their lives. Granted that the boy may not be a fully grown sexual being, but he most likely possesses a gun or a knife, clearly approved extensions of male sexuality and power.

Mitchell elucidates on the symbolical representation of the boy:

The twelve-year-old in the subway becomes an urban "everyman" whose violence is contained by the "tunnel" image now suggested in the "straight up brick walls" of the city tenements. The "youn man fulla his power" emerges in relief against the limp, powerless "women hanging outta windows/like ol silk stockings."[7]

The fear of rape, whether it be in a slum in Harlem or a supermarket in the suburbs, hangs threateningly in the back of most women's mind. This in turn curtails the freedom of movement in addition to the oppressive weight this burden entails in women's subconscious.

If ideological and economic considerations structure Moraga's and Lizárraga's rape narratives, it is the theme of loss of innocence that predominates in Sandra Cisneros' short story "Red Clowns."[8] In this vignette we encounter Esperanza, the innocent and naive protagonist who is accompanying her older and street savvy friend Sally to the carnival. Sally disappears with her boyfriend and Esperanza, alone in the amusement park, is attacked by a group of boys. The narrative begins with the bitter recriminations of a disillusioned and traumatized Esperanza after the sexual transgression has occurred where, in a monologue full of hurt and despair, she mourns her loss of innocence: "Sally, you lied. It wasn't what you said at all. What he did. Where he touched me. I didn't want it, Sally. The way they said it, the way it's supposed to be, all the storybooks and movies, why did you lie to me?" (93). The diatribe is directed not only at Sally the silent interlocutor but at the community of women who keep the truth from the younger generation of women in a conspiracy of silence. The protagonist discovers a conspiracy of two forms of silence: silence in not *denouncing* the "real" facts of life about sex and its negative aspects in violent sexual encounters, and *complicity* in embroidering a fairy-tale-like mist around sex, and romanticizing and idealizing unrealistic sexual relations.

The protagonist confronts the hard truth and spits it out at what she perceives to be the perpetrators of the sex-is-glamorous myth:

> You're a liar. They all lied. All the books and magazines, everything that told it wrong. Only his dirty fingernails against my skin, only his sour smell again. The moon that watched. The tilt-a-whirl. The red clowns laughing their thick-tongue laugh (94).

The theme of the silent, voiceless victim, the woman that is afraid to denounce her attackers, is reiterated in Cisnero's story: "Sally, make him stop. I couldn't make them go away. I couldn't do anything but cry. I don't remember. It was dark. I don't remember. I don't remember. Please don't make me tell it all" (93). This response to block out the rape scene and, to become silent and withdrawn is common in victims of sexual assault.[9]

The Texas-Mexican author, Estela Portillo Trambley takes a different tangent in her metaphoric construct of the rape scene in her narratives. The rape theme appears in two of her short stories published in the anthology *Rain of Scorpions*[10] and in her play "The Day of the Swallows".[11] In both the play and in the story "If It Weren't for the Honeysuckle" the attempted rape leads to a closer relationship with women, although in the play the lesbian bond that ensues between the two woman (the victim of the attempted rape and the woman that saves her from it) is presented as contributing to the eventual tragedy that unfolds. In the short story, on the other hand, the threat of sexual violation of the young girl, significantly enough named Lucretia, unites the women and together they murder their oppressor, the drunk Robles. The dangerous violent male principle is eliminated and the women live together in harmony with nature, each other and the cosmos.[12]

Possibly the most complicated structurization of the rape motif appears in Portillo Trambley's "The Trees." In this short story the main structuring agent is the paradise lost motif. Nina, the main protagonist, incarnates the archetypal Eve who rains death and destruction and the loss of a paradisiacal world on the Ayala family, prosperous owners of the Ayala apple orchard ranch.

Tomás Vallejos rightly perceives that "even before Nina's arrival, the Ayala's "Eden" was inherently flawed. Its very structure, a patriarchal order, is inequitable and thus doomed to final disintegration."[13] Indeed the story describes the family political structure in the following manner:

> The family, with its elementary tie to the earth, had established a working patriarchal order. The father and sons lived for a fraternal cause, the apple orchards. Their women followed in silent steps, fulfilled in their ways. If ambition or a sense of power touched the feminine heart, it was a silent touch. The lives were well patterned like the rows of apple trees and the trenches that fed them. Men and women had a separate given image until Nina came. (13)

Nina in her archetypal role of Eve is portrayed as causing the downfall of the Ayala family. Sexual transgression structures the destruction of the wealthy, apple-growing family. The first violation occurs when Nina as a child is sold into prostitution by her stepmother, and four drunks who "bought" her sexually abuse her: "Nina remembered the four drunk men who held her. They had bought her from the stepmother. The room over the tavern . . . the many voices that drowned out her screams. The disgust . . . the long, long vomiting . . . the dark alley . . . the fatigue and numbness of the damned" (19). The assault is forever imprinted in the young girl's mind and it is this violent act that germinates years later into the tragic events described in the narrative. For it is Nina's sense of economic insecurity and psychological vulnerability that leads her to undertake the drastic steps she did that led to the tragedy.

Nina's problems begin when the patriarch of the family dies and she perceives her husband at a disadvantage with regard to the family inheritance. She decides to right the situation by "proving" to her husband that his brothers are untrustworthy. Nina proceeds to seduce her brother-in-law Rafael, the self proclaimed Don Juan of the Ayala family. After the seduction she leads everyone to believe she has been raped.

If rape is a weapon used against women, in the story "The Trees" the female protagonist inverts the male-violates-woman motif and empowers herself with the construct using it to battle the patriarchal structure that threatens her economic and psychological security.

Nina is successful in destroying the patriarchal structure but in the process destroys everything around her, including herself, for, unable to bear the tragedy that unfolds (the brothers shoot each other, and thinking that the family has left the house, Nina sets fire to it, trapping and killing the entire family within), she jumps to her death from the top of a cliff.

Elizabeth Ordóñez perceptively associates the theme of rape dominating Chicana poetry with the archetypal Malinche figure. She posits:

> For if rape has become a powerful image of woman's helplessness and subjugation before the sheer brute force of the male, then that universal trauma for all women becomes exacerbated in the Chicana experience by those remnants of the collective physical and cultural rape which she carries buried within her collective unconscious. The Chicana's attitude toward her own sexuality must be colored by that original rape by European culture, as well as by the sexual violence which often exists in her immediate personal environment. Several Chicana poets have captured these feelings of anger and vengeance, as well as the strength and integrity that this act of sexual violence engenders in *la mujer*.[14]

Indeed many Chicana poets employ the rape motif in their creative writings and, although the La Malinche myth is one of many vectors structuring the rape scene in Chicana literature, I believe economic, social, and political circumstances are more instrumental in influencing Chicanas to utilize sexual assault as a recurring metaphor in their works. It is not surprising, for instance, that other minority women in similar economic and socio-political circumstances, such as Black women, incorporate rape as an important structuring motif in their novels and poetry. These writers essentially share the same socio-political and economic conditions that Chicanas have. On the other hand, Mexican women writers in Mexico have generally not utilized the rape motif.

The structurization of the rape scene in literature provides significant insights both into the dynamics of male-female relations and into the creative process as undertaken by either sex. Since the rape motif appears in the literary writings of both sexes, analysis of its portrayal can yield important information with regard to gender and its impact on creative literature.

It is significant that short story writers have not, to a significant extent, incorporated the rape motif in their writing. Writes Martha Foley in her *200 Years of Great American Short Stories:* "Rape is the most devastating of crimes but, unlike murder and other offenses, practically never figures in the modern short story, although for literary purposes it presents great dramatic and characterization opportunities."[15] It is a shame that Foley did not include any Chicana short story writers, for she would have seen how Mexican American women are challenging the canon and making rape an important literary motif in American literature.

NOTES

1. Elaine Marks and Isabelle de Courtivron, *New French Feminism* (New York: Schocken Books, 1981), 194–95.

2. See Elaine Marks and Isabelle de Courtivron; Mary Daly, *Gyn/Ecology: The Metaethics of Radical Feminism* (Boston: Beacon Press, 1978); Susan Griffin, *The Politics of Consciousness* (San Francisco: Harper & Row Publishers, 1986); Anna Clark, *Women's Silence, Men's Violence: Sexual Assault in England 1770–1845* (New York: Pandora, 1987); London Rape Crisis Center, *Sexual Violence: The Reality for Women* (London: The Women's Press, 1984).

3. See Patricia Monaghan, *The Book of Goddesses and Heroines* (New York: E.P. Dutton, 1981).

4. *Giving Up the Ghost* (Los Angeles: West End Press, 1986), 36.

5. "Silver Lake Road," in *Requisa Treinta y Dos,* Ed. Rosaura Sánchez (La Jolla, CA: Chicano Research Publications, 1979).

6. *for colored girls who have considered suicide/when the rainbow is enuf* (New York: MacMillan, 1977), 29.

7. "A Laying of Hands: Transcending the City in Ntozake Shange's *for colored*

girls . . .," in *Women Writers and the City,* Ed. Susan Merrill Squier (Knoxville: University of Tennessee Press, 1986), 233–34.

8. "Red Clowns," in *The House on Mango Street* (Houston: Arte Público Press, 1984).

9. See Elizabeth Ordóñez, "Sexual Politics and The Theme of Sexuality in Chicana Poetry," in *Women in Hispanic Literature: Icons and Fallen Idols,* Ed. Beth Miller (Berkeley: University of California Press,1983), 316–39.

10. *Rain of Scorpions* (Berkeley: Tonatiuh International, 1975).

11. "The Day of the Swallows," *El Grito: A Journal of Contemporary Mexican American Thought* 4:3 (Spring, 1971), 4–47.

12. See María Herrera-Sobek, "La unidad del hombre y el cosmos: Reafirmación del proceso vital en Estela Portillo Trambley,' *La Palabra* 4/5:1–2 (primavera/otoño, 1982/3), 127–41.

13. "Estela Portillo Trambley's Fictive Search for Paradise," *Contemporary Chicano Fiction: A Critical Survey,* Ed. Vernon E. Lattin (Binghamton, N.Y.: Bilingual Press/Editorial Bilingüe, 1986), 270.

14. "Sexual Politics," 328.

15. *200 Years of Great American Short Stories,* Ed. Martha Foley (New York: Galahad Books, 1982), 914.

Bibliography

MARÍA HERRERA-SOBEK

Abrego, Carmen. "A Conversation." In *Chicana Lesbians: The Girls Our Mothers Warned Us About,* ed. Carla Trujillo, 63. Berkeley: Third Woman Press, 1991.
———. *Women in My Lost Dreams.* n.p., 1985.
Acosta, Teresa Palomo. *Passing Time.* n.p., 1984.
Adler, Rana and Hy. "How a Plucky Woman Foiled a Governor." *Impact/ Albuquerque Journal Magazine,* Feb. 10, 1981.
Agosín, Marjorie and Patricia Montenegro, eds. *Midwest-East, Midwest-West.* Bloomington, Ind.: A Chicano-Riqueño Studies Publication, 1980.
Aguilar-Henson, Marcela. "Angela de Hoyos and Ricardo Sánchez: A Thematic, Stylistic and Linguistic Analysis of Two Chicano Poets." Ph.D. diss. University of New Mexico, 1982.
Aguilar-Henson, Marcela. *Figura cristalina,* ed. Norma Cantú. San Antonio: M & A Editions, 1983.
Aguirre, Lydia R. "The Meaning of the Chicano Movement." *Social Case Work.* 1971. Rpt. in *We Are Chicanos: An Anthology of Mexican-American Literature,* ed. Philip D. Ortego, 121–27. New York: Washington Square Press, 1973.
Alarcón, Norma. "Cognitive Desires: An Allegory for Chicana Critics." In *Listening to Silences: New Essays in Feminist Criticism,* ed. Elaine Hedges and Shelley Fisher Fishkin. New York: Oxford University Press, 1994.
———. "Making 'Familia' from Scratch: Split Subjectivities in the Work of Helena María Viramontes and Cherríe Moraga." *The Americas Review* 15:3–4 (Fall-Winter, 1987): 147–59.
———. "The Sardonic Powers of the Erotic in the Work of Ana Castillo." In *Breaking Boundaries: Latina Writing and Critical Readings,* ed. Asunción Horno-Delgado et al, 94–107. Amherst: University of Massachusetts Press, 1989.
———. "The Theoretical Subject(s) in *This Bridge Called My Back* and Anglo-American Feminism." In *Making Face, Making Soul: Haciendo Caras,* ed. Gloria Anzaldúa, 356–69. San Francisco: Aunt Lute, 1990.
———. "Traddutora, Traditora: A Paradigmatic Figure of Chicana Feminism." *Cultural Critique.* Fall, 1989: 57–87.
———. "What Kind of Lover Have You Made Me Mother?" In *Women of Color: Perspectives on Feminism and Identity,* ed. Audrey T. McCluskey, Occasional Papers Series 1:1. Bloomington: Women's Studies Program, Indiana University, 1985.

Alarcón, Norma, Ana Castillo, Cherríe Moraga, eds. *Third Woman: The Sexuality of Latinas.* Berkeley: Third Woman Press, 1989.

Alcalá, Kathleen. *Mrs. Vargas and the Dead Naturalist.* Corvallis, Or: Calyx Books, 1992.

Almaguer, Tomás. "Class, Race, and Chicano Oppression." *Socialist Revolution* 5 (1975), 71–99.

Alurista. "Portillo, Valdez y Castillo: ¡Se acabó la patriarquía!" *Culturas Hispanas de los Estados Unidos de América,* ed. María de Jesús Buxó Rey y Tomás Calvo Buezas, 519–28. Madrid: Ediciones de Cultura Hispánica, 1990.

Alvarado de Ricord, Elsie, Lucha Corpi and Concha Michel. *Fireflight,* trans. Catherine Rodríguez-Nieto. n.p. Oyez, 1976.

Álvarez, Lynne. *The Dreaming Man.* Seattle: Waterfront Press, 1984.

———. *Hidden Parts.* Maplewood, N.J.: Waterfront Press, 1987, 1988.

———. *Living With Numbers.* Maplewood, N.J.: Waterfront Press, 1988.

Alvírez, David, Frank D. Bean, and Dorie Williams. "The Mexican American Family." In *Ethnic Families in America,* ed. C. H. Mindel and R. W. Habenstein. New York: Elsevier, 1981.

Anton, Ferdinand. *La mujer en la América antigua.* México: Editorial Extemporáneos, 1975.

———. *Women in Pre-Columbian America.* New York: Abner Schram, 1973.

Anzaldúa, Gloria. *Borderlands/La Frontera. The New Mestiza.* San Francisco: Spinsters/Aunt Lute, 1987.

———. "La Historia de una Marimacho." *Third Woman: The Sexuality of Latinas,* ed. Norma Alarcón et al, 64–68.

———. *Making Face, Making Soul: Haciendo Caras.* San Francisco: Aunt Lute, 1990.

Anzaldúa, Gloria and Cherríe Moraga, eds. *This Bridge Called My Back: Writings by Radical Women of Color.* Boston: Persephone Press, 1981. Second edition, New York: Kitchen Table Press, 1983.

Apodaca, María Linda. "The Chicana Woman: An Historical Materialist Perspective." *Latin American Perspectives,* 4:1–2, 1977.

Arellano, Angela. "Untitled." *Chicana Lesbians: The Girls Our Mothers Warned Us About,* ed. Carla Trujillo, 62. Berkeley: Third Woman Press, 1991.

Arellano, Anselmo F. *Los Pobladores Nuevo Mexicanos y Su Poesía, 1889–1950.* Albuquerque: Pajarito Press, 1976.

Arellano, Esteban. "La Poesía Nuevo Mexicana: Su Desarrollo y Su Transición Durante Los Fines Del Siglo Diez y Nueve." Unpublished paper, 1985.

Arizona Federal Writers Project. State History Archives, Phoenix, Az. "Martina Díaz," coll. Rosalía Gómez. "Isabel Hernández," coll. Rosalía Gómez. "Apolonia Mendoza," coll. Rosalía Gómez. "Lola Romero," coll. Rosalía Gómez.

Ashley, L. M. "Self, Family, and Community: The Social Process of Aging among

Urban Mexican-American Women." Ph.D. diss., University of California, Los Angeles, 1985.

Augenbraum, Harold and Ilan Stavans, eds. *Growing Up Latino: Memoirs and Stories.* New York: Houghton Mifflin, 1993.

Baca-Zinn, Maxine. "Chicano Family Research: Conceptual Distortions and Alternative Directions." *Journal of Ethnic Studies* 7 (1979), 59–71.

———. "Chicano Men and Masculinity." *Journal of Ethnic Studies* 10 (1982), 9–44.

———. "Employment and Education of Mexican American Women: The Interplay of Modernity and Ethnicity in Eight Families." *Harvard Educational Review* 50 (1980), 47–62.

———. "Political Familism: Toward Sex Role Equality in Chicano Families." *Aztlán* 6 (1975), 13–26.

Barrera, Mario. *Race and Class in the Southwest: A Theory of Racial Inequality.* South Bend: University of Notre Dame Press, 1979.

Barrera, Mario, Albert Camarillo, and Francisco Hernández, eds. *Work, Family, Sex Roles, Language.* Berkeley: Tonatiuh-Quinto Sol International, 1980.

Barrett, Michéle. *Women's Oppression Today.* London: Verso Editions, 1980.

Beauvoir, Simone De. *The Second Sex.* New York: Random House, 1974.

Behar, Ruth. *Translated Woman: Crossing the Border with Esperanza's Story.* Boston: Beacon Press, 1993.

Beltrán, Carmen Celia. "La Cuna Vacía." Unpublished play.

———. *Remanso Lírico.* Published privately.

Best New Chicano Literature, 1986. Binghamton, New York: Bilingual Press/Editorial Bilingüe, 1986.

Binder, Wolfgang. *Contemporary Chicano Poetry: An Anthology.* Erlanger Studien. Nürnberg, Germany: Verlag Palm and Enke Erlander, 1986.

———. *Partial Autobiographies: Interviews with 20 Chicano Poets.* Nürnberg, W. Germany: Verlag Palm and Enke Erlander, 1986.

Blanco, Iris. "La mujer En Los Albores De La Conquista de México." *Aztlán* II (1980), 11.

Blea, Irene. *Celebrating, Crying and Cursing.* Pueblo, Co: Pueblo Poetry Project, 1980.

Bonifaz de Novelo, María Eugenia. *Análisis histórico sobre la mujer mexicana.* México, 1975.

Boone, Margaret S. "The Uses of Traditional Concepts in the Development of New Urban Roles: Cuban Women in the United States." *A World of Women,* ed. E. Bourguignon. New York: Praeger, 1980.

Bornstein-Somoza, Miriam. *Bajo Cubierta.* Tucson: Scorpion Press, 1977.

———. *Siete Poetas.* Tucson: Scorpion Press, 1978.

Boxer, C.R. *Women in Iberian Expansion Overseas: Some Facts, Fancies and Personalities.* New York: Oxford University Press, 1975.

Boza, María del Carmen, Beverly Silva and Carmen Valle, eds. *Nosotras: Latina Literature Today.* Binghamton, N.Y.: Bilingual Review/Press, 1986.

Brinson Curiel, Bárbara. *Speak To Me From Dreams.* Berkeley: Third Woman Press, 1989.

Brinson-Pineda, Bárbara. *Nocturno.* Berkeley: El Fuego de Aztlán. Vol. 2, no. 2, 1978.

———. *Nocturno.* Oakland, Calif.: Milagro Books, 1979.

———. "Poets on Poetry: Dialogue with Lucha Corpi," *Prisma* Spring, 1979.

———. *Vocabulary of the Dead.* Oakland, Calif.: Nomad Press, 1984.

Broyles González, Yolanda. "Toward a Re-vision of Chicano Theater History: The Women of El Teatro Campesino." In *Making a Spectacle: Feminist Essays on Contemporary Women's Theater,* ed. Lynda Hart, 209–38. Ann Arbor: University of Michigan Press, 1989.

———. "Women in El Teatro Campesino: 'Apoco estaba molacha la Virgen de Guadalupe?'" *Chicana Voices,* ed. Teresa Córdova et al, 162–87. Center for Mexican American Studies, University of Texas, Austin, 1986. Albuquerque: University of New Mexico Press, 1993.

Bruce-Novoa, Juan. "Canonical and Noncanonical Texts: A Chicano Case Study." *Redefining American Literary History,* ed. A. LaVonne Brown Ruoff and Jerry W. Ward, Jr., 196–209. New York: Modern Language Association of America, 1990.

———. *Chicano Authors: Inquiry by Interview.* Austin: University of Texas Press, 1980.

———. *Chicano Poetry: A Response to Chaos.* Austin: University of Texas Press, 1982.

———. *Retrospace: Collected Essays on Chicano Literature.* Houston: Arte Público, 1990.

Bullough, Vern L. *The Subordinate Sex: History of Attitudes Toward Women.* New York: Penguin Books, 1974.

———.

Buss, Fran Leeper. *La Partera: Story of a Midwife.* Ann Arbor: University of Michigan Press, 1980.

Cabeza de Baca, Fabiola. *The Good Life.* Santa Fe: Museum of New Mexico Press, 1982.

———. *Historic Cookery.* Las Vegas, N.M.: La Galería de los Artesanos, 1970; originally published in 1949.

———. *We Fed Them Cactus.* Albuquerque: University of New Mexico Press, 1954.

Calderón, Hector and José David Saldívar, eds. *Criticism in the Borderlands: Studies in Chicano Literature, Culture, and Ideology.* Durham: Duke University Press, 1991.

Calvillo, Jaime Darío. "Between Heaven and Earth: Actos of El Teatro Campesino." Ph.D. diss. University of Minnesota, 1982.

Calvillo-Craig, Lorenza. "Soy Hija de Mis Padres." *El Grito* 7:1, 1973.

Camarillo, Lydia. "Mi Reflejo." *La Palabra* 2:2, 1980.

Candelaria, Cordelia. *Chicano Poetry, A Critical Introduction.* Westport, CT, London, England: Greenwood Press, 1986.

———. *Ojo de la Cueva.* Colorado Springs, Colorado: Maize Press, 1984.

———, ed. *The Wild Zone: Essays in Multi-Ethnic Literature.* Boulder: University of Colorado, 1989.

Casillas, A. *La mujer en dos comunidades de emigrantes (Chihuahua).* México: Secretaría de Educación Pública, 1986.

Castañeda, Antonia. "Memory, Language and Voice of Mestiza Women on the Northern Frontier: Historical Documents as Literary Text." In *Recovering the U.S. Hispanic Literary Heritage,* ed. Ramón Gutiérrez and Genaro Padilla, 265–77. Houston: Arte Público Press, 1993.

———. "The Political Economy of Nineteenth Century Stereotypes of Californians." *Between Borders: Essays on Mexicana/Chicana History,* ed. Adelaida R. Del Castillo, 213–36. Encino, Calif.: Floricanto Press, 1990.

Castellano, Olivia. *Blue Horse of Madness.* Sacramento, Calif.: Crystal Clear, 1983.

———. *Blue Mandolin, Yellow Field.* Berkeley: Grito del Sol, quarterly books, year five, book three, 1980.

———. *Spaces That Time Missed.* Sacramento, Calif.: Crystal Clear, 1986.

Castellanos, Rosario. *Album de Familia.* 2nd. ed. México: J. Mortiz, 1975.

Castillo, Ana. *i close my eyes (to see).* Spokane: Washington State University Press, 1975.

———. *The Invitation.* n.p.: 1979.

———. *Massacre of the Dreamers: Essays on Xicanisma.* University of New Mexico Press, 1994.

———. *The Mixquiahuala Letters.* Binghamton, N.Y.: Bilingual Press/Editorial Bilingüe, 1986.

———. *My Father Was a Toltec.* Novato, Calif.: West End Press, 1988.

———. *My Father Was a Toltec and Selected Poems.* New York: W. W. Norton, 1995.

———. *Otro Canto.* Chicago: Alternativa Publications, 1977.

———. *Sapogonia.* Tempe: Bilingual Press/Review, 1989. New York: Doubleday/ Anchor Books, 1994.

———. *So Far From God.* New York: W.W. Norton, 1993.

———. *Women Are Not Roses.* Houston: Arte Público Press, 1984.

———. *Zero Makes Me Hungry.* Glenbrook, Ill: Scott, Foresman, 1975.

Castillo, Debra A. *Talking Back: Toward a Latin American Feminist Literary Criticism.* Ithaca: Cornell University Press, 1992.

Castro, Carrie. "The Night Filled With Faint Cries." *Morena,* 23–24. Santa Barbara, 1980.

Catacalos, Rosemary. *Again For The First Time.* Santa Fe, N. M.: Tooth of Time Books, 1984, 1972.

Cazemajou, Jean. *Les Minorités Hispaniques en Amérique Du Nord (1960–1980).* Bordeaux, France: Presses Universitaires de Bordeaux, 1985.

Cervantes, Irma H. *Sparks, Flames, and Cinders.* Scottsdale, Az: Five Windmills Publishing Company, 1982.

Cervantes, Lorna Dee. *Emplumada.* Pittsburgh: University of Pittsburgh Press, 1981.

———. *From the Cables of Genocide: Poems on Love and Hunger.* Houston: Arte Público, 1991.

———. "Para Un Revolucionario." *The Third Woman: Minority Women Writers of the United States,* ed. Dexter Fisher, 381–82. Boston: Houghton Mifflin, 1980.

Chabram-Dernersesian, Angie. "I Throw Punches for My Race, but I Don't Want to Be a Man" Writing Us—Chica-nos (Girl, Us)/Chicanas—into the Movement Script." *Cultural Studies,* eds. L. Grossberg, Cary Nelson, Paula Treichler, 81–95. New York: Routledge, 1992.

Chacón, María, et al. *Chicanas in Postsecondary Education.* Stanford, Calif.: Center for Research on Women, Stanford University, 1982.

Chávez, Denise E. *Face of an Angel.* New York: Farrar, 1994.

———. *The Last of the Menu Girls.* Houston: Arte Público Press, 1986. Second printing: 1987.

———. *Life is a Two-Way Street.* Las Cruces, N.M.: Rosetta Press, 1980.

Chávez, Fray Angélico. *New Mexican Roots, Ltd., 1678–1869.* Santa Fe, N.M., 1982.

Cherry, L. "The Preschool Teacher-Child Dyad: Sex Differences in Verbal Interaction." *Child Development* 46 (1975), 532–35.

Chispas! Cultural Warriors of New Mexico. February 15, 1992. Phoenix: The Heard Museum.

Cisneros, Sandra. *Bad Boys.* San José, Calif.: Mango Publications, 1980. (The Chicano Chapbook Series, no.8)

———. "Down There." *Third Woman: The Sexuality of Latinas,* ed. Norma Alarcón et al, 19–23. Berkeley: Third Woman Press, 1989.

———. *The House on Mango Street.* Houston: Arte Público Press, 1983.

———. *The House on Mango Street.* 2nd, revised edition. Houston: Arte Público Press, 1988.

———. *The House on Mango Street.* New York: Random House, 1992.

———. *Loose Woman.* New York: Random House, 1994.

———. *My Wicked, Wicked Ways.* Berkeley: Third Woman Press, 1987. New York: Turtle Bay, 1992.

———. *My Wicked, Wicked Ways.* New York: Vintage Books/Random House, 1992.

———. "Una Anciana." *Growing Old in America.* 2nd ed., ed. B. Hess. New Brunswick, N.J.: Transaction Books, 1980.

———. *Woman Hollering Creek and Other Stories.* New York: Random House, 1991, 1992 (paper).

Córdova, Josephine. *No Lloro Pero Me Acuerdo.* Dallas: Taylor Publishing Co., 1976.

Córdova, Teresa, Norma Cantú, Gilberto Cárdenas, Juan García, Christine M. Sierra, eds. *Chicana Voices: Intersections of Class, Race and Gender.* Austin: Tex: The Center for Mexican American Studies, 1986. Albuquerque: University of New Mexico Press, 1993.

Corpi, Lucha. *Cactus Blood.* Houston: Arte Público Press, 1995.

——— . *Delia's Song.* Houston: Arte Público Press, 1989.

——— . *Eulogy for a Brown Angel.* Houston: Arte Público Press, 1992.

——— . *Palabras de Mediodía/Noon Words.* Berkeley: El Fuego de Aztlán, 1980.

——— . "The Protocol of Vegetables," *Prisma* (Spring, 1979). Translation by Catherine Rodríguez-Nieto.

——— . *Variations Sobre Una Tempestad/Variations on a Storm.* trans. from original English/Spanish. Catherine Rodríguez-Nieto. Berkeley: Third Woman Press, 1990.

Cortés, Carlos E. "Chicanas in Film: History of an Image." *Chicano Cinema: Research, Reviews, and Resources,* ed. Gary D. Keller, 94–108. Binghamton, N.Y.: Bilingual Press/Editorial Bilingüe, 1985.

Cota-Cárdenas, Margarita. "Lírica Fanática." In *Infinite Divisions: An Anthology of Chicana Literature,* ed. Tey Diana Rebolledo and Eliana Rivero, 299. Tucson: University of Arizona Press, 1993.

——— . "Malinche's Discourse." *Infinite Divisions: An Anthology of Chicana Literature,* ed. Tey Diana Rebolledo and Eliana Rivero, 203–7. Tucson: University of Arizona Press, 1993.

——— . *Marchitas de Mayo.* (Sones Pa'l Pueblo). Austin: Relámpago Press, 1989.

——— . *Noches despertando inconsciencias.* Tucson: Scorpion Press, 1977.

——— . *Puppet.* Austin: Relámpago Books Press, 1985.

Cotera, Martha P. *The Chicana Feminist.* Austin: Information Systems Development, 1977. ——— . *Diosa y Hembra, The History and Heritage of Chicanas in the U.S.* Austin: Information Systems Development, 1976.

——— . *Profile on the Mexican American Women.* Austin: Information Systems Development, 1976.

Cunningham, Veronica. "ever since." *Capirotada.* Los Angeles: Fronteras, 1976.

De Colores 2:3 (1975).

De Colores 4:3 (1978).

de la Guerra, María de las Angustias. *Occurrences in California,* trans. Francis Price and William Ellison. Washington: Academy of American Franciscan History, 1956.

De la Peña, Terri. *Latin Satins.* Seattle: Seal Press, 1994.

——— . *Margins.* Seattle: Seal Press, 1992.

de la Torre, A., and L. Rush. "The Determinants of Breastfeeding for Mexican Migrant Women." *International Migration Review* (1987) 21, no. 3:728–42.

Del Castillo, Adelaida R., ed. *Between Borders: Essays on Mexicana/Chicana History.* Encino, Calif.: Floricanto Press, 1990.

Del Castillo, Adelaida, and Magdalena Mora, eds. *Mexican Women in the United States: Struggles Past and Present.* Los Angeles: Chicano Studies Research Center Publications, 1980.

del Fuego, Laura. *Maravilla.* Los Angeles: Floricanto Press, 1989.

Delgado, Holly. *The Junk City Journal.* Albuquerque, N.M.: Holly Delgado, Inc., 1977.

Diamond, Betty Ann. " 'Brown-Eyed Children of the Sun': The Cultural Politics of El Teatro Campesino." Ph.D. diss. University of Wisconsin, Madison, 1977.

Domínguez, Sylvia Maida. *La Comadre María: Una comedia.* Austin: American Universal Artforms Corporation, 1973.

El Grito: A Journal of Contemporary Mexican-American Thought. Vol. 4, No. 3, (Spring 1971).

——— . Vol. 7, No. 1 (1973).

Elsasser, Nan, Kyle MacKenzie, and Yvonne Tixier y Virgil. *Las Mujeres: Conversations from a Hispanic Community.* New York: McGraw Hill, 1980.

Enríquez, Evangelina and Alfredo Mirandé. "Chicana Feminism." In *La Chicana: The Mexican-American Woman.* Chicago: University of Chicago Press, 1979. 202–44.

Escajeda, Josefina. "Tales from San Elizario." *Puro Mejicano,* ed. Frank Dobie. Austin: The University of Texas Press Society, 1935. Rpt. in *We Are Chicanos: An Anthology of Mexican-American Literature,* ed. Philip D. Ortego, 40–47. New York: Washington Square Press, 1973.

Espinosa, Carmen. *Shawls, Crinolines, Filigree. The Dress and Adornment of the Women of New Mexico, 1739–1900.* El Paso: Texas Western Press, 1970.

Estes, Clarissa Pinkola. *Women Who Run With the Wolves: Myths and Stories of the Wild Woman Archetype.* New York: Ballantine Books, 1992.

Evans, Francis B., and James G. Anderson. "The Psychocultural Origins of Achievement and Achievement Motivation: The Mexican American Family." *Sociology of Education* (1973) 46:396–419.

Farris, Buford, and Norval Glenn. "Fatalism and Familism among Anglos and Mexican Americans in San Antonio." *Sociology and Social Research* (1976) 60: 393–402.

Fernández, Roberta. *Intaglio: A Novel in Six Stories.* Houston: Arte Público Press, 1990.

Fisher, Dexter. *The Third Woman: Minority Women Writers of the United States.* Boston: Houghton Mifflin, 1980.

Flores, Gloria Amalia. *And Her Children Lived.* San Diego: Toltecas en Aztlán Publications, Centro Cultural de la Raza, 1974.

Flores-Ortiz, Yvette. "The Impact of Acculturation on the Chicano Family: An

Analysis of Selected Variables." Ph.D. diss., University of California, Berkeley, 1978.

Fontes, Montserrat. *First Confessions.* New York: W. W. Norton, 1991.

Fourth Chicano Literary Prize (1977–1778). Irvine, California: Department of Spanish and Portuguese, 1978.

Fregoso, Rosa Linda. *The Bronze Screen: Chicana and Chicano Film Culture.* Minneapolis: University of Minnesota Press, 1993.

Frontiers. Summer 1980. "Chicanas en El Ambiente Nacional/Chicanas in the National Landscape." (Special issue on Chicanas).

Gaitán, Marcela T. *Chicano Themes: Manita Poetry.* Minneapolis: Chicano Studies Department, University of Minnesota, 1975.

Gandara, Patricia. "Passing through the Eye of the Needle: High Achieving Chicanas." *Hispanic Journal of Behavioral Sciences* (1982) 4, no. 2:167–79.

García, Céline Frémaux. *Céline: Remembering Lousiana, 1850–1871.* Athens: University of Georgia Press, 1988.

García, Ignacio M. *La Mexicana/Chicana: Renato Rosaldo Lecture Series Monograph.* Vol. 1 Series 1983–84. (Summer, 1985). Tucson: Mexican American Studies and Research Center, University of Arizona.

García, John A., Theresa Córdova and Juan R. García, eds. *The Chicano Struggle, Analyses of Past and Present Efforts.* Binghamton, N. Y.: Bilingual Press/Editorial Bilingüe, 1984.

García, Nasario. *Abuelitos: Stories of the Río Puerco Valley.* Albuquerque: University of New Mexico Press, 1992.

———. *Recuerdos de Los Viejitos: Tales of the Río Puerco.* Albuquerque: University of New Mexico Press, 1987.

Gaspar de Alba, Alicia. "Beggar on the Córdova Bridge." In *Three Times a Woman.* ed. Alicia Gaspar de Alba, María Herrera-Sobek, and Demetria Martínez. Tempe, Arizona: Bilingual Review/Press, 1989.

———. "Juana Inés." In *New Chicana/Chicano Writing 1,* ed. Charles M. Tatum, 1–15. Tucson: The University of Arizona Press, 1992.

———. "Literary Wetback," *The Massachusetts Review* 29:2.

———. *The Mystery of Survival and Other Stories.* Tempe: Bilingual Review Press, 1993.

Goldsmith, Raquel Rubio. "Shipwrecked in the Desert: A Short History of the Adventures and Struggles for Survival of the Mexican Sisters of the House of the Providence in Douglas Arizona During Their First Twenty-two years of Existence (1927–1949). *La Mexicana/Chicana: Renato Rosaldo Lecture Series Monograph 1983–84.* Tucson: Mexican American Studies and Research Center, University of Arizona, 1985.

Gómez, Alma, Cherríe Moraga and Mariana Romo-Carmona, eds. *Cuentos: Stories by Latinas.* New York: Kitchen Table Press, 1983.

Gómez, Elvira. "Open." *Odes of March* I (March 1965). Rpt. in *We Are Chicanos: An Anthology of Mexican-American Literature,* ed. Philip D. Ortego, 179–80. New York: Washington Square Press, 1973.

Gonzales, Gloria. "There is Nothing." In *Las Mujeres Hablan: An Anthology of Nuevo Mexicana Writers,* ed. Tey Diana Rebolledo, Erlinda Gonzales-Berry and Teresa Márquez, 184. Albuquerque: El Norte Publications, 1988.

González, Jovita. "Don Tomás." "Among My People." *Southwest Review* 2 (Winter 1932). Rpt. in *We Are Chicanos: An Anthology of Mexican-American Literature,* ed. Philip D. Ortego, 48–52. New York: Washington Square Press, 1973.

Gonzales, María Dolores. "Dolores." In *Las Mujeres Hablan: An Anthology of Nuevo Mexicana Writers,* ed. Tey Diana Rebolledo, Erlinda Gonzales-Berry and Teresa Márquez, 186. Albuquerque: El Norte Publications, 1988.

Gonzales, Rebecca. *Slow Work to the Rhythm of Cicadas.* Fort Worth: Prickly Pear Press, 1985.

Gonzales, Sylvia Alicia. *La Chicana Piensa, The Social-Cultural Conscious of a Mexican-American Woman.* s.l.: Sylvia A. González, 1974.

Gonzales-Berry, Erlinda. "Carlota Gonzales." In *Nuestras Mujeres, Hispanas of New Mexico: Their Images and Their Lives,* ed. Tey Diana Rebolledo, 35–36. Albuquerque: El Norte Publications, 1993.

———. "Rosebud." In *Las Mujeres Hablan: An Anthology of Nuevo Mexicana Writers,* ed. Tey Diana Rebolledo, Erlinda Gonzales-Berry and Teresa Márquez, 27–31. Albuquerque: El Norte Publications, 1988.

Gonzales-Berry, Erlinda, ed. *Paletitas de Guayaba.* Albuquerque: El Norte Publications, 1991.

———. *Pasó Por Aquí. Critical Essays on the New Mexican Literary Tradition, 1542–1988.* Albuquerque: The University of New Mexico Press, 1989.

Gonzales-Berry, Erlinda, and Tey Diana Rebolledo, "Growing Up Chicano: Tomás Rivera and Sandra Cisneros." In *International Studies in Honor of Tomás Rivera,* ed. Julián Olivares, 109–19. *Revista Chicano-Riqueña,* 13 (3–4).

González, Beatriz. *The Chosen Few.* San Antonio: M & A Editions, 1983.

González, Deena. "Gender Relations in the Spanish Borderlands." In *Encyclopedia of the North American Colonies.* New York: Scribner's, 1993.

———. *The Spanish-Mexican Women of Santa Fe: Patterns of Their Resistance and Accommodation, 1820–1880.* Ph.d. diss. University of California, Berkeley, 1985.

González, Ray. "A Chicano Verano." *The Nation* 7 June 1993, pp. 772–74.

Griswold del Castillo, Richard. *La Familia: Chicano Families in the Urban Southwest, 1848 to the Present.* South Bend: University of Notre Dame Press, 1984.

Gutiérrez, Ramón A. "Marriage and Seduction in Colonial New Mexico." In *Between Borders: Essays on Mexicana/Chicana History,* ed. Adelaida R. Del Castillo, 448–58. Encino, Calif.: Floricanto Press, 1990.

————. *When Jesus Came, The Corn Mothers Went Away: Marriage, Sexuality and Power in New Mexico, 1500–1846*. Stanford: Stanford University Press, 1991.

Gutiérrez, Ramón and Genaro Padilla eds. *Recovering the U.S. Hispanic Literary Heritage*. Houston: Arte Público Press, 1993.

Gutiérrez Spencer, Laura. "Fairy Tales and Opera: The Fate of the Heroine in the Work of Sandra Cisneros." *Bilingual Review*, forthcoming.

Hahner, June. *Women in Latin American History: Their Lives and Views*. Los Angeles: UCLA Latin American Center Publications, University of California, 1976.

Halfon, S., et al. *Campesinas: Women Farmworkers in the California Agricultural Labor Force*. Sacramento: California Commission on the Status of Women, 1978.

Hernández, Inés. "Chicana Writers." In *Women in Texas*, ed. Rose Marie Cutting and Bonnie Freeman. Austin: University of Texas Press, 1977

————. *Con Razón, Corazón*. San Antonio: Caracol, 1977. Revised edition, San Antonio, TX: M & A Editions, 1987.

————. "The Feminist Aesthetic in Chicano Literature." In *The Third Woman: Minority Women Writers of the U.S.*, ed. Dexter Fisher. Boston: Houghton Mifflin, 1980.

Third Chicano Literary Prize(1976–1977). Irvine, Calif.: Department of Spanish and Portuguese, 1977.

————. "Testimonio de Memoria." *New Chicana/Chicano Writing 2*, ed. Charles M. Tatum, 17. Tucson: University of Arizona Press, 1993.

————. "Untitled." *Caracol* 4:3 (November, 1977) n.p.

Hernández, Irene, B. *Across the Great River*. Houston: Arte Público Press, 1989, 1990.

————. *Heartbeat-Drumbeat*. Houston: Arte Público Press, 1992.

Hernández, Lisa and Tina Benítez, eds. *Palabras Chicanas: An Undergraduate Anthology*. Mujeres en Marcha. Berkeley: University of California Press, 1988.

Hernández, Salomé. "Nueva Mexicanas as Refugees and Reconquest Settlers, 1680–1696." In *New Mexico Women: Intercultural Perspectives*, ed. Joan M. Jensen and Darlis A. Miller, 17–41. Albuquerque: University of New Mexico Press, 1986.

————. *The Present-day U.S. Southwest: Female Participation in Official Spanish Settlement Expeditions: Specific Case Studies in the Sixteenth, Seventeenth, and Eighteenth Centuries*. Ph.D. diss. University of New Mexico, 1987.

Herrera-Sobek, María. "The Acculturation Process of the Chicana in the Corrido." *De Colores Journal*, 6 (1982), 7–16. Also published in *Proceedings of the Pacific Coast Council of Latin American Studies*, 9 (1982), 25–34.

————. *Beyond Stereotypes: The Critical Analysis of Chicana Literature*. Binghamton, N.Y.: SUNY Bilingual Review Press, 1985.

————. "Canon Formation and Chicano Literature." *Recovering the U.S. Hispanic Literary Heritage*, ed. Ramón Gutiérrez and Genaro Padilla, 209–19. Houston: Arte Público Press, 1993.

————. "Chicana Writers: A Regional Experience." *Hispanorama,* Feb. 1990, pp. 103–106.

————. "Crossing the Border: Three Case Studies of Mexican Immigrant Women in Orange County in the 1980s." In *Second Lives: The Contemporary Immigrant/ Refugee Experience in Orange County,* ed. Valerie Smith and Michael Bigelow. Costa Mesa, Calif.: South Coast Repertory, 1983.

————. "Josephina Niggli: A Border Precursor of Chicano/a Literature." In *Mexican Village* by Josephina Niggli. Albuquerque: University of New Mexico Press, 1994. Pp. xv-xxxi.

————. "La Chicana: Nuevas perspectivas." *La Opinión Literary Supplement* No. 10 (June 22, 1980), 14-15.

————. " 'La Delgadina': Incest and Patriarchal Structure in a Spanish/Chicano Romance-Corrido." *Studies in Latin American Popular Culture Journal* 5 (Spring, 1986), 90-107.

————. "La imagen de la madre en la poesía Chicana." *Mujer y Socieded an América Latina,* ed. Lucía Guerra-Cunningham, 253–61. Chile: Editorial del Pacífico, 1980. Rep. in *La Opinión* (Suplemento Cultural). Los Angeles: April 27, 1980, 10–11.

————. "La mujer traidora: Arquetipo estructurante en el corrido." *Cuadernos Americanos.* 235 (marzo-abril, 1981), 230–42.

————. "La unidad del hombre y del cosmos: reafirmación del proceso vital en Estela Portillo Trambley." *La Palabra* 4/5 (Spring and Fall, 1982–83), 127–41.

————. *The Mexican Corrido: A Feminist Analysis.* Bloomington: Indiana University Press, 1990.

————. "Mi Poesía." *Chasqui.* February-May, 1980.

————. "Mothers, Lovers, and Soldiers: Images of Women in the Mexican Corrido." *Keystone Folklore Journal* 23, No. l (1979), 53–77.

————. "Naked Moon/Luna Desnuda." In *Three Times a Woman.* Tempe: Bilingual Review/Press, 1989.

————. "Poema." *Infinite Divisions:An Anthology of Chicana Literature,* ed. Tey Diana Rebolledo and Eliana Rivero, 297. Tucson: University of Arizona Press, 1993.

————. "The Politics of Rape: Sexual Transgression in Chicana Fiction." In *Chicana Creativity and Criticism: Charting New Frontiers in American Literature,* ed. María Herrera-Sobek and Helena María Viramontes. Houston: Arte Público Press, 1988.

————. "Protesta social, folklore e ideología feminista en escritoras chicanas." *El poder hispano.* Alberto Moncada Lorenzo, Carmen Flys Junquera and José Antonio Gurpegui Palacios. Alcalá de Henares, Spain: Universidad de Alcalá, Centro de Estudios Norteamericanos, 1994. Pp. 455–63.

————. "The Street Scene: Metamorphic Strategies in Two Contemporary

Chicana Poets." In *Chicana Writers: On Word and Film,*[1] ed. María Herrera-Sobek and Helena María Viramontes. Berkeley: Third Woman Press, 1995.

———. "Systems In Conflict: Myth, Family and Industrial Society." *1987 Hispanic Playwrights Project.* Costa Mesa, Calif.: Southcoast Repertory, 1987. pp. 17–19.

———. "Transformaciones Culturales: La Tradición Oral Mexicana y la Literatura de Escritoras Chicanas." *Foro Hispánico.* Forthcoming.

———. "The Treacherous Woman Archetype: Structuring Agent in the *Corrido.*" *Aztlán: International Journal of Chicano Studies Research* 13 (Spring, 1982), 136–47.

Herrera-Sobek, María, ed. *Reconstructing a Chicano/a Literary Heritage: Hispanic Colonial Literature of the Southwest.* Tucson: University of Arizona Press, 1993.

Herrera-Sobek, María and Helena María Viramontes, eds. *Chicana Creativity and Criticism: Charting New Frontiers in American Literature. The Americas Review.* 15 (3–4). 1987.

———. *Chicana Writers: On Word and Film.* Berkeley: Third Woman Press, 1995.

Hoberman, Louise S. "Hispanic American Women as Portrayed in the Historical Literature: Types and Archetypes." *Revista/Review Interamericana,* 4 (Summer 1974), pp. 136–37.

Holden, William Curry. *Teresita* (Life of Teresa Urrea). Owings Mills, MD: Stemmer House, 1978.

Horno-Delgado, Asunción, Eliana Ortega, Nina M. Scott, and Nancy Saporta Sternbach. *Breaking Boundaries: Latina Writing and Critical Readings.* Amherst: University of Massachusetts Press, 1989.

Howard, Gerald, letter to Ray Gonzales regarding Ana Castillo's *So Far From God. The Nation* 19 July 1993, p. 86.

Howard, Melissa. "The First Woman to Govern New Mexico." *Impact/Albuquerque Journal Magazine* (Nov. 2, 1982).

Hoyos, Angela de. *Arise Chicano and Other Poems.* San Antonio: M & A Editions, 1975.

———. *Chicano Poems for the Barrio.* San Antonio: M & A Editions. 1977.

———. *Selected Poems/Seleccións.* San Antonio: Dezkalzp Press, 1979.

———. *Women, Women.* Houston: Arte Público Press, 1985.

Hurtado, Aída. "Feminismo Chicano: Una perspectiva." *Culturas Hispanas de los Estados Unidos de América,* ed. María de Jesús Buxó Rey y Tomás Calvo Buezas, 125–42. Madrid: Ediciones de Cultura Hispánica, 1990.

Jaquette, Jane S. "Women in Revolutionary Movements in Latin America." *Journal of Marriage and the Family,* Vol. 35 (May 1973), pp. 344–54.

Jara, René and Hernán Vidal. *Testimonio y Literatura.* Minneapolis: Institute for the Study of Ideologies and Literature, 1986.

Jaramillo, Cleofas. *Cuentos del Hogar.* El Campo, Texas: Citizen Press, 1939.

————. *The Genuine New Mexico Tasty Recipes.* Rev. ed. Santa Fe: Seton Village, 1942; originally published in 1939.

————. *Romance of a Little Village Girl.* San Antonio: Naylor, Co., 1955.

————. *Shadows of the Past.* Santa Fe: Seton Village Press, 1941.

————. *Shadows of the Past.* Santa Fe, N.M.: Ancient City Press, 1980.

Jensen, Joan M. "Women Teachers, Class, and Ethnicity: New Mexico, 1900–1950." *Southwest Economy and Society* (1978–1979) 4:1, 3–13.

Jensen, Joan M. and Darlis A. Miller, eds. *New Mexico Women: Intercultural Perspectives.* Albuquerque: University of New Mexico Press, 1986.

Jiménez, Francisco, ed. *The Identification and Analysis of Chicano Literature.* New York: Bilingual Press/Editorial Bilingüe, 1979.

Kaminsky, Amy K. *Reading the Body Politic: Feminist Criticism and Latin American Women Writers.* Minneapolis: University of Minnesota Press, 1993.

Keefe, Susan E. "Real and Ideal Extended Familism among Mexican Americans and Anglo Americans: On the Meaning of 'Close' Family Ties." *Human Organization* (1984) 43:65–70.

Keefe, Susan E., Amado M. Padilla, and Manuel L. Carlos. "The Mexican-American Extended Family as an Emotional Support System." *Human Organization* (1979) 38:144–52.

Kendrix, H. D. *Mary of Agreda. The Life and Legend of a Spanish Nun.* London: Routledge and Kegan Paul, 1967.

Korte, Manuel. "Theoretical Perspectives in Mental Health and the Mexicano Elders." In *Chicano Aging and Mental Health,* ed. M. Miranda and R. Ruiz. Rockville, Md.: National Institute of Mental Health, 1980.

Kozikowski, Janusz. "Agueda Martínez—Weaver of Many Seasons," *New Mexico Magazine* (August 1979), 44–46.

La Chrisx. "La Loca de la Raza Cósmica." *Comadre 2* 1978: 5–9.

La Cosecha/The Harvest: The Chicana Experience. Special issue of *De Colores* Vol. 4, No.3. Albuquerque: Pajarito Publications, 1978.

Lafaye, Jacques. *Quetzalcóatl and Guadalupe: The Formation of Mexican National Consciousness 1531–1813.* Chicago: University of Chicago Press, 1976.

Larvin, Asunción, ed. *Latin American Women: Historical Perspectives.* Westport, Conn.: Greenwood Press, 1978.

Lawhn, Juanita. "El Regidor and La Prensa: Impediments to Women's Self Definition" In *Third Woman: The Sexuality of Latinas,* ed. Norma Alarcón, Ana Castillo, and Cherríe Moraga, 134–42.Berkeley: Third Woman Press, 1989.

————. "Women Publishing in La Prensa, 1913–1920," Unpublished paper, 1985.

Lecompte, Janet. "The Independent Women of Hispanic New Mexico, 1821–1846." In *New Mexico Women: Intercultural Perspectives,* ed. Joan M. Jensen and Darlis A. Miller, 71–93. Albuquerque: University of New Mexico Press, 1986.

León-Portilla, Miguel. "Afrodite Y Tlazolteotl," *Vuelta* 71 (Oct. 1982).

———. "The Chalco Cihuacuicatl of Aquiauhtzin: Erotic Poetry of the Nahuas," *New Scholar* 5:2 (1978) 256–62.

———. "Las Alegradoras de Tiempos Pre-hispánicos," *Cuadernos del Viento* 45–46 (1964), 708.

Leonardi, Susan J. "Recipes for Reading: Summer Pasta, Lobster a la Riseholme, and Key Lime Pie." *PMLA* 104 (1989): 340–47

Levinson, Daniel. *Seasons of a Man's Life.* New York: Ballantine, 1978.

Limón, Jane. "incongruity." *Odes of March* I (March 1965). Rpt. in *We Are Chicanos: An Anthology of Mexican-American Literature,* ed. Philip D. Ortego, 174. New York: Washington Square Press, 1973.

Littlefield, C., and C. L. Stout. "A Survey of Colorado's Migrant Farmworkers: Access to Health Care." *International Migration Review* (1987) 21, no. 3:688–708.

Lizárraga, Sylvia. "The Gift?" In *Infinite Divisions: An Anthology of Chicana Literature,* ed. Tey Diana Rebolledo and Eliana S. Rivero, 91. Tucson: University of Arizona Press, 1993. First published in Spanish in *Caracol,* 1973.

———. "Monarquía." In *Requisa Treinta y Dos,* ed. Rosaura Sánchez, 133–34. La Jolla, Calif.: Chicano Research Publications, 1979.

Lomas, Clara. "The Articulation of Gender in the Mexican Borderlands, 1900–1915." In *Recovering the U.S. Hispanic Literary Heritage,* ed. Ramón Gutiérrez and Genaro Padilla, 293–308. Houston: Arte Público Press, 1993.

———. "Mexican Precursors of Chicana Feminist Writing." In *Wild Zone: Essays on Multi Ethnic American Literature,* ed. Cordelia Candelaria, 21–33. Boulder: University of Colorado, 1989.

López, Natasha. "From Between Our Legs." In *Chicana Lesbians: The Girls Our Mothers Warned Us About,* ed. Carla Trujillo, 156. Berkeley: Third Woman Press, 1991.

López, Tiffany Ann, ed. *Growing Up Chicana/o.* New York: William Morrow & Co., 1993.

López-Medina, Sylvia. *Cantora: A Novel.* Albuquerque: University of New Mexico Press, 1992. New York: One World, Ballatine Books, 1993.

Lucero, Helen. *Hispanic Weavers of North Central New Mexico: Social/Historical and Educational Dimensions of a Continuing Artistic Tradition.* Ph.D. diss. Albuquerque: University of New Mexico, 1986.

Lucero, Marcela Christine. "The Socio-historical Implication of the Valley as a Metaphor in Three Colorado Chicana Poets." Ph.D. diss. University of Minnesota, 1981.

Lucero-White Lea, Aurora. "Our Treasury of Spanish Folklore," *New Mexico Folklore Research,* (1954–55) Vol. 4, 15–19.

Luera, Yolanda. *Solitaria J.* La Jolla, Calif.: Lalo Press Publications, 1986.

Luna Robles, Margarita. *TRIPTYCHS: Dreams, Lust and Other Performances.* Los Angeles: Lalo Press, 1993.

————. *The Broken Web: The Educational Experience of Hispanic American Woman,* ed. Teresa McKenna and Flora Ida Ortiz. Encino, Calif: Floricanto Press, 1988.

MacLachlan, Colin. "Modernization of Female Status in Mexico: The Image of Women's Magazines." *Revista/Review Interamericana* 4 (Summer 1974), pp. 246–57.

Madsen, William. *The Mexican-Americans of South Texas.* New York: Holt, Rinehart and Winston, 1964.

Magnus, P. D. "Breastfeeding among Hispanics." *American Journal of Public Health* (1983) 73, no. 5: 597.

Marín, Christine. "La asociación Hispano-Americana de Madres de España: Tucson's Mexican American Women in World War II." *La Mexicana/Chicana: Renato Rosaldo Lecture Series Monograph 1983–84.* Tucson, Arizona: Mexican American Studies and Research Center, University of Arizona, 1985.

Martínez, Demetria. *Mother Tongue.* Tempe: Bilingual Review/Press, 1994.

————. "Turning." In *Three Times a Woman.* Tempe: Bilingual Review/Press, 1989.

Martínez, Joe L. *Chicano Psychology.* New York: Academic Press, 1977.

Martínez, María. *Sterling Silver Roses.* San Luis Obispo, Calif.: La Morenita Publishers, 1981.

McCluskey, Audrey., ed. *Women of Color: Perspectives On Feminism and Identity.* Occasional Papers Series, Vol. 1, No. 1. Bloomington: Women's Studies Program, Indiana University, 1985.

Meier, Matt and Feliciano Ribera. *Mexican Americans/American Mexicans: from Conquistadors to Chicanos.* Revised edition. New York: Hill and Wang, 1993.

Melville, Margarita, ed. *Twice a Minority: Mexican American Women.* St. Louis: Mosby, 1980.

Messinger Cypress, Sandra. *La Malinche in Mexican Literature: From History to Myth.* Austin: University of Texas Press, 1991.

Mestizo: Anthology of Chicano Literature. Special issue of *De Colores,* Vol. 4, Nos. 1 & 2. Albuquerque: Pajarito Publications, 1978.

Meyer, Doris L. "The Language Issue in New Mexico, 1880–1900: Mexican American Resistance Against Cultural Erosion." *The Bilingual Review/La Revista Bilingüe* (1977) 4:2, 99–106.

Michie, Helena. *The Flesh Made Word: Female Figures and Women's Bodies.* New York: Oxford University Press, 1987.

Miguélez, Armando. *Antología Histórica del Cuento Literario Chicano, 1877–1950.* Ann Arbor: University Microfilms, 1981.

Miller, Beth, ed. *Women in Hispanic Literature, Icons and Fallen Idols.* Berkeley, Los Angeles, London: University of California Press, 1983.

Miller, Darlis A. "Cross-Cultural Marriages in the Southwest. The New Mexico Experience, 1846–1900." In *New Mexico Women: Intercultural Perspectives,* ed. Joan M. Jensen and Darlis A. Miller, 72–94. Albuquerque: The University of New Mexico Press, 1986.

Miller, Michael V. "Variations in Mexican American Family Life: A Review Synthesis of Empirical Research." *Aztlan* (1978) 9:209–31.

Mirandé, Alfredo, and Evangelina Enríquez. *La Chicana: The Mexican American Woman.* Chicago: University of Chicago Press, 1979.

Mujeres en revolución. La Habana: Editorial de Ciencias Sociales, 1978.

Montes, Ana. "Adelita." *Comadre II* 1978, 23.

Moore, Joan W., with Harry Pachon. *Mexican Americans.* 2nd ed. Englewood Cliffs, N.J.: Prentice-Hall, 1976.

Mora, Pat. ———. *Borders.* Houston: Arte Público Press, 1986.

———. *Chants.* Houston: Arte Público Press, 1984, 1985 (second printing).

———. *Communion.* Houston: Arte Público Press, 1991.

———. "Hands," *Revista Chicano-Riqueña* 10:33, 1982. 33–36.

———. "The Named, the Namer, the Naming," *Cuentos del Zaguán.* Unpublished book.

———. *Nepantla: Essays from the Land in the Middle.* Albuquerque: University of New Mexico Press, 1993.

Moraga, Cherríe. *Giving Up the Ghost.* Los Angeles: West End Press, 1986.

———. *The Last Generation: Poetry and Prose.* Boston: South End Press, 1993.

———. *Loving In the War Years: Lo que nunca pasó por sus labios.* Boston: South End Press, 1983.

———. *Three Plays: Giving Up the Ghost, Shadow of a Man, Heroes & Saints.* Albuquerque: West End Press, 1993.

Moraga, Cherríe and Gloria Anzaldúa, eds. *This Bridge Called My Back: Writings by Radical Women of Color.* New York: Kitchen Table: Women of Color Press, 1983.

Morales, Sylvia. "Chicano-Produced Celluloid Mujeres." *Chicano Cinema: Research, Reviews, and Resources.* ed. Gary D. Keller, 89–93. Binghamton, New York: 1985.

Moreno, Dorinda. *La Mujer Es La Tierra/ La Tierra de Vida.* Berkeley: Casa Editorial, 1975.

———, ed. *La mujer en pie de lucha.* México: Espina del Norte publications, 1973.

Niggli, Josephina. *Mexican Folk Plays.* Chapel Hill: University of North Carolina Press, 1938.

———. *Mexican Village.* With an Introduction by María Herrera-Sobek. Albuquerque: University of New Mexico Press, 1994. Originally published by the University of North Carolina Press, 1945.

———. *Step Down Elder Brother.* New York: Rinehart, 1947.

Oñate, María del Pilar. *El feminismo en la literatura española.* Madrid: Espasa-Calpe, 1983.

Ordóñez, Elizabeth. "Body, Spirit and the Text: Alma Villanueva's *Life Span.*" In *Criticism in the Borderlands: Studies in Chicano Literature, Culture, and Ideology,* ed. Héctor Calderón and José David Saldívar, 61–71. Durham: Duke University Press, 1991.

————. "Sexual Politics and the Theme of Sexuality in Chicana Poetry." In *Women in Hispanic Literature: Icons and Fallen Idols,* ed. Beth Miller, 7–16. Berkeley: University of California Press, 1984.

Ornelas, Berta. *Come Down From the Mound.* Phoenix: Miter Publishing Co., 1975.

Ortego, Philip D., ed. *We Are Chicanos: An Anthology of Mexican-American Literature.* New York: Washington Square Press, 1973.

Ortiz Vásquez, Dora. *The Enchanted Dialogue of Loma Parda and Cañada Bonita.* Chacón, N.M.: n.p., 1990.

————. *Enchanted Temples of Taos: My Story of Rosario.* Santa Fe: The Rydal Press, 1975.

O'Sullivan-Beare, Nancy. *Las mujeres de los conquistadores. La mujer española en los comienzos de la colonización americana. Aportaciones para el estudio de la transculturación.* Madrid: Compañía Bibliográfica Española, 1956.

Otero-Warren, Nina. "Count La Cerda's Treasure." *Old Spain in Our Southwest.* New York: Harcourt Brace Jovanovich, 1936. Rpt. in *We Are Chicanos: An Anthology of Mexican-American Literature,* ed. Philip D. Ortego, 36–40. New York: Washington Square Press, 1973.

————. *Old Spain in Our Southwest.* New York: Harcourt Brace Jovanovich, 1936.

Padilla, Genaro M., "Imprisoned Narrative? Or Lies, Secrets and Silence in New Mexico Women's Autobiography." In *Criticism in the Borderlands: Studies in Chicano Literature, Culture, and Ideology,* ed. Héctor Calderón and José David Saldívar, 43–60. Durham: Duke University Press, 1991.

————. *My History, Not Yours: The Formation of Mexican American Autobiography.* Madison: University of Wisconsin Press, 1994.

————. "Recovering Mexican-American Autobiography." In *Recovering the U.S. Hispanic Literary Heritage,* ed. Ramón Gutiérrez and Genaro Padilla, 153–78. Houston: Arte Público Press, 1993.

————. "The Recovery of Chicano Nineteenth-Century Autobiography," *The American Quarterly* 42 (1988): 287–98.

La Palabra. 2:2 (1980).

Palacios, Mónica. "La Llorona Loca: The Other Side." In *Chicana Lesbians: The Girls Our Mothers Warned Us About,* ed. Carla Trujillo, 49–51. Berkeley: Third Woman Press, 1991.

Palley, Julian. *Best New Chicano Literature, 1986.* Binghamton, New York: Bilingual Press/Editorial Bilingüe, 1986.

Palomo Acosta, Teresa. *Passing Time* Austin: n.p., 1984.

Panich, Paula. "Spirits in the Material World." *Spirit. The Magazine of Southwest Airlines* (1990), 38–42.

Paredes, Raymond, "The Evolution of Chicano Literature." In *Three American Literatures,* ed. Houston A. Baker, Jr. New York: Modern Language Association, 1982.

Paz, Octavio. *The Labyrinth of Solitude Life and Thought in Mexico.* New York: Grove Press, 1961.

———. *Sor Juana Inés de la Cruz o las trampas de la fe.* Madrid: Seix Barral Biblioteca Breve, 1982.

Peden, Margaret Sayers, trans. *A Woman of Genius: the Intellectual Autobiography of Sor Juana Inés de la Cruz.* Salisbury, Ct.: Lime Rock Press, 1982.

Peñalosa, Fernando. "Toward an Operational Definition of the Mexican American." *Aztlan* (Spring 1970) 1: 1–12.

Pérez, Emma. "Sexuality and Discourse: Notes from a Chicana Survivor." In *Chicana Lesbians: The Girls Our Mothers Warned Us About,* ed. Carla Trujillo, 159–84. Berkeley: Third Woman Press, 1991.

Pérez, Eulalia. "Una Vieja y Sus Recuerdos," Manuscript in the Bancroft Library. Translated by Ruth Rodríguez. (C-D 139).

Pérez-Torres, Rafael. *Movements in Chicano Poetry: Against Myths, Against Margins.* Cambridge: Cambridge University Press, 1995.

Pescatello, Ann. *Female and Male in Latin America.* Pittsburgh: University of Pittsburgh Press, 1973.

———. *Power and Pawn: The Female in Iberian Families, Societies, and Cultures.* Newport, Connecticut: Greenwood Press, 1976.

Pesquera, Beatriz M. "Compromiso e identidad con el trabajo entre las trabajadoras chicanas." *Culturas Hispanas de los Estados Unidos de América,* ed. María de Jesús Buxó Rey y Tomás Calvo Buezas, 157–68. Madrid: Ediciones de Cultura Hispáncia, 1990.

———. "Work and Family: A Comparative Analysis of Professional, Clerical, and Blue Collar Chicana Workers." Ph.D. diss., University of California, Berkeley, 1985.

Pettit, Arthur G. *Images of the Mexican American in Fiction and Film.* College Station: Texas A & M University Press, 1980.

Phillips, Rachel. "Marina/Malinche: Masks and Shadows." In *Women in Hispanic Literature: Icons and Fallen Idols,* ed. Beth Miller, 97–114. Berkeley: University of California Press, 1983.

Pico, María Inocenta. "Reminiscences of California," 1878. Manuscript in the Bancroft Library. (C-D 34).

Pineda, Cecile. *Face.* New York: Viking, 1985.

———. *Frieze.* New York: Viking, 1986. New York: Penguin Books, 1987.

Ponce, Mary Helen. *Hoyt Street. An Autobiography.* Albuquerque: University of New Mexico Press, 1993. New York: Anchor, 1995.

———. *Recuerdo: Short Stories of the Barrio.* Tujunga, Calif.: Adams & Associates, 1983.

———. *Taking Control.* Houston: Arte Público Press, 1987.

———. *The Wedding.* Houston: Arte Público Press, 1990.

Ponce, Merrihelen. "The Lives and Works of Five Hispanic New Mexican Women Writers, 1878–1991." Working Paper #119. Albuquerque: Southwest Hispanic Research Institute, 1992.

Ponce-Montoya, Juanita. *Grief Work*. Hicksville, N.Y.: Exposition Press, 1978.

Poole. Stafford, C. M. *Our Lady of Guadalupe: The Origins and Sources of a Mexican National Symbol, 1531–1797*. Tucson, University of Arizona Press, 1995.

Portes, Alejandro, and Robert L. Bach. *Latin Journey: Cuban and Mexican Immigrants in the United States*. Berkeley: University of California Press, 1985.

Portillo-Trambley, Estela "The Day of the Swallows." In *We Are Chicanos: An Anthology of Mexican-American Literature,* ed. Philip D. Ortego, 224–71. New York: Washington Square Press, 1973.

———. "The Day of the Swallows." In *Contemporary Chicano Theater,* ed. Roberto J. Garza. South Bend: University of Notre Dame Press, 1976.

———. *Rain of Scorpions and Other Writings*. Berkeley: Tonatiuh International, 1975.

———. *Sor Juana and Other Plays*. Ypsilanti, Mich.: Bilingual Press/Editorial Bilingüe, 1983.

———. *Trini*. Binghamton, New York: Bilingual Press/Editorial Bilingüe, 1986.

Powers, Edith. *Singing for My Echo: Memories of Gregoria Rodríguez, A Native Healer of Santa Fe*. Santa Fe: Cota Editions/Ocean Tree Services, 1987.

Pratt, Annis. *Archetypal Patterns in Women's Fiction*. Bloomington: Indiana University Press, 1981.

Preciado Martin, Patricia. *Days of Plenty, Days of Want*. Tempe, Ariz.: Bilingual Review/Press, 1988.

———. *Del Rancho al Barrio. The Mexican Legacy of Tucson*. Tucson: Arizona Historical Society, 1983.

———. *Images and Conversations: Mexican Americans Recall a Southwestern Past*. Tucson: University of Arizona Press, 1983.

———. *Songs My Mother Sang to Me*. Tucson: University of Arizona Press, 1993.

Quezada, Naomí. *Amor y Magia Amorosa Entre Los Aztecas*. México: UNAM, 1975.

Quintana, Alvina E. "Ana Castillo's *The Mixquiahuala Letters:* The Novelist as Ethnographer." In *Criticism in the Borderlands: Studies in Chicano Literature, Culture and Ideology,* ed. by Héctor Calderón and José David Saldívar, 72–83. Durham: Duke University Press, 1991

———. "Women: Prisoners of the Word." In *Chicana Voices: Intersections of Class, Race and Gender,* ed. Teresa Córdova, et al, 208–19. Austin: Center for Mexican American Studies, 1986. Albuquerque: University of New Mexico Press, 1993.

Quiñónez, Naomi. "The Confession." In *Infinite Divisions: An Anthology of Chicana Literature,* ed. Tey Diana Rebolledo and Eliana Rivero, 300–302. Tucson: University of Arizona Press, 1993.

———. *Sueño de Colibrí: Hummingbird Dream*. Los Angeles: West End Press, 1985.

Quiñónez, Naomi, ed. *Invocation*. Los Angeles: West End Press, 1990.

Quirarte, Josefina Lomelí, "Condición social de la mujer." *México Prehispánico*. Mexico: Editorial Emma Hurtado, 1946.

Ramos, Luis Arturo. *Angela de Hoyos, A Critical Look*. Albuquerque: Pajarito Publications, 1979.

Ranck, Katherine Quintana. *Portrait of Doña Elena*. Berkeley: Tonatiuh-Quinto Sol International, 1982.

Rebolledo, Tey Diana.

———. "The Bittersweet Nostalgia of Childhood in the Poetry of Margarita Cota-Cárdenas." *Frontiers* 5:2 (1980) 31–35.

———. "Comience La Danza: La Poesía Nahuatl de Macuilxóchitl, 5 Flor." *Revista Interamericana de Bibliografía* 27: 3 (1978), 283–89.

———. "From Coatlicue to Doña Luz: Mitotes in Chicana Literature." In *To Speak or Be Silent,* ed. Lina Ross, 210–25. Wilamette, Ill.: Chiron Publications, 1993.

———. "Las Escritoras: Romances and Realities." In *Pasó por Aquí:Critical Essays on the New Mexican Literary Tradition, 1542–1988,* ed. Erlinda Gonzales-Berry, 199–214. Albuquerque: University of New Mexico Press, 1989.

———. "The Maturing of Chicana Poetry: The Quiet Revolution of the 1980s." In *For Alma Mater: Theory and Practice in Feminist Scholarship,* ed. Paula A. Treichler, Cheris Kramarae, and Beth Stafford, 143–58. Chicago: University of Illinois Press, 1985.

———. "Narrative Strategies of Resistance in Hispana Writing." *The Journal of Narrative Technique,* 20 (20): 134–46.

———, ed. *Nuestras Mujeres. Hispanas of New Mexico: Their Images and Their Lives, 1582–1992* . Albuquerque: El Norte Publications, 1993.

———. "Tradition and Mythology: Signatures of Landscape in Chicana Literature." In *The Desert is No Lady,* ed. Vera Norwood and Janice Monk, 98–124. New Haven: Yale University Press, 1987.

———. "Walking the Thin Line. Humor in Chicana Literature." In *Beyond Stereotypes: The Critical Analysis of Chicana Literature,* ed. María Herrera-Sobek, 91–105. Tempe, Ariz.: Bilingual Review Press, 1985.

———. "Witches, Bitches and Midwives: The Shaping of Poetic Consciousness in Chicana Literature." In *The Chicano Struggle: Analysis of Past and Present Efforts,* ed. García, John A., Teresa Córdova, and Juan R. García. Binghamton: Bilingual Press, 1984. Pp. 166–177.

———. *Women Singing in the Snow: A Cultural Analysis of Chicana Literature*. Tucson: University of Arizona Press, 1995.

Rebolledo, Tey Diana, and Eliana S. Rivero. *Infinite Divisions: An Anthology of Chicana Literature*. Tucson: University of Arizona Press, 1993.

Rebolledo, Tey Diana, Erlinda Gonzales-Berry and Teresa Márquez, eds. *Las Mujeres Hablan: An Anthology of Nuevo Mexicana Writers*. Albuquerque: El Norte Publications, 1988.

Reiter, Rayana R. *Toward an Anthropology of Women*. New York: Monthly Review Press, 1975.

Reincourt, Amaury de. *Sex and Power in History*. New York: Dell Publishing, Co., 1974.

Revista Chicano-Riqueña. 7:2 (1978).

Revista Mujeres. 6:1, (Jan. 1989).

Reyna, Dorotea. "Voice." In *New Chicana/Chicano Writing 1*, ed. Charles M. Tatum, 172–174. Tucson: University of Arizona Press, 1992.

Richardson, B.D. "The Vicissitudes of Breastfeeding." *Journal of Tropical Pediatrics* (1986) 32, no. 3: 102–3.

Ríos, Isabella. *Victuum*. Ventura, Calif.: Diana-Etna Incorporated, 1976.

Rivera, Marina. "Mestiza." English translation in *Infinite Divisions: An Anthology of Chicana Literature*. ed. Tey Diana Rebolledo and Eliana Rivero, 97–101. Tucson: University of New Mexico Press, 1993.

———. *Mestiza*. Tucson: Grilled Flowers, 1977.

———. *Sobra*. San Francisco: Casa Editorial, 1977.

Rivero, Eliana. "Escritoras Chicanas: Fronteras de La Lengua y La Cultura," *Anales del Pacífico* (forthcoming).

———. "Escritura Chicana: Introducción y Contexto." *Areíto* 5 (18): 38–52.

———. "Escritura Chicana: La Mujer." *La Palabra* 2 (2): 2–9.

———. "*The House on Mango Street:* Tales of Growing Up Female and Hispanic." SIROW Working Paper Series, no. 21 (University of Arizona-Southwest Institute for Research on Women, 1986), pp. 2–19.

———. "Poesía en Arizona: Las Voces de *Mestiza. La Palabra* 1 (1): 26–33.

Robinson, Cecil. *Mexico and the Hispanic Southwest in American Literature*. Tuscon: University of Arizona Press, 1977.

Robles, Mireya. *En esta aurora*. San Antonio: M & A Edition, 1978.

Rocard, Marcienne. "*Faultline:* como una metáfora estructural en la novela de Sheila Ortiz Taylor *Faultline*." *Culturas Hispanas de los Estados Unidos de América*, ed. María de Jesús Buxó Rey y Tomás Calvo Buezas, 547–54. Madrid: Ediciones de Cultura Hispánica, 1990. Rocha, Rina García. *Eluder*. Chicago: Alexander Books Ltd., 1980.

Rodríguez, Andrés and Roberto G. Trujillo, eds. *Literatura Chicana, Creative and Critical Writings Through 1984*. Oakland, Calif.: Floricanto Press, 1985.

Rodríguez, María Guadalupe. *Morena, 66*.

Rodríguez, Gregorita. *Singing For My Echo*. As told to Edith Powers. Santa Fe, New Mexico: Cota Editions, Ocean Tree Services, 1987.

Rodríguez Baños, Roberto, Patricia Trejes de Zepeda, and Edilberto Soto Angli. *Virginidad y machismo en México.* México: Editorial Posada, 1973.

Romano-V., Octavio Ignacio, and Herminio Ríos. C., eds. *El Espejo—The Mirror. Selected Chicano Literature.* Berkeley: Quinto Sol Publications, 1969.

Romero, Lin. *Happy Songs, Bleeding Hearts.* San Diego, Calif.: Toltecas en Aztlán Publications, 1974. (*Rostros de Amerindiana: A Series of Indigenous Xicano Journeys*)

Rowbotham, Sheila. *Women, Resistance and Revolution: A History of Women and Revolution in the Modern World.* New York: Random House, 1974.

Roybal, Rose Marie. *From La Llorona to Envidia . . . A Few Reflections.* Denver: Southwest Clearinghouse for Minority Publications, 1973.

Rubel, Arthur J. *Across the Tracks.* Austin: University of Texas Press, 1966.

Ruiz, Vicki L. "Obreras y Madres: Labor Activism Among Mexican Women and Its Impact on the Family." *La Mexicana/Chicana: Renato Rosaldo Lecture Series Monograph 1983–84.* Tucson: Mexican American Studies and Research Center, University of Arizona, 1985.

Ruiz de Burton, María Amparo. *The Squatter and the Don,* ed. and with an introduction by Rosaura Sánchez and Beatrice Pita. Houston: Arte Público Press, 1992.

Rule, Janice. *Lesbian Images.* London: Peter Davies, 1975.

Ryan, Bryan, ed. *Hispanic Writers: A Selection of Sketches from Contemporary Authors.* London: Gale Research, 1991.

Saguaro. Vol. 2, 1985.

Saldívar, Ramón. *Chicano Narrative: The Dialectics of Difference.* Madison: University of Wisconsin Press, 1990.

Saldívar-Hull, Sonia. *Feminism on the Borders.* Berkeley: University of California Press, forthcoming.

Sánchez, Elba. "Mirror Image: Womanpoetry," In *New Chicana/Chicano Writing 1,* ed. Charles M. Tatum, 50. Tucson: University of Arizona Press, 1992.

Sánchez, Margarita Virginia. "Escape." *Regeneración* I:5. Rpt. in *We Are Chicanos: An Anthology of Mexican-American Literature,* ed. Philip D. Ortego, 208. New York: Washington Square Press, 1973.

———. "La Raza." *Regeneración* I:5. Rpt. in *We Are Chicanos: An Anthology of Mexican-American Literature,* ed. Philip D. Ortego, 208–10. New York: Washington Square Press, 1973.

Sánchez, Marta. "Chicana Prose Writers: The Case of Gina Valdés and Sylvia Lizárraga." In *Beyond Stereotypes: The Critical Analysis of Chicana Literature,* ed. María Herrera-Sobek. Tempe, Ariz.: Bilingual Review Press, 1985. Pp. 61–70.

———. *Contemporary Chicana Poetry: A Critical Approach to An Emerging Literature.* Berkeley: University of California Press, 1985.

Sánchez, Pilar. *Symbols.* San Francisco: Casa Editorial Publications, 1975.

Sánchez, Rita. "Chicana Writer Breaking Out of Silence." *De Colores* 3, No. 3, 1977.

Sánchez, Rosaura. *Essays on la mujer.* Los Angeles: Chicano Studies Center Publications, University of California, 1977.

————. "The Hubert H. Bancroft Collection." In *Recovering the U.S. Hispanic Literary Heritage.* ed. Ramón Gutiérrez and Genaro Padilla, 279–92. Houston: Arte Público Press, 1993.

————. *Requisa Treinta y Dos.* La Jolla, Calif.: Chicano Research Publications, 1979.

Santana-Bejar, Patricia. "In the Toolshed." *Maize* 4:1–2 (1981).

Sapia, Yvonne. *Valentino's Hair.* Boston: Northeastern University Press, 1987.

Schmidt, Adeny, and Amado M. Padilla. "Grandparent-Grandchild Interaction in a Mexican American Group." *Hispanic Journal of Behavioral Sciences* (1983) 5:181–98.

Schmidt, Lorenza Calvillo. *Poems.* In *First Chicano Literary Prize 1974–75.* Irvine: Dept. of Spanish and Portuguese, University of California, 1975.

Segura, Denise A. "Chicana and Mexicana Immigrant Women in the Labor Market: A Study of Occupational Mobility and Stratification." Ph.D. diss., University of California, Berkeley, 1986.

————. "Chicanas y mexicanas en el mundo laboral: Barreras para el empleo y la movilidad social." *Culturas Hispanas de Los Estados Unidos de América.* ed. María de Jesús Buxó Rey y Tomás Calvo Buezas, 143–57. Madrid: Ediciones de Cultura Hispánica, 1990.

————. "Labor Market Stratification: The Chicana Experience." *Berkeley Journal of Sociology* (Spring 1984) 29:57–91.

Sen, G., and C. Grown. *Development, Crisis, and Alternative Visions: Third World Women's Perspectives.* New York: Monthly Review Press, 1987.

Sena-Rivera, Jaime. "Extended Kinship in the United States: Competing Models and the Case of La Familia Chicana." *Journal of Marriage and the Family* (1979) 41: 121–129.

Senour, María Nieto. "Psychology of the Chicana." *Chicana Psychology,* ed. Joe Martínez, 329–43. New York: Academic Press, 1977.

Serrano, Nina. *Heart Songs, The Collected Poems of Nina Serrano (1969–1979).* San Francisco: Editorial Pocho-Che, 1980.

Serros, Michelle. *Chicana Falsa and Other Stories of Death, Identity and Oxnard.* Santa Monica, Calif: Lalo Press, 1995.

Shirley, Paula W. "Josefina Niggli." *Dictionary of Literary Biography Yearbook.*

Siete Poetas. Tucson: Scorpion Press, 1978.

Silva, Beverly. *The Cat and Other Stories.* Tempe, Arizona: Bilingual Press/Editorial Bilingue, 1986.

————. *The Second St. Poems.* Ypsilanti, Mich.: Bilingual Press/Editorial Bilingüe, 1983.

Smith, J.C., et al. "Trends in the Incidence of Breastfeeding for Hispanics of

Mexican Origin and Anglos on the U.S. Border." *American Journal of Public Health* (1982) 72, no. 1:54–61.

Soto, Gary, ed. *Pieces of the Heart: New Chicano Fiction.* San Francisco: Chronicle Books, 1993.

Sotomayor, Marta. "A Study of Chicano Grandparents in an Urban Barrio." Ph.D. diss., University of Denver, 1973.

Soustelle, Jacques. *La vida cotidiana de los Aztecas.* México: Fondo de Cultura Económica, 1977.

Sponsler, Lucy A. *Women in the Medieval Spanish Epic and Lyric Traditions.* Lexington: University Press of Kentucky, 1975.

Stephens, Sandra L., "The Women of the Amador Family, 1860–1940." In *New Mexico Women: Intercultural Perspectives,* ed. Joan M. Jensen and Darlis A. Miller, 257–77. Albuquerque: University of New Mexico Press, 1986.

Stevens, Evelyn P. "Marianismo: The Other Face of Machismo" In *Female and Male In Iberoamerica,* 2d ed. Ann Pescatello, ed. Pittsburgh: University of Pittsburgh Press.

———. "Mexican Machismo: Politics and Value Orientation." *Western Political Quarterly.* Vol. 18, No.4 (December, 1965), p. 848–57.

Straw, Mary J. *Loretto. The Sisters and their Santa Fe Chapel.* Santa Fe: Loretto Chapel, 1983.

Swadesh, Frances Leon. *Los Primeros Pobladores.* Notre Dame: University of Notre Dame Press, 1974.

Tafolla, Carmen. *Curandera.* San Antonio, Texas: M & A Editions, 1983.

———. "Federico y Elfiria." In *Third Woman: The Sexuality of Latinas,* ed. Norma Alarcón, Ana Castillo, Cherríe Moraga. Berkeley: Third Woman Press, 1989. Pp. 105–12.

———. *Get Your Tortillas Together.* n.p., 1976.

———. *Patchwork/Colcha.* Flagstaff, Ariz.: CEE Publications, 1987.

———. *Sonnets From A Human Being.* Santa Monica, Calif.: Lalo Press, 1993.

———. *Sonnets To Human Beings and Other Selected Works.* Santa Monica, Calif.: Lalo Press, 1992.

———. *To Split a Human: Mitos, Machos y la Mujer Chicana.* San Antonio: Mexican American Cultural Center, 1985.

Tatum, Charles M. *Chicano Literature.* Boston: Twayne Publishers, 1982.

Tatum, Charles M., ed. *New Chicana/Chicano Writing 1.* Tucson: University of Arizona Press, 1992.

———, ed. *New Chicana/Chicano Writing 2.* Tucson: University of Arizona Press, 1993.

———, ed. *New Chicana/Chicano Writing 3.* Tucson: University of Arizona Press, 1993.

———. "Some Considerations on Genres and Chronology for Nineteenth

Century Hispanic Literature." In *Recovering the U.S. Hispanic Literary Heritage,* ed. by Ramón Gutiérrez and Genaro Padilla, 199–208. Houston: Arte Público Press.

Taylor, J. E. "Undocumented Mexico-U.S. Migration and the Returns to Households in Rural Mexico." *American Journal of Agricultural Economics* (August, 1987) 69, no. 3: 626–38.

Taylor, Sheila Ortiz. *Faultline.* Tallahassee, Fla.: Naiad Press, 1982.

———. *Spring Forward/Fall Back.* Tallahassee, Fla.: Naiad Press, 1985.

Tinajero, Sara G., "The Role of a Mexican American Woman Poet in the Southwestern United States." MA thesis: Laredo State University, 1988.

Torres, Olga Beatrice. *Memorias de Mi Viaje.* Introduction and translation by Juanita Luna Lawhn. Albuquerque: University of New Mexico Press, 1994.

Treviño, Gloria. "Early Chicana Prose Fiction Writers. In Search of a Female Space." Paper presented at the Modern Language Association, December, 1985.

Trujillo, Carla, ed. *Chicana Lesbians. The Girls Our Mothers Warned Us About.* Berkeley: Third Woman Press, 1991.

Trujillo-Gaitán, Marcela. *Chicano Themes: Manita Poetry.* Minneapolis: Chicano Studies, University of Minnesota, 1975.

———. "The Dilemma of the Modern Chicana Artist and Critic." *De Colores* 3:3 (1977), 38–48. Reprinted in *Heresies 8* (1979), 5–10 and in *The Third Woman,* ed. Dexter Fisher, 324–32. Boston: Houghton Mifflin, 1980.

Turner, Frederick. "Los efectos de la participación femenina en la revolución de 1910." *Historia mexicana,* Vol. 16, No. 4 (abril-junio 1967), pp. 601–20.

201: Homenaje a la ciudad de Los Angeles: Latino Experience in Literature and Art. Los Angeles: Los Angeles Latino Writers Association, 1982.

Velásquez, Gloria L. *I Used to Be a Superwoman.* Santa Monica, Cal: Santa Monica College Press, 1994.

Valdés, Gina. "Josefina's Chickens," *Caracol* March 1979: 15–20.

———. *Comiendo Lumbre/Eating Fire.* Colorado Springs: Maize Press, 1986.

———. *Puentes y Fronteras: Coplas Chicanas.* Los Angeles: Castle Lithograph, 1982.

———. *There Are No Madmen Here.* San Diego: Maize, 1981.

———. "Weeping With Laughter." In *Infinite Divisions: An Anthology of Chicana Literature,* ed. Tey Diana Rebolledo and Eliana Rivero, 368–69. Tucson: University of Arizona, 1993.

Valdés-Fallis, Guadalupe. "A Liberated Chicana—A Struggle Against Tradition." *Women: A Journal of Liberation* 3, No. 4, 1974, pp. 20–21.

Van Hooft, Karen S. and Gabriela Mora, eds. *Theory and Practice of Feminist Literary Criticism.* Ypsilandti, Mich.: Bilingual Press/Editorial Bilinque, 1982.

Vásquez, Melba J.T. "Confronting Barriers to the Participation of Mexican American Women in Higher Education." *Hispanic Journal of Behavioral Sciences* (1982) 4, no. 2:167–79.

Vásquez-Castro, Javier. *Acerca de Literatura (Diálogo Con Tres Autores Chicanos)*. Con introducción de Luis Arturo Ramos. San Antonio: M & A Editions, 1979.

Vigil, Evangelina. *The Computer is Down*. Houston: Arte Público Press, 1987.

———. *Nade y Nade*. San Antonio: M & A Editions, 1978.

———. *Thirty an' Seen a Lot*. Houston: Arte Público Press, 1982, 1985.

Vigil, Evangelina, ed. *Woman of Her Word: Hispanic Women Write*. Houston: Arte Público Press, 1984.

Villanueva, Alma Luz. *Bloodroot*. Austin: Place of Herons Press, 1977, 1982.

———. "La Chingada." In *Five Poets of Aztlán,* ed. Santiago Daydí-Tolson. Tempe, Ariz.: Bilingual Review, 1985.

———. *La Chingada*. Tempe, Ariz.: Bilingual Review/Press, 1985.

———. "Dark Roots." *Haight Ashbury Literary Journal* I:3 (1981).

———. "The Food" (prose) and "Bloodline." *ChismeArte* (Summer 1981). Special Women's Issue.

———. "Golden Glass" (short story), "Siren," and "The Ceremony of Orgasm" (poems). In *Hispanics in the United States: An Anthology of Creative Literature. Vol. II,* ed. Francisco Jiménez and Gary D. Keller, 70–72; 101–3. Ypsilanti, MI: Bilingual Press, 1982.

———. "Her Choice" (short story). *Maize* (Spring-Summer 1981).

———. "The Icicle." *Somos.* (Dec. 1978), pp. 22–23.

———. "Legacies and Bastard Roses." In *I Sing a Song To Myself,* ed. David Kherdian. New York: William Morrow, 1978.

———. *Life Span*. Austin: Place of Herons Press, 1985.

———. "The Love of It," "On Recognizing the Labor of Clarity," "A la vida," "Island." *ChismeArte* 1:4 (1977), pp. 12–13.

———. "Mother May I." In *Contemporary Chicana Poetry: A Critical Approach to an Emerging Literature,* Marta Sánchez. Berkeley: University of California Press, 1985. Pp. 277–366.

———. *Mother, May I?* Pittsburgh, PA: Motheroot Publications, 1978.

———. "My Mecca" (poem). In *Hispanics in the United States: An Anthology of Creative Literature,* ed. Gary D. Keller and Francisco Jiménez, 110. Ypsilanti, Mich.: Bilingual Press, 1980.

———. "Myth of Isla Mujeres." *Somos* (April 1979), p. 11.

———. *Naked Ladies*. New York: Anchor Press/Doubleday, 1993.

———. *Naked Ladies*. Tempe, Ariz.: Bilingual Press, 1993.

———. "Passion," "The Labor of Buscando la Forma." *Metamorfosis* (Spring 1982).

———. "Pyramids and Such." *Somos* (Oct. 1978), p. 37.

———. "To Jesús Villanueva, With Love" and three untitled poems. In *The Next World,* ed. Joseph Bruchac. New York: Crossing Press, 1978.

———. *The Ultraviolet Sky*. Tempe, Ariz.: Bilingual Press/Editorial Bilingüe, 1988.

———. "Wild Pollen." In *Contemporary Women Poets,* ed. Jennifer McDowell. San José, Calif.: Merlin Press, 1977.

———. "Windy Women." In *Beyond Rice,* ed. Geraldine Kudaka. San Francisco: Noro Press, 1979.

Villegas de Magnón, Leonor. *The Rebel.* Edited by Clara Lomas. Houston: Arte Público Press, 1994.

Viramontes, Helena María. *Chicana Writes On Word and Film.* Berkeley: Third Woman Press, 1995.

———. *The Moths and Other Stories.* Houston: Arte Público Press, 1985, 1993. Second edition, 1995.

———. *Under The Feet of Jesus.* New York: Dutton, 1995.

Weigle, Marta. *New Mexicans in Cameo and Camera.* Albuquerque: University of New Mexico Press, 1985.

———, ed. *Two Guadalupes. Hispanic Legends and Magic Tales From Northern New Mexico.* Santa Fe: Ancient City Press, 1987.

Wilbur-Cruce, Eva Antonia. *A Beautiful, Cruel Country.* Tucson: University of Arizona Press, 1987.

Xelina. *KU.* San Antonio: Caracol, 1977.

Yarbro-Bejarano, Yvonne. "Chicana Literature From a Chicana Feminist Perspective." In *Feminisms,* ed. Robyn R. Warhol and Diane Price Herndl, 731–37. New Brunswick, NJ: Rutgers University Press, 1991.

———. "De-constructing the Lesbian Body: Cherríe Moraga's *Loving in the War Years.*" In *Chicana Lesbians: The Girls Our Mothers Warned Us About,* ed. Carla Trujillo, 143–55. Berkeley: Third Woman Press, 1991.

———. "The Female Subject in Chicano Theatre: Sexuality, 'Race' and Class." *Theatre Journal* (December 1986), 389–407.

———. "Insider/Outsider. Multiple Cultural Critiques in Chicana Art and Literature." Unpublished Paper.

Ybarra, Lea. "When Wives Work: The Impact on the Family." *Journal of Marriage and the Family* (1982) 2:169–77.

Ybarra, Lea, and Carlos H. Arce. "Entra Dicho y Hecho Hay Gran Trecho: The Division of Household Chores in the Chicano Family." Paper presented at the National Association for Chicano Studies conference, Riverside, Calif., April 1981.

Ybarra-Frausto, Tomás. "Rasquachismo: A Chicano Sensibility." In *Chicano Art: Resistance and Affirmation, 1965–1985.* Los Angeles: Wright Art Gallery UCLA, 1991.

———. *Rasquachismo.* Phoenix: MARS (Movimiento Artístico del Río Salado), 1989.

Zamora, Bernice. *Releasing Restless Serpents.* Tempe: Bilingual Review Press, 1993.

———. *Restless Serpents.* Menlo Park, Calif.: Diseños Literarios, 1976.

Zavella, Patricia. "El efecto del trabajo en las fábricas sobre las familias chicanas en las que trabajan ambos cónyuges." *Culturas Hispanas de los Estados Unidos de América.* ed. María de Jesús Buxó Rey y Tomás Calvo Buezas, 169–80. Madrid: Ediciones de Cultura Hispánica, 1990.

————. *Women, Work and the Chicano Family: Cannery Workers of the Santa Clara Valley.* Ithaca, N.Y.: Cornell University Press, 1987.

Zepeda, M. "Las Abuelitas." *Agenda* (1979) 9:10–13.

————. "Selected Maternal Care Practices of Spanish-Speaking Women." *JOGN Nursing* (1982) 11, no. 6:371–74.

Zimmerman, Bonnie. "What Has Never Been. An Overview of Lesbian Feminist Literary Criticism." In *Feminisms,* ed. Robyn R. Warhol and Diana Price Herndl. Pp. 117–37.

BIBLIOGRAPHIES

Anzaldúa, Mike. *Mexican American Literature: A Preliminary Bibliography of Literary Criticism.* Austin: Institute of Latin American Studies, 1981.

Dwyer, Carlota Cárdenas de. *Chicano Literature: An Introduction and An Annotated Bibliography.* Austin: Department of English and Center for Mexican American Studies, University of Texas at Austin, 1977.

Eger, Ernestina N. *A Bibliography of Criticism of Contemporary Chicano Literature.* Berkeley: Chicano Studies Library Publications: University of California, Berkeley:, 1982, 1980. (Chicano Studies Library Publications Series, no. 5)

Lomelí, Francisco A. and Donaldo Urioste. *Chicano Perspectives in Literature: A Critical and Annotated Bibliography.* Albuquerque: Pajarito Publications, 1976.

Martínez, Julio A., and Francisco A. Lomelí, eds. *Chicano Literature, A Reference Guide.* Westport, C.T., London: Greenwood Press, 1985.

Parcero, María de la Luz. *La Mujer en el Siglo XIX en México: Bibliografía.* México: Instituto Nacional de Antropología e Historia, 1982.

Rojas, Guillermo, com. "Toward a Chicano/Raza Bibliography: Drama, Prose, Poetry." *El Grito: A Journal of Contemporary Mexican-American Thought.* 7:2 (1973). Berkeley: Quinto Sol Publications, 1973.

Scott, Frank, César Caballero and Ida González. *Chicano Literature: A Selective Bibliography.* El Paso: University of Texas, El Paso, 1977.

Trujillo, Roberto G. and Raquel Quiróz de González. "A Comprehensive Bibliography (1970–1979)." *A Decade of Chicano Literature (1970–1979): Critical Essays and Bibliography.* Santa Barbara: Editorial La Causa, 1982. Pp. 107–28.

————. "An Essay on Collection Development and Bibliography of Chicano Literature Published 1980–1984." By Robert G. Trujillo with assistance from

A. A. Rodríguez and Richard Kiy. *Lector* 3:1 (July/August 1984) Berkeley: Hispanex, formerly the California Spanish Language Data Base, 1984. Pp. 20–28.

————. *Literatura Chicana: A Comprehensive Bibliography (1980-June 1984).* Stanford: Stanford University Libraries, Collection Development Program, Chicano Collections, 1984. (Working Bibliography Series, no.1)

Contributors

Laura Aguilar is a Chicana photographer from the San Gabriel Valley, California. Of Mexican and Irish descent, much of her work is concerned with the tension of her duel cultural heritage. She received her training at East Los Angeles Community College and has exhibited extensively since 1985.

Norma Alarcón is Associate Professor, Chicano/Ethnic Studies, University of California, Berkeley. She is editor and publisher of Third Woman Press. She has translated *This Bridge Called My Back* into Spanish and has published numerous seminal articles on Chicana literature and Latin American women writers.

Gloria Enedina Álvarez is a poet, teacher, and a cultural ambassador creating bridges between Central American women and Chicanas. She continues to teach bilingual poetry workshops based in the Latino/a community and has published her first collection of poetry title *The Excuse/La Excusa*.

Alma E. Cervantes is a graduate from the Havana Film School. Her training in scriptwriting has redirected her imagery in poetry. A poet springing from her E.L.A. experience, Cervantes's poems have been published in anthologies such as *Invocation: L. A. Urban Multicultural Poetry.*

Lorna Dee Cervantes is the author of two collections of poetry, the classic *Emplumada* published in 1981 by the University of Pittsburg Press, and *From the Cables of Genocide,* which has received both the Patterson Poetry Award and the poetry award of the Institute of Latina American Writers. She is currently completing her third collection titled *Bird Ave.* Cervantes teaches Creative Writing at the University of Colorado in Boulder.

Yreina Cervántez is a muralist, painter, teacher of art, and community healer through the arts. Her imagery often reflects a complex symbolism that arises from her political, cultural, and personal beliefs and traditions. She is a recipient of numerous grants and awards including a Certificate of Distinguished Recognition from the National Association of Chicano Studies and the Vesta Award for Excellence in the Arts. Currently painting a mural with Alma Lopez for the Huntington Beach Arts center titled "La Historia adentro, la Historia afuera," she is also an instructor at Rancho Santiago.

Denise Chávez, novelist, poet, and playwright, is the author of *Face of an Angel* (Farrar, Straus and Giroux, 1994), *La Mujer Que Sabia El Idioma de Los Animales,* and *The Last of the Menu Girls.* She is the recipient of the American Book Award, the Premio Aztlan, the Mesilla Valley Writer of the Year Award, and the Steele Jones Award. She has received a National Endowment for the Arts grant and a Rockefeller Playwright grant. A native of Las Cruces, New Mexico, Chávez sees herself as a community-oriented performance writer.

Lucha Corpi is author of two poetry collections, *Palabras de Mediodía: Noon Words* and *Variations*. In addition, she wrote two mystery novels, *Eulogy for a Brown Angel,* which one the PEN/Oakland Josephine Miles award, and *Cactus Blood*. She is the recipient of several awards for fiction including an NEA and was past president of Centro Chicano de Escritores. When not writing she teaches English in the Oakland City public schools. She is currently working on her third mystery novel.

Roberta Fernández is a professor in the Department of Modern and Classical Languages, University of Houston. Her novel *Intaglio: A Novel in Six Stories* was selected by Multicultural Publishers Exchange as Best Fiction of 1991. She is editor of *In Other Word: Literature by Latinas in the United States* and has edited numerous novels for Arte Público Press.

Carmen Lomas Garza is considered one of the best known Chicana artists in the Untied States. Her work has been exhibited in a one-woman art show and appears on checks as well as galleries. She has collaborated with Harriet Rohmer to create *Family Pictures: Cuadros de familia,* which depicts in bilingual and visual text her childhood upbringing in Kingsville, South Texas.

María Herrera-Sobek, a Cultural Studies and Chicana literature scholar, is a full professor in the Department of Spanish and Portuguese, University of California, Irvine and is Director of the Chicano/Latino Studies Program. She has edited *Beyond Stereotypes: Critical Analysis of Chicana Literature* and *Chicana Writes: On Word and Film* and has written numerous scholarly books, most notably *The Mexican Corrido: A Feminist Analysis* and *Northward Bound: The Mexican Immigrant Experience in Ballad and Song*. A fine poet, Herrera-Sobek's poetry has been published in anthologies such as *Three Times a Woman.*

Rosa M. is a native of Ascensión, Chihuahua. She was raised in southern California and has spent most of her adult life in the northeast. She received her art training at the Rhode Island School of Design. While her main creative focus is on painting, she has also worked in other media. She has exhibited widely over the past five years.

Julián Olivares is Full Professor of Hispanic and Classical Languages, University of Houston. He is the author of *The Love Poetry of Francisco de Quevedo* and has edited *International Studies in Honor of Tomás Rivera.*

Naomi Quiñónez is currently a faculty fellow at West Virginia Graduate College and is working on her Ph. D. She has co-edited *Invocation L.A.: Urban Multicultural Poetry* with Sesshu Foster and Michelle Clinton and is author of a collection of poetry titled *Hummingbird Dream*. From her years as a poet, educator, and activist, Quiñónez has developed a substantial range of themes.

Tey Diana Rebolledo is Full Professor of Spanish, University of New Mexico. She has edited and co-edited numerous anthologies that deal with women and their creative expression, such as *Las Mujeres Hablan*. Her cultural analysis of Chicana literature titled *Women Singing in the Snow* and her anthology *Infinite Divisions* have been hailed as landmark studies.

Evangelina Vigil-Piñón has edited *Woman of Her Word: Hispanic Women Write*. Her first collection of poetry, *Thirty an' Seen a Lot* was awarded the Before Columbus Book Award. She is an NEA recipient and a winner of many literary awards. A committed advocate for community based art, Vigil-Piñón currently hosts a Community Service Program broadcasting out of Houston.

Sheila Ortiz Taylor is a Professor of English at Florida State University. She has written several novels and one book of poetry. Her novel *Faultline,* published in 1982, won a Book of the Year award and has been translated into German and Spanish.

Helena María Viramontes is a writer and editor and has written one teleplay, which was filmed by Ana María García and produced by the American Film Institute. She is the author of one collection of short stories, *The Moths and Other Stories,* and one novel, *Under the Feet of Jesus.* She is currently an Assistant Professor of Creative Writing, Cornell University.

Yvonne Yarbro-Bejarano is Associate Professor, Department of Spanish, and director of the Chicano Fellows Program at Stanford. She has just completed her collection of published and unpublished essays on Cherríe Moraga titled *Voices From the Borderlands.* She is expanding her research to include visual art, popular culture, and film/video by Chicanas and will write on Chicana cultural production from an interdisciplinary and comparative point of view.

Credits